Riding and Schooling The Western Performance Horse

Riding and Schooling The Western Performance Horse

G.F. Corley, D.V.M.

PRENTICE HALL PRESS
New York   London   Toronto   Sydney   Tokyo

Published in 1986 by Prentice Hall Press
A Division of Simon & Schuster, Inc.
Gulf + Western Building
One Gulf + Western Plaza
New York, N. Y. 10023

Originally published by Arco Publishing, Inc.

PRENTICE HALL PRESS is a trademark of
Simon & Schuster, Inc.

Library of Congress Cataloging-in-Publication Data
Corley, G. F.
    Riding and schooling the western performance
horse.
    Includes index
    1. Western riding.   2. Horse-shows—Western
division and classes.   3. Horse-training.   I. Title
II. Title: Western performance horse.
SF309.3.C.67   78.2'3   81-3550
ISBN 0-668-05083-7   AACR2

Manufactured in the Unites States of America

10   9   8   7   6   5

CONTENTS

LIST OF ILLUSTRATIONS

Chapter 1

Chapter 2

Chapter 3

Chapter 4

Chapter 6

LIST OF TABLES

ACKNOWLEDGMENTS

My greatest thanks to:

The photographers: Peggy Humphrey Corley, Sedona, Ariz.; Patricia Mansmann, West Chester, Pa.; Todd Macklin, Lawrence, Kans.; and Luis Schleiniger, Sedona, Ariz.—for doing all of Peggy Corley's developing and printing.

The riders: Carlie Beisel, Peggy Humphrey Corley, Darlene Dale, Chris Liewher, Jessica Newberry Ranshausen, Chuck Smallwood, Lloyd Donley, Casey Hinton, Doug Lilly, Trisha Taylor, Paul Reed, and Marilyn Camarillo.

Dick and Jeannie Bangham, Milpitas, Calif.; Johnson County Community College, Overland Park, Kans.; Park College, Parkville, Mo.; Pretty Penny Ranch, Scottsdale, Ariz.; and Richard Young, Win-Rich Farm, Warrenton, Va.—for the use of their facilities and personnel. Also thanks to Michele Slater and Susan Lajewski.

Peggy Humphrey Corley for technical assistance, for verification of portions of the content of this book, and for her help in writing the chapter on the rider's correct position.

Lloyd Donley for taking the time to discuss some of the higher-level movements with me, and for sharing with me some of his longtime experience with western performance horses.

Doug Lilly for his demonstrations of advanced riding and schooling techniques in several of the photographs used here.

V. S. Littauer for the seven, the four, nonabuse of the horse, logical thought, an open mind and much, much more.

Chuck Smallwood not only for his time in the saddle, but for his encouragement and astute discussion about portions of the rough draft of this text.

Other Authors: Suzanne Norton Jones, *The Art of Western Riding;* V. S. Littauer, *Commonsense Horsemanship;* W. Museler, *Riding Logic;* and the AAHPER Affiliated National Riding Committee, *Riding Standards,* all of whom have helped me enormously through their writing—the beginning of better riding and schooling.

INTRODUCTION

This book details a system of riding and schooling for the western performance horse. By reading and studying this book and then applying what you have learned to actual riding situations, you will improve your present levels of riding, schooling and perhaps teaching. If you are a motivated rider or an astute amateur, this book is for you. Not only should your riding improve, but your horses should perform better, and their overall quality of movement should likewise improve. If you ride professionally or teach riding, I believe that you will be able to do these things even better if you apply the concepts of this book. Very likely, many of you will be able to upgrade your overall professional activities.

Today the state of modern western riding, its theory and active practice at the higher levels of riding and schooling, rests in the hands of a relatively few talented individuals—artists, in a sense. Many colleges, universities and even secondary schools offer good riding programs. A national organization—the Affiliated National Riding Commission, a joint commission of the National Association of Girls and Women in Sport (NAGWS) and the National Association of Sport and Physical Education (NASPE)—provides rigorous examinations of a rider's theoretical and practical level of riding and schooling. Additionally, many people well trained in riding share their knowledge with their own pupils and with the general public through clinics and articles in the popular "horse press." Yet for all of this potential expertise, riding and schooling for the western horse is usually still nothing more than a conglomeration of helpful tips, hints and suggestions. Western riding has suffered and continues to suffer economically and in status from this.

The point is this. If you and I do not apply a system of riding and schooling to our own activities, including teaching, then how can we expect the beginner to develop logically his or her own riding? How can we expect the student to improve in both riding and schooling if these activities are based only on a scrambled pile of helpful hints? What can we possibly expect from the western horses this beginner will school later on? And what about the time, even later in this same beginner's life, when he or she comes to the show ring as an approved judge? Or begins teaching professionally? The application of a system of riding is essential. Better and more effective riding, schooling, teaching and judging can result from such an application. The credibility of western riding can be enhanced, and judging can be improved.

The system of riding presented in this book can be called *modern western riding* or, for schooling purposes, *modern western schooling*. This system is a logical progression of ideas and techniques beginning at the elementary level of riding and schooling and progressing through a high-intermediate level for both of these activities. Also, later in the book, the advanced level of riding is treated, and you will find out why the entire subject of advanced riding and schooling is a touchy one. The system of riding presented centers on three things:

1. The rider's position astride the moving horse
2. The control techniques employed by the rider
3. The actual schooling of the modern western performance horse

Although this is not a book on how to teach western riding, you may well choose to model your teaching on it. I strongly suggest that you consider teaching a system of riding; this should definitely be to your economic benefit, provided you are experienced in teaching and that you can actually ride at the levels described in this book. Of course sizable portions of the text deal with the actual "how to's" of riding and schooling. You will also find sizable portions, and even full chapters, dealing primarily with riding theory and the mechanics of motion—the necessary background for a successful technique.

Theory and practice realistically go hand in hand. For example, improved riding does not merely consist of learning the correct use of aids. Rather, it consists of learning both the correct and efficient use of aids. You will find that in order to be both correct and efficient, you must first understand a good deal of theory. If you teach, you will find that your credibility as an instructor will improve if you teach theory as well as the actual practice of riding. The mechanics of motion in the horse should be understood so that you can most effectively coordinate your aids with the efforts of the horse in performing exercises and show ring movements. In short, you will find that knowing all of the "how to's" is really of little consequence unless you also understand the theory behind them—and apply this theory to each riding and schooling situation.

One of the biggest problems in presenting a system of riding and schooling to riders who have never known, or ridden, a particular system is that you, the rider, will often say to yourself, "If his method is useful and works well, then mine must be useless and does not produce good results. If I agree with his particular point of view, my point of view must not be valid." Nothing could be further from the truth. Learning something new should be exciting, not a blow to your ego. You should continually argue the system and its applications with me, as well as with yourself and other riders. Take a fiendish delight in finding the limitations to this system of riding. No book is ever perfect, and no book will take every rider to the highest level that he wishes to achieve. Improve this system. Add refinements. If you teach, then teach it; but also rehash it periodically, and then teach it again with your own improvements.

This book is not as easy to read as some. The text is definitely not written on the "ain't riding fun" level. While learning and applying a system of riding and schooling to your individual situation is not difficult, learning such a system so that it is second nature takes a lot of work. You will not be terribly effective if you must periodically dismount in order to review this chapter or that. A system of riding must become largely second nature if it is to be effective. For this reason, you will have to study. As you progress through each chapter, you must think as you read. As you continue to incorporate a system of riding and schooling into your activities, you should continually argue its methods and logic. As you argue and explore the points you may become increasingly dissatisfied with certain popular vogues in riding, schooling, teaching and showing. Illogical methods of riding may begin to annoy you more and more.

The goals and levels of knowledge which I have set for you (and for myself) in this book are high. My ultimate aim in this book is to influence a large number of western riders. I hope this book will encourage more riders to become "educated horsemen" and to replace their base of helpful tips and hints with a workable system of riding and schooling. I hope most of you are willing to advance theory, to consider change when warranted and to correlate riding, schooling and teaching principles—to work within a system of riding to improve the western horse and rider.

Please join with me in continuing to improve riding, schooling and teaching for the western performance horse.

G. F. Corley
Sedona, Arizona

Chapter 1

THE MECHANICS OF MOTION FOR THE PERFORMANCE HORSE

Mechanics is simply that branch of physics which studies the motion of bodies, and the results of certain forces acting upon bodies.

How a runner moves forward, a vehicle negotiates a curve at high speed, a coin is balanced on edge—all of these things are part of the study of mechanics. Certainly, I am not asking that you become a physicist in order to read this chapter, but I am asking you to understand the principles of motion for the horse: how he moves forward, how he negotiates a sharp turn at high speed, how he balances himself and much more. All of these things have a very direct bearing upon the effectiveness of your riding, schooling and teaching. To a somewhat lesser extent, these same things also are relevant to judging the western performance horse.

The subjects of this chapter are the following:

1. The balance of the horse, standing still and moving forward
2. The balancing gestures of the horse's head and neck
3. The location of the horse's center of balance, at rest and in motion
4. The sequence of legs (succession of hoof beats) at the various gaits, including the walk, trot, canter and rein back (backing up)
5. The inflexibility of the horse's back, and why he cannot literally bend his entire body around a circle or turn
6. The horse's performance of circles and turns, particularly at high speeds
7. The horse's forward motion and how both slow and fast forward speeds are generated and maintained

THE BALANCE OF THE HORSE

The idea of balance is applied to the horse in many different ways. For example, we talk about a horse that is forward balanced or one more centrally balanced, carrying more of his weight rearward toward the hindlegs. We talk about a stop being well balanced or not. Many instructors talk about the horse's center of balance in attempting to explain why a rider should sit astride the horse in a particular way, and there are even more ways in which the word is applied to different riding situations. A rider is said to be in balance or not in balance with his horse. A saddle may be described as well balanced, and people speak of the balancing gestures of the horse's head and neck. All of these uses of the word *balance* have importance for riding, and you will encounter nearly all of them as you read this book. But for now, I would like you to take an overview of the whole business of balance. Take a look at two particular types of balance: two ways in which the word *balance* can be applied to any horse. The first of these is *static balance* and the second is *dynamic balance*. Dynamic balance is also referred to by many riders and instructors as *balance in motion*.

Static balance deals only with the balance of the horse at rest, his balance while standing still at the halt. This is not a terribly exciting situation, and obviously little riding or schooling takes place at the halt. Nevertheless, the concept of static balance is important. If we first understand the nature of static balance, we are in a better position to understand how the balance of the horse might change as he begins to move forward, as he performs different events and as he is ridden by riders of different abilities. We have a reference point from which to gauge his changes in balance as he begins to move under various circumstances.

The horse standing motionless bears approximately 3/5 of his total body weight on the front limbs and the remaining 2/5 on the rear limbs. This division of weight assumes that the horse maintains a natural carriage of the head and neck—the head and neck carriage you see as the horse stands relaxed but alert in his stall, or as he stands relaxed but attentive in practically any show ring lineup. The division of weight between the hindquarters and the forehand is uneven by nature. This approximate weight division applies so long as the horse maintains a naturally extended and relaxed carriage of the head and neck.

You can verify this weight division by placing the horse's front feet on one set of scales and his back feet on another. You can see intuitively that it is true by simply mentally dividing the horse in half between the front and rear legs as I have done in Picture 1, a mental exercise analogous to placing the front feet on one set of scales and the back feet on another. As you look at this picture, you will correctly surmise that the excess weight normally borne by the horse's front legs is the weight of the head and neck—a rather heavy pendulum extending ahead of the forelegs, but whose weight must nevertheless be borne mostly by these same legs.

As you look at Picture 1, you may also guess that if the horse were to drastically alter the natural carriage of the head and neck, a change in his static balance would occur. If he were to extend the head and neck or lower them substantially, some additional shifting of his weight forward would follow. In this case the front limbs might bear even more than their normal load. On the other hand, if the horse were to raise the head and neck drastically, or flex the head back toward his chest, a shifting of his weight rearward would occur. In this case the front limbs would bear less than their normal load while the hind limbs would bear an increased amount of the horse's total body weight.

The point is that the normal state of static balance divides the horse's weight about 60 to 40 percent between the front and rear limbs. If the carriage of the head and neck are altered from their natural position, a shifting of this normal weight

Picture 1. Balance at the halt. *The horse with a relaxed and natural carriage of the head and neck bears about 60 percent of his weight on the front limbs and only about 40 percent of his weight on the rear limbs, so long as he remains motionless.*

Picture 2. Balance in motion. *The horse is in motion. At this moment his balance has been lost to the front. His entire mass is balanced upon one leg. This purposeful loss of balance to the front is how forward speed is achieved.*

distribution occurs. The usual way in which the carriage of the head and neck is altered is by setting the horse in motion.

Only when the horse begins to move forward can we talk about his balance in motion—his dynamic balance. Balance in motion is the ability of the horse to continuously cope successfully with his constant loss of equilibrium as he moves forward. In fact, the horse cannot even move forward unless he does continually lose and regain his balance as the bulk of his body passes forward and over the legs which support him.

If you look at Picture 2, you will see the essence of balance in motion, dynamic balance. Here you can see a quarter horse at the full gallop with only his leading leg in contact with the ground. The forward thrust of his body literally carries him over this leading leg, and at this very moment his balance has been badly lost to the front. It remains for this horse to regain this loss of balance by extending the opposite foreleg to contact the

ground, and thus successfully coping with the momentary loss of equilibrium.

V. S. Littauer has summed up dynamic balance:

"The forward movement of all animals is the result not only of the propulsive actions of the rear legs, but of a necessary recurrent loss [and regaining] of equilibrium to the front as well. For instance, a man when walking, first shifts his weight forward, taking it off the foot which is still on the ground, losing his balance to the front and catching it again on the leg being put down in front of the body; he usually aids himself with the balancing gestures of the arms [analogous to the balancing gestures of the horse's head and neck at the walk and canter]. The bigger the steps, the more pronounced is the shifting of weight forward—that is, the bigger the momentary loss of equilibrium in the front. Similarly, the forward movement of the horse consists of continually alternating movements of stability and instability. Balance is the skill to cope with this phenomenon efficiently [and this skill must be relearned by the horse in coping with the added weight of the rider during all early schooling].''

THE BALANCING GESTURES OF THE HEAD AND NECK

There are three facts of immediate concern in understanding how the horse uses his head and neck to aid his natural balance.

1. The horse uses his head and neck as a free-moving pendulum (up and down) in order to retain his balance during forward movement. The head and neck are repeatedly moved up and down (and to a much lesser degree from side to side). It is this repetitive up-and-down movement of the head and neck which above all else assists the horse in balancing himself during forward movement. The horse's head and neck are his balancers, just as our arms are ours. The balancing gestures are greatest at the walk and the canter. The balancing gestures of the head and neck are minimized, or nearly absent, at the trot. Head and neck gestures up and down are easily seen in the horse moving free in nature or ridden on loose reins at either the walk or the canter.

2. At any moment while the horse is moving forward, his weight is shifting from the front of his body toward the rear, and then to the front again. This cycle of weight shifting continues as long as the horse is in motion, and it occurs once each stride. Like the balancing gestures of the head and neck, the extent of the horse's weight shift backward and forward is greatest at the gaits of the walk and canter. The faster the speed at which these gaits are executed, the greater the horse's need to shift his weight back and forth efficiently in order to retain his balance. Very slow gaits, with the horse's head and neck substantially raised and the head flexed back toward the chest, tend to minimize this shifting of weight back and forth as well as minimizing the balancing gestures of the head and neck. Minimizing both of these factors, weight shifting and balancing gestures, is one of the important characteristics of semicollected gaits, as explained in Chapter 4.

3. Because the horse is constantly losing and regaining his balance in order to move forward, his legs ultimately catch him, and reestablish a base

from which balance is momentarily regained (before being lost again). The horse, as I have said, is actually incapable of forward movement without a loss of balance to the front.

V. S. Littauer (the first person to discuss at length, in print, and to include in his teaching the terms *static* and *dynamic balance*) has written in one of his letters that ''the French, early in this century, were the first to recognize that the system of the head and neck is the balancer of the horse (Le Balancier). You can read about it in the Fort Riley publication of an abominable translation of *Les allures, le cavalier* by L. de Sevy (circa 1918).''

De Sevy himself was a French cavalry officer (rank *capitaine*) whose real name was de Beauregard. He used the pen name de Sevy in all of his writings. Why would a professional horseman, attempting the honest pursuit of raising the level of his profession, choose to write under an assumed name? The answer is quite simple.

At the time *Les allures, le cavalier* was published, the idea that a horse required free use of his head and neck to retain his natural balance and perform well at a variety of tasks was revolutionary. The so-called educated horsemen, officers and civilians alike, looked down upon anything less than a fixed and stiff carriage of the horse's head and neck as a crude form of horsemanship. The fact that a horse in a collected attitude (head and neck maintained in a stiff and raised position) was in a frame to do little else than appear light in various rather inconsequential ring exercises seemed to be of little interest. In this way perhaps, the conservative approach and reluctance of professional horsemen to change was not much different from the conservative approach and attitude of the professional western horseman competing in the arena today. At any rate, Capitaine de Beauregard, without benefit of a pen name, would probably have soon been signing his writings and investigations as Corporal de Beauregard.

Following are five photographs which I hope will help you see the nature and importance of the balancing gestures of the horse's head and neck. In Picture 3 you will see a green horse experiencing the weight of a rider for the first time. The horse's head and neck are held in a low, stiff and unnaturally extended position. He can barely catch his balance under the new weight of the rider. The balancing gestures of his head and neck are at a

Picture 3. The unbalanced green horse. *Even at the walk, the young horse experiences considerable unbalance whenever he is mounted and ridden for the first time. Since the normal balancing gestures of the horse's head and neck are upset due to his inexperience in balancing the new weight of a rider, a low stiff carriage of the head and neck usually occurs. Additionally, a stiff gait in front is common, coupled with a reluctance to reach forward with the hind legs.*

Picture 4. Becoming accustomed to the rider's weight. *After becoming accustomed to the weight of a rider during forward motion, the head and neck of the green horse will quite naturally elevate. As the head and neck rise, and a normal carriage of these structures is reestablished, then normal balancing gestures of the head and neck will also be restored. Additionally, as the horse feels more in control of his balance as he moves forward under the weight of a rider, the stride in front will become more flexible and the horse will no longer be as reluctant to engage his hind legs well forward.*

minimum; he experiences considerable unbalance during any type of forward movement. In Picture 4 the same gelding is shown about 15 days later. His head and neck carriage have returned to normal, and he now utilizes the balancing gestures of his head and neck during forward movement.

Picture 5. Balancing gestures at the walk. *A continuous-light photograph illustrating the nature and magnitude of the balancing gestures of the head and neck at the walk.*

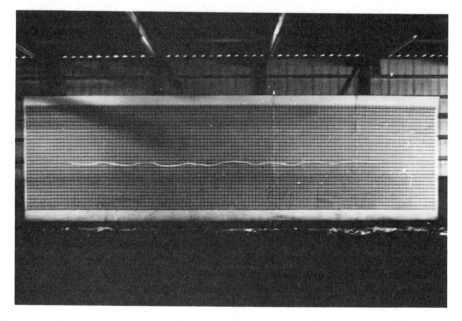

Picture 6. Balancing gestures at the trot. *This continuous-light photograph illustrates the minimal nature of the balancing gestures of the head and neck at the trot. Balancing gestures at the trot are substantially less than those for the walk and canter.*

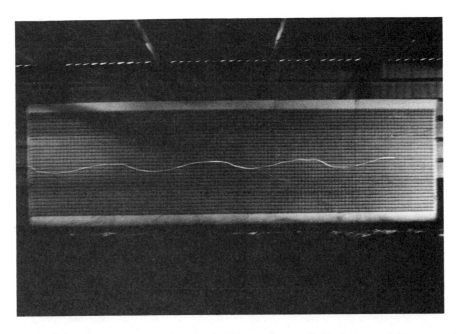

Picture 7. Balancing gestures at the canter. *This continuous-light photograph illustrates the nature and substantial magnitude of the balancing gestures of the head and neck at the ordinary canter.*

With the reestablishment of the balancing gestures as he employed them before ever being mounted and ridden for the first time, he has become well balanced at all gaits and during circles and turns. Pictures 5, 6 and 7 illustrate both the nature and relative magnitudes of the balancing gestures at the three gaits: the walk, trot and canter. An older, more experienced horse was used for these photographs. The horse had a bright light source attached to his bridle just behind his ears. A long exposure was used for each photograph, and the horse and rider were rendered invisible on the final developed photos. The graphic background, consisting of individual four-inch squares, gives you a good idea of the magnitude of the normal balancing gestures at each of the three gaits. At the ordinary walk the balancing gestures of the head and neck are considerable. At the canter they are even greater. During the trot, on the other hand, balancing gestures are at a minimum.

THE CENTER OF BALANCE

Knowing where the center of balance is and how it changes in the moving horse are important prerequisites for understanding later chapters.

In the stationary horse, the center of balance lies along a line passing vertically downward through the horse's chest cavity. As you view the horse from the side, this line passes downward through the chest at about the level of the sixth thoracic vertebra (the third thoracic vertebra is generally considered that part of the backbone representing the highest point of the withers). The sixth thoracic vertebra is located to the rear of the highest portion of the withers, and lies along the back at about the same level as the saddle horn. If you skip ahead to Picture 19, you will find the sixth thoracic vertebra labeled T6.

When you view the horse from the side, you are seeing what is, in effect, a two-dimensional figure. Viewed from the side, the line describing the location of the horse's center of balance is shown in Picture 8. If you were strong and large enough, you could place a single finger tip underneath the horse in line with his center of balance, and lift the horse above your head balanced on this single finger tip. If the horse would cooperate by not wiggling about, he would remain balanced upon your finger, and he would tip neither forward nor backward.

Of course, the horse is not a two-dimensional figure, so the line describing his center of balance does not simply pass downward along the side of the chest. Rather, this line passes downward and through the chest, dividing the horse left to right

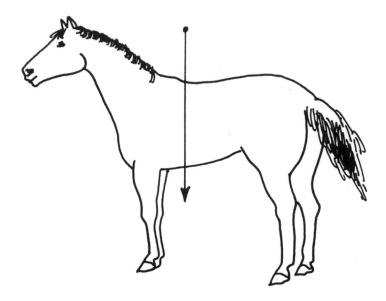

Picture 8. Center of balance of the horse, side view. *The arrow divides the horse into equal halves by total body weight. If the horse were to raise the head and neck, flex the head rearward, or even lower the croup—or do any combination of these three possibilities—the arrow in the diagram would move somewhat rearward.*

Picture 9. Center of balance of the horse, top view. *The line which describes the center of balance of the horse not only divides his length from front to back as in Picture 8, but also divides him from side to side.*

as well as front to back. Picture 9 illustrates the way you would view the tip of the line describing the horse's center of balance, if you were sitting astride the horse and looking down.

Now that you know the location of the center of balance for the horse at rest, I will tell you its significance.

The line describing the center of balance, unevenly divides the horse lengthwise, in terms of distance head to tail. But the division is made so that one-half of his total body weight is in front of this line and the remaining half is behind the line. As the horse begins to move, his anatomical shape begins to change, and his center of balance also begins to shift from the place it occupied as the horse stood motionless. As the moving horse raises his head and neck, his overall body length shortens. His center of balance moves rearward. If at the same time the horse flexes his head just behind the poll, this shortens the body length even more as the head is brought rearward toward the chest. With flexion of the head rearward, the center of balance moves even farther toward the hindquarters. On the other hand, should the horse inadvertently stumble or move the head and neck forward in a long and extended position for any reason, his center of balance will move forward and to the front of its normal position as described for the horse at rest.

The center of balance for any horse constantly changes position as the horse moves. As his head, neck, legs and croup move, the horse's anatomical shape changes. In response to these bodily changes in shape, the center of balance moves forward or backward. As the center of balance moves forward ahead of its position for the resting horse, the horse becomes heavy on the forehand—he supports more of his total weight farther to the front, over the front limbs. On the other hand, when the horse effectively moves his center of balance rearward (by raising the head and neck, flexing the head toward the chest or lowering the croup), he has in effect lightened his forehand. He has moved more of his total body weight to the rear. The rear limbs then support an increased load. As the forehand is lightened, the horse becomes "handier," working more off the hindquarters.

One final point. The rider too may influence the location of the horse's center of balance. When mounted, horse and rider in effect become one

physical system. The horse must bear the burden of the rider by distributing this weight load among his four limbs in some manner. If the rider leans forward, the horse's center of balance moves forward. If the rider leans backward behind the vertical, the horse's center of balance is displaced to the rear. Because the forelegs of the horse are located nearer the saddle than the rear limbs are, a rider is more likely to produce a horse which is heavy on the forehand by leaning forward, than by leaning back to produce a horse which works off his hindquarters.

Forward inclination of the rider's upper body is not always undesirable, by any means. The essence of forward speed, as you will remember, is the efficient loss of balance to the front by the horse. Some overleaning to the front by the rider encourages this loss of balance, very desirable whenever fast forward speeds are required. By comparison, only a relatively small displacement of the horse's center of balance to the rear can be achieved by a rider's inclining his upper body backward, or behind the vertical. In this case, the sacrifice of the rider's position design simply is not warranted by the slight tendency of the horse to lighten his forehand. However, sitting up straight, in conjunction with the horse's efforts to lighten his forehand through some elevation of the head and neck as well as flexion behind the poll, is a worthwhile effort on the rider's part toward encouraging a more centrally balanced horse.

THE SEQUENCE OF LEGS AT THE WALK

The sequence of legs, or succession of hoofbeats, at the walk is diagrammed for you in Picture 10. Envision the horse as moving toward the top of the page as you look at this picture.

At the walk, the horse uses substantial balancing gestures of the head and neck in order to maintain his balance as he moves forward. The balancing gestures of the head and neck are pronounced at the walk because the gait is a lateral one. The legs on one side only of the horse's body support his weight at any one time as he moves forward at the walk—1 and 2 on the right side of his body first, and then 3 and 4 on the left side. You can appreciate the process if you kneel on all fours, and then raise both your right hand and right knee off the floor as you attempt to balance yourself on

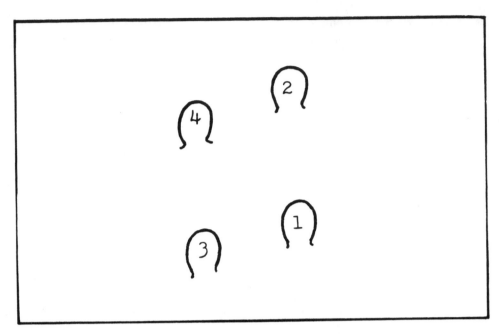

Picture 10. Sequence of legs at the walk. *The walk is a four-beat gait. Each leg is moved forward in the sequence shown by the numbered hoofprint.*

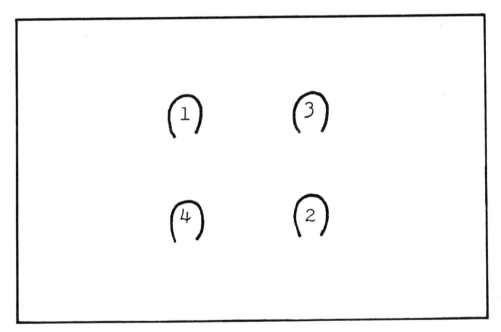

Picture 11. Sequence of legs at the walk. *This is the sequence if you begin counting with the left front foot.*

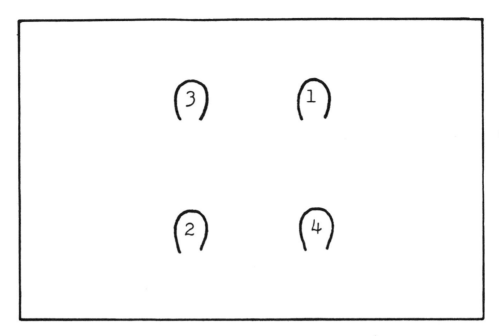

Picture 12. Sequence of legs at the walk. *Here we begin counting with the right front foot.*

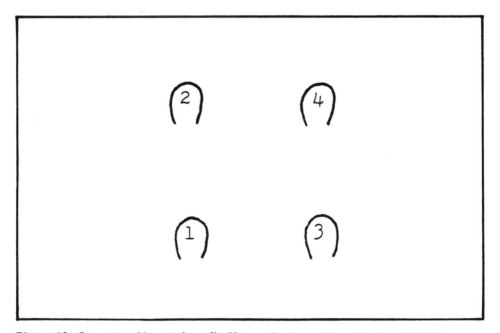

Picture 13. Sequence of legs at the walk. *Here we begin counting with the left hind foot.*

your left hand and left knee alone. If you skip ahead to Picture 25, you can see the lateral nature of the walk.

The walk is really rather complicated. Very often, if we cannot start counting the sequence of legs beginning with the right rear (number 1 in the previous diagram), we become momentarily confused about which leg is next in the sequence. Perhaps this will help: suppose that you wish to start counting the sequence of legs as the horse's left front foot contacts the ground. The sequence is then numbered as shown in Picture 11.

If you wish to recognize the correct sequence of legs at the walk, but start counting as the right front is in contact with the ground, refer to Picture 12.

Finally, if you wish to recognize the correct sequence of legs at the walk, but start counting as the left hindfoot touches with the ground, refer to Picture 13.

In all of these diagrams the sequence of legs has not changed from that shown by the original diagram (Picture 10). If you abbreviate right front as RF, and left rear as LR, and so on, then you will see that the sequence of legs at the walk is always RR, RF, LR, LF, RR, RF, LR, LF, RR, RF, LR and so on.

THE SEQUENCE OF LEGS AT THE TROT

At the trot, the horse uses diagonal pairs of legs to propel himself forward. First, one foreleg and its opposite hindleg are advanced as a pair (both swinging forward at the same instant). As this first pair of legs are grounded and subsequently begin their backward flight, the opposite foreleg and its diagonal hindleg are advanced. The trotting sequence of legs is illustrated by Picture 14.

The use of diagonal pairs of legs in moving forward makes the trot the most stable gait possessed by the horse in terms of maintaining his balance in motion. At all times, the horse moving at the trot literally has a leg on each side of his body to support his weight and catch his balance as he moves. Shifting his weight back and forth or from side to side in order to maintain his balance becomes a minimal requirement at this gait. Because of this stability, the horse has little need to make the balancing gestures of the head and neck which are so prominent at the walk and canter. If you skip ahead to Picture 28, you can see diagonal pairs of legs moving forward at the trot.

The Jog Trot

The mechanics of the jog trot (slow trot) are no different from those of the trot at medium or even very fast speeds. The actual sequence of legs remains the same (diagonal pairs). However, the nature of the stride differs considerably from that at faster speeds of the trot. If you skip ahead to Pictures 26, 28 and 29, you can directly compare the nature of the horse's stride at the jog trot and at medium and faster speeds of the trot. At the jog trot, the forward stride of both the front and back legs is considerably shortened, as you can check by measuring the separation of the hindlegs in Pictures 26, 28 and 29. The slower speeds of the jog also exhibit both a greater flexion or bending of the knees and hock joints, as well as an increased cadence or rhythm of the legs themselves. It is the slow forward speed of the jog trot, along with its rhythm, that makes this gait so comfortable to sit. Regardless of the type of trot, however, the sequence of legs always remains the same; only the length of stride, the flexion of the joints and the cadence differ.

THE SEQUENCE OF LEGS AT THE CANTER

The sequence of legs occurring at each stride of the canter is shown by Picture 15. Note that the canter is a distinct three-beat gait, as opposed to the two-beat gait of the trot and the four-beat gait of the walk.

The hoofprint labeled 1 in Picture 15 represents the leading foreleg at each full stride of the canter. The hoofprint labeled 2 is the outside hind. It is the leg which is diagonally opposite to the leading foreleg. The hoofprints labeled 3 represent the diagonal pair of legs moved forward and backward in unison, just as they move at the trot. The three beats of the canter are as follows: First, the leading foreleg comprises one beat as it is grounded. The second beat occurs when the opposite hind limb is advanced and its foot hits the ground. Finally, the diagonal pair, moving in unison, are advanced and their feet strike the ground at the same instant, in the single third beat of the canter.

The canter possesses both instants of great instability and instants of stability, insofar as the horse's balance in motion is concerned. Great instability, with its accompanying loss of balance to the front, occurs as the leading leg moves under the horse and to the rear. At this moment, the

Picture 14. Sequence of legs at the trot. *The trot is a two-beat gait. The legs are moved forward and backward as diagonal pairs.*

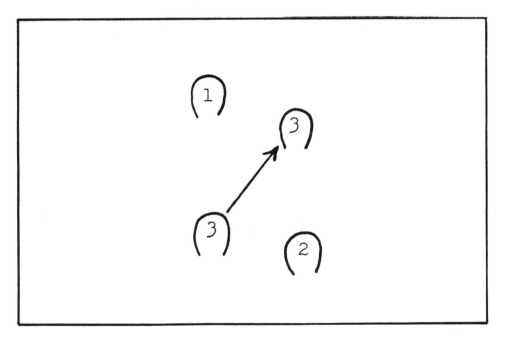

Picture 15. Sequence of legs at the canter. *The sequence of legs at the canter comprises a distinctly three-beat gait. The leading leg and its opposite hind limb are advanced. They hit the ground independently, at different moments. The opposite foreleg and its diagonal hind limb are then advanced and contact the ground at the same instant—a diagonal pair of legs used in the same manner as at the trot.*

horse must support his entire weight on this limb. For a fraction of a second, this is the only limb actually touching the ground. The horse must literally balance himself on this one limb as the entire mass of his body continues to travel forward and over this leading leg. On the other hand, as the diagonal pair is advanced forward and backward, a moment of very good stability is provided for the horse as a leg on both the right and left side of the horse provides support.

The stability afforded by the hindleg opposite the leading foreleg is on the order of the leading leg itself. This hind limb (hoofprint 2) momentarily balances the entire weight of the horse, also. For an instant during each stride at the canter, it becomes (like the leading leg at a different instant) the only leg whose foot is in contact with the ground.

While the mechanical sequence of legs at the canter cannot actually change, some riders prefer to assign the following numbers to the succession of beats (Picture 16). They prefer to start counting as the outside hindleg is grounded, rather than as the leading foreleg is grounded (and for good reason, as you will see later).

The Lope

The mechanics of the lope (slow canter) are no different from those of any other speed at the canter. The sequence of legs remains the same. At the lope, however, the forward stride of all legs is considerably shortened, and a slower rhythm or cadence is established. The balancing gestures of the head and neck are usually increased over those at faster speeds at this same gait. This increase in balancing gestures can be directly attributed to the fact that the forward speed is slow: the horse must balance himself upon one leg (the leading leg and the outside hind alternately) for longer periods of time. Whenever the forward speed of the lope becomes too slow, the canter will degenerate into a four-beat gait, not really a canter at all.

THE SEQUENCE OF LEGS AT THE GALLOP

The gallop is not a fast canter; the mechanics of producing it are not the same. The gallop is a distinct four-beat gait, while the canter produces only three beats. The sequence of legs at the gallop are shown by Picture 17.

As the horse increased speed at the canter and assumes the gallop, the normal cantering sequence of legs becomes slightly out of sequence. The diagonal pair of legs at the canter become unsynchronized as speed increases; they begin to strike and leave the ground at slightly different times, the hindleg striking first and the opposite foreleg later. Thus, the four distinct beats of the gallop occur.

THE SEQUENCE OF LEGS DURING BACKING

I will often use the term *rein back*, both here and later in the book, to signify a horse's backing up. The correct sequence of legs for the horse executing the rein back is shown by Picture 18. The horse uses diagonal pairs of legs in order to back properly. Although the direction of movement is obviously different for the trot and the rein back, the sequence of legs is actually the same. The horse should use diagonal pairs of legs in backing, just as he does in trotting forward. The horse which only walks backward one leg at a time is executing a rein back of poor quality. The use of diagonal pairs is considered the better movement. Simply walking backward is generally seen in young, lazy or resistive horses.

IMPORTANCE OF KNOWING THE SEQUENCE OF LEGS

Although this is not a "how to" chapter, you should recognize some specific things about riding, schooling and teaching as they relate to the sequence of legs at the various gaits.

The Walk

At the walk, the sequence of legs becomes important for you to understand if you are to

1. teach the horse the rollback from the walk efficiently, without placing the horse in a disadvantaged position from which to learn this movement (such as asking for a rollback to the left when in fact the left rear foot is off the ground or behind the horse).
2. obtain square halts.
3. ask for a canter on the correct lead, reliably.
4. lengthen the stride at the walk.

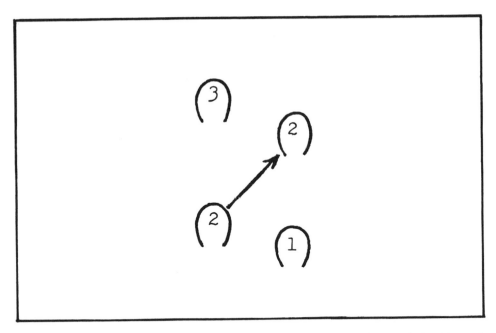

Picture 16. Sequence of legs at the canter. *Here numbering begins with the right hind leg and the leading leg (the left foreleg) is numbered 3.*

Picture 17. Sequence of legs at the gallop. *The gallop is a four-beat gait. Each leg of the diagonal pair of legs at the canter actually strikes, and then leaves, the ground at a slightly different time.*

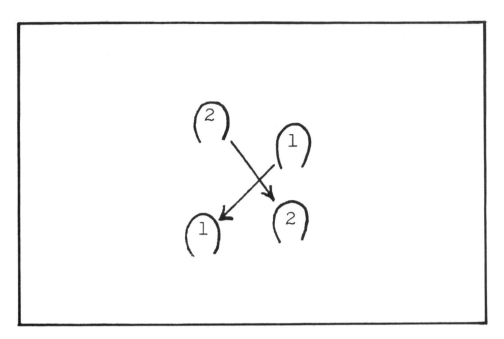

Picture 18. Sequence of legs during backing. *The horse should use diagonal pairs of legs when backing. In essence, he trots backward.*

The Trot

At the trot, knowing the sequence of legs becomes important if you are to

1. understand something of the stability of this gait, and the relative absence of the balancing gestures as the trot is executed.
2. understand why you should *not* school the horse for a rollback from the trot.

The Canter

At the canter, knowing the sequence of legs becomes important if you are to

1. teach the horse the rollback from the canter efficiently, without placing him in a disadvantaged position from which to learn and perform the movement.
2. determine the correct lead as the horse canters away after performing the rollback.
3. teach a reliable flying change of leads.
4. add greater promptness and smoothness to every canter departure.

At this point you need only understand that the sequence of legs may be important to you. Later,

in the chapters on schooling and primarily Chapter 7 which deals with schooling at the intermediate level, you will begin to understand why it is important to use your own legs or hands at very specific points within the horse's sequence of legs at the different gaits. If you teach, I believe that it is merely a matter of good teaching to inform your students as to the sequence of legs at the different gaits. If you are not completely satisfied with your understanding of the sequence of legs at the various gaits, take the time to stand at the rail and watch horses moving at the walk, trot, canter and rein back. Later, ride and concentrate upon the position of the horse's legs underneath you as you move at each of the gaits.

THE INFLEXIBILITY OF THE BACK

The horse's back is incapable of any degree of bending to the side which might prove useful in turning or circling. The back is a rigid structure designed to support the mass of the chest, abdomen and pelvic cavity. While the neck and tail of the horse are capable of bending to the side, the back is not. Many good riding instructors, including those who have updated their thinking on this point, still speak of "bending the horse around the rider's leg." Such phrases, while representing something which is actually a physical impossibility for both horse and rider, do serve a useful purpose in the riding classroom.

Suzanne Norton Jones writes in her excellent book, *The Art of Western Riding,* that "The ability of a horse to bend properly to the circle is vital for changing leads and for the rollback, for barrel racing, and for cutting and roping in the arena or on the range." In his dressage book, *Creative Horsemanship,* Charles de Kunffy concludes that "the systematic, consistent and logical gymnastisizing of a horse is also called dressage. . . . These exercises are designed to increase the horse's ability to bend longitudinally [lengthwise] and laterally [to the side]."

Both of these authors have a long list of credits and many hours in the saddle riding and schooling. Jones is a western rider, while de Kunffy is a classical rider. Both are educators, exhibitors, clinicians and respected judges in their fields. What, then, is the problem with our thinking? Why do so many of us refer to the bending of the horse, as if the back bends as well as the neck? Whenever a noted authority such as Jones or de Kunffy or one of scores of others equally well qualified refers to bending the horse, we tend to imagine the horse's back actually bending to the side, which is literally quite impossible.

Perhaps the problem is this. All of us seemingly have participated in, or at least perpetuated in our language and writing, what V. S. Littauer deemed a "mass hypnosis." We see, or at least express in words, what does not really exist.

As R. H. Smythe, an English veterinarian of the Royal College of Veterinarians, has explained, "The horse has an almost rigid spine, incapable of any useful degree of bending." I have personally dissected several horses and have also studied the vertebral column in the laboratory, with and without its muscles and ligaments attached. I have found the following to be true:

1. The horse's neck is flexible. It is perfectly capable of bending from side to side.
2. The horse's back is largely inflexible.
    a. However, a small degree of side-to-side flexibility may be present around the twelfth and thirteenth thoracic vertebrae, a location far to the rear of the rider's normal leg position.
    b. A somewhat larger degree of flexibility in the vertebral column probably exists at the sacroiliac junction—the junction of the last lumbar vertebra and sacrum, the area just ahead of the croup. However, this flexibility is primarily up and down rather than side to side. I don't believe that it assists the horse at all in bending around obstacles, turns or circles.
3. The horse's tail is flexible from side to side, but this, of course, is a small point.
4. While the ribs of the horse do in fact move backward and forward as well as outward and upward, during normal breathing, a rider cannot possibly hope to bend the ribs inward with pressure from his own legs. Even if the horse were to cooperate by standing still and permitting the rider to apply maximum pressure with either of his legs, the ribs simply could not be pushed inward. Neither would any bending of the horse's barrel around the rider's leg occur by the physical efforts of the rider or by the physical and mental cooperation of the horse.

Moving on the Line

Should you then discard "bending" exercises because they simply cannot help us to achieve the goal of bending the horse's body and his back? Not at all. Simply stop trying to teach the horse to bend around your leg. Instead, teach the horse the most ideal way, the most efficient way, in which to move along the arc of a circle or turn. This ideal, and physically possible movement is termed *moving on the line.* Moving on the line, detailed in Chapter 4, requires that the horse look in the direction of his turns and that his hindfeet travel along the same path described by the front feet. The horse bends his neck in the direction of the turn to be made, and at the same time he neither allows the shoulders to pop inward nor allows the haunches to skid inward or outward along the arc of the turn.

Picture 19 illustrates the areas of the spinal column which have been discussed and shows those limited areas of the back where some small

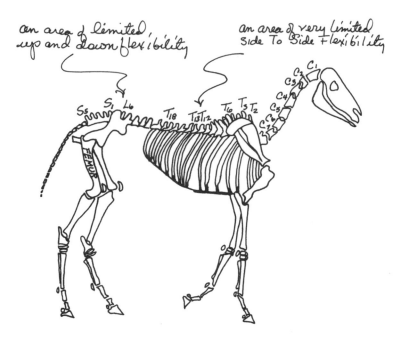

Picture 19. The skeleton of the horse.

degree of flexibility exists. Please note that any areas of the back which possess the potential for flexibility are quite far to the rear of the rider's normal leg position. In this illustration the vertebrae are numbered. Those of the neck are preceded with a capital letter C for *cervical* vertebrae). Those of the back carry the letters T, L and S (for *thoracic, lumbar* and *sacral* vertebrae, respectively).

Pictures 20 and 21 show a horse moving in two different circular patterns. As you can see, the back is not bending.

TURNING QUICKLY AT FAST FORWARD SPEEDS

The primary concern here is horses that must make sharp turns or circles at fast speeds: barrel racers, pole benders, roping horses and, to a lesser extent, reining and cutting horses and those worked outdoors on cattle.

Look at Picture 20 of a rather nice barrel-racing horse during a tight turn at high speed. It is obvious that the horse's back has not undergone any bending in order to negotiate the turn. However, you see a sizable lean to the inside of the turn. It is

this very substantial leaning, and not any bending of the back, which permits the horse to negotiate a high speed turn with success. Leaning is the key to sharp, fast turns. In this same picture, also note that the horse's inside leg is shortened due to the flexing or bending of the knee joint. The outside leg, on the other hand, is maintained in a straight, or extended, attitude. Because of this lopsided arrangement of the legs, the horse's weight falls inward and toward the shorter of the two legs at this instant. Thanks to this leaning, the turn can be accomplished successfully without any bending of the horse's back.

Another facet of turning and one which is not so obvious photographically, or even to an observer, is the rotation of the chest downward and away from the actual direction of the turn. The front limbs of the horse have no actual bony attachment to the sides of the chest. The shoulder blades, or scapuli, are merely attached to the sides of the body by soft tissue structures. This particular tissue, strong enough to hold the limbs in place against the sides of the chest, has a good deal of give and take. The elasticity of this tissue permits the barrel of the horse to actually rotate between the two front limbs. During sharp turns, particularly when they are performed at high speeds,

Picture 20. Turning at high speed.

Picture 21. Inflexibility of the horse's back while turning. *Although the saddle constitutes a visual obstacle of sorts, it is apparent that the horse's back does not bend during a turn.*

the entire barrel of the horse undergoes considerable rotation. As you view this rotation from astride the horse while turning sharply, the horse's barrel rotates counterclockwise during left turns and clockwise during right turns.

As the barrel of the horse rotates between the front limbs, its direction of rotation is downward and toward the outside of the turn. Considerable force, due simply to the weight of the horse's chest and barrel, is directed downward and toward the ground. The ground surface, in turn, imparts a force directed upward and against the direction in which the chest is rotating (Picture 22). It is this upward force, pushing against the soles of the horse's feet, which tends to stabilize him, preventing him from slipping as the turn is made. As the horse leans sharply in the direction of the turn the reaction of the ground surface against the soles of his feet permits him to accelerate around a sharp turn without slipping and falling on his side.

These mechanical considerations related to turning sharply are the same for any turn or circle, even those performed along the arc of a very wide turn or large circle, and even if the horse's speed is rather slow. In these cases, of course, the leaning and the rotation of the chest go relatively unnoticed.

Those of you interested in learning more about how the chest is suspended between the two front limbs should consult any good equine anatomy text. The most complete text to my knowledge is the *Anatomy of Domestic Animals* by Sisson and Grossman, published by W. B. Saunders. Also, if you would care to know more about the properties of circular motion, any good noncalculus physics text should meet your needs. The relevant portions of the text will be those dealing with centripetal and centrifugal accelerations and forces and with friction.

FORWARD SPEED

For purposes of riding and schooling the western horse, there are three primary influences on forward speed:

1. The ground surface over which the horse moves
2. The anatomy of the horse's body, his weight distribution and his ability to lose or prevent the loss of his balance to the front
3. The position of the rider astride the horse

An understanding of these three influences will not only contribute to your education as a rider,

Picture 22. The mechanism of stability during high-speed turns. *(A) Rotation of the chest; (B) force transmitted down through the grounded limb; (C) opposing force of ground surface against this limb.*

but will also allow you to school your speed horses and your pleasure horses more effectively.

Influence of the Ground Surface

We usually think of the muscular efforts of the horse's limbs, coupled with their directional movements backward against the ground surface, as the way in which forward movement and speed are produced. We recognize that the rear limbs are the primary source of propulsion, but of course, we should also recognize that the front limbs make their own small contribution to producing forward speed. Most horsemen correctly place their emphasis upon the hindlegs as the largest contributors to forward speed, but they recognize the front limbs as also playing a role. For example, most race horses are shod with toe grabs on the front and back shoes.

The limbs are a crucial but not the only factor in producing forward motion. In order for the horse to move forward at any speed, the ground surface itself must literally exert a force forward and against the soles of the horse's feet. This force opposes the backward movement of the limbs and feet against the ground. Imparted by the ground surface against the soles of the feet, it is just as responsible for propelling the horse forward as are the muscular and directional movements of the limbs themselves. The name given to this propulsive force—an inherent property of the ground itself—is the force of *friction*.

Frictional force, coupled with the horse's own muscular efforts, enables him to move forward and at very fast speeds. Without both of these elements forward movement is impossible. The propulsive nature of the ground's frictional force is shown in Picture 23.

Different types of bearing surfaces possess different degrees of push. Think of the tremendous muscular efforts that a horse might make as he attempts to move forward across a very slick and frozen lake bed. He might well expend the effort required to run a good race or even to set a new track speed record, but still he would be unable to move forward effectively—he might be unable to move forward at all. The missing ingredient here is the sufficient frictional force to provide a forward push.

Every year race horse trainers and enthusiasts travel thousands of miles with their racing stock and spend large sums of money, attempting to find a "fast" track—one on which their horses will be able to run a fast AAA or TAAA speed. When the particular track finally materializes, the horse is actually capable of running no faster than he could previously, but he now turns in a faster race simply because the surface of this track is different from those on which he had run before. The "fast" track possesses a greater frictional force in its surface composition than the "slow" tracks on which he had been competing.

Reining classes are won and lost on the quality of the horse's sliding stop—again, a matter of frictional force (schooling aside for the moment). Horses entered in reining classes are usually meticulously shod with sliding plates on their hind feet in an effort to assist them in manipulating (to their advantage) the frictional forces of the surfaces on which they compete. Arena surfaces are composed of different materials or varying percentages of the same materials. Therefore, frictional forces vary from arena to arena. This is seen in the increased or decreased sliding distance for the same horse (putting in the same effort) as he moves from arena to arena during the show season.

Remember the discussion of turning sharply at high speed. The barrel racer was able to turn the barrel, and even to accelerate as he did so, without great likelihood of slipping. As the horse's chest rotated downward and toward the ground, the ground itself pushed against the soles of the horse's feet, providing a stable base of support in order to prevent slippage—a matter of frictional force again.

You will not receive a blue ribbon or trophy just for understanding how forward motion is produced, but you will get a certain intuitive feel for what is occurring beneath you as you ride. Some understanding of the facts which govern how forward motion is produced is simply a matter of educated riding. If you teach, the whole matter can take on an even greater significance, one that directly relates to how qualified you are to teach, particularly at the higher levels of riding.

Anatomy, Weight Distribution and Loss of Balance

As the horse raises his head and neck and perhaps flexes his head back toward his chest, he effectively alters his anatomical shape. In doing so

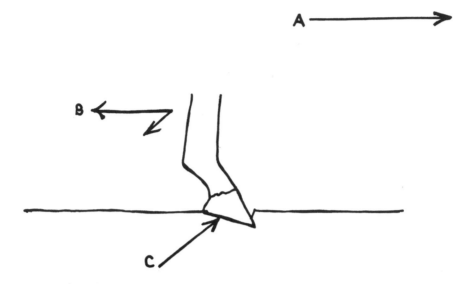

Picture 23. Forces producing forward speed. *Pushing against the ground with the limbs is useless in propelling the horse forward unless the surface over which he travels possesses sufficient frictional force to permit him to move forward. (A) Direction of the horse's forward movement; (B) directional movement of the limb backward and against the ground surface; (C) direction in which the force of friction is applied in response to the directional movement of the limb backward and against the ground's surface: a force responsible for propelling the horse forward.*

he shifts his weight rearward, moving his center of balance. The back legs bear increasingly more weight than the front legs. Faster forward speeds become more difficult for the horse to achieve. He cannot efficiently lose his balance to the front: slower forward speeds naturally result. (Incline your own upper body rearward and try to walk forward. You will find it is difficult to walk with any substantial speed.)

As the horse lowers the head and neck and extends his head forward, he alters his anatomical shape again. In this case he shifts his weight forward, altering his center of balance. The front legs bear increasingly more weight, the rear legs less. With this anatomical arrangement, the horse redistributes his weight to the front, and faster forward speeds are readily achieved. With his weight moved forward, he can now efficiently lose his balance to the front. Efficient loss of balance to the front is a prime consideration in producing rapid forward speed.

In order for a horse to move forward at fast speeds at any gait, the forehand must be weighted efficiently by both the horse (primarily through lowering and extending the head and neck) and by the rider (by the forward inclination of the rider's upper body). To produce slow forward speeds at any gait, just the opposite is true. Slow forward gaits with some energy about them are produced by weighting the hindquarters efficiently—by some elevation of the head and neck, flexion at the poll (bringing the horse's head back toward the vertical) and even a lowered croup, if the horse is executing a particularly high-level movement (see Picture 182).

Position of the Rider

The effective rider, whether assisting the horse to move at fast or slow speeds, adjusts his position to best suit the type of forward speed desired. The jockey leans forward to assist the horse in the efficient loss of his balance to the front. The dressage rider sits back and toward the vertical to assist the horse in moving his center of balance to the rear, to assist the horse in maintaining slow but energetic forward speed by preventing the efficient loss of balance to the front. Regardless of whether you ever ride either of these two types of horses, the same principles relating to the rider's position still apply. Even if you lean to the front or rear, the horse himself must still make appropriate adjustments in his anatomical shape to temporarily permit him to increase or decrease his speed efficiently. The rider, using his reins, legs and weight, can help the horse alter his frame in such a way as to promote faster or slower speeds. The riding techniques involved are discussed in several later chapters.

To understand the role of the rider's position in forward speed, you must recognize a fundamental physical law:

The force of friction which acts to propel the horse forward is directly dependent upon the weight borne between the two surfaces in contact. The horse's feet (soles and frogs) and the ground surface itself.

This really means that if you lean forward, adding weight to the horse's front limbs, they will be capable of better pushing to obtain faster forward speeds. If you lean backward, the back limbs will be weighted more, and in turn they, rather than the front limbs, will be capable of better pushing to attain fast forward speeds. Now, think about the jockey's position and that of the dressage rider in relation to the type of speed desired by each. You will note what seems to be a paradox. The hind limbs are the primary driving limbs, and they are the greatest contributors to forward speed. Why doesn't the jockey then lean to the rear to more effectively weight the hind limbs— the primary driving limbs? Why does the dressage rider attempt to weight the back limbs by inclining his upper body rearward? Wouldn't it make more sense to lean forward to unburden the rear limbs so that the force of friction on the rear feet would be minimized?

The answer is this. The dressage rider's position supports the horse's own anatomical efforts: the rider's upper body is inclined somewhat rearward, while the horse elevates his head and neck, flexes at the poll and distributes his weight toward the hindquarters. True, this type of increased weighting of the hind limbs does make them more efficient at pushing, and you would at first think that faster, rather than slower, forward speeds should result. But remember that if the hind limbs are weighted more effectively, the front limbs are

less effectively weighted. This unweighting of the front legs, or lightening of the forehand, results in inefficient pushing and an inefficient forward movement of the front limbs. Certainly the hindquarters cannot travel forward any faster than the front of the horse can. It is the inefficient, slow movement of the front limbs and not the increased pushing ability of the hind limbs which results in slow forward speeds for the dressage horse.

As for the position of a jockey, he or she leans forward in an effort to encourage the most efficient loss of balance to the front by the horse. By leaning forward he helps the horse to lose his balance to the front, while at the same time weighting the forelimbs a little more in order that they can push more efficiently than they normally might. All the while, the horse himself continually raises and lowers his head and neck to achieve the best compromise between weighting the hind limbs for efficient pushing and weighting the front limbs for a better, more rapid, loss of balance to the front.

Look at Table I. Consider what would be the appropriate position of your upper body in relation to each type of gait or movement listed—forward or more toward the vertical. To make the point even clearer apply a particular performance event to each of the gaits or events listed, and consider how you would use your body position to weight or unweight the forehand for a slower or faster speed.

TABLE I
SPEEDS AT THE VARIOUS GAITS

Ordinary walk	4–6 *miles per hour*
Jog trot	4–6 *miles per hour*
Ordinary trot	8 *miles per hour*
Lope	7–8 *miles per hour*
Ordinary canter	10–12 *miles per hour*
Semicollected walk	3–4 *miles per hour*
Semicollected trot	4–6 *miles per hour*
Semicollected canter	6–8 *miles per hour*
Fully collected walk	2–3 *miles per hour*
Fully collected trot	0–4 *miles per hour*
Fully collected canter	5–6 *miles per hour*
Pole bending (21-foot spacing)	16 *miles per hour* (average start to finish)
Reining horse (gallop to end of arena)	18–22 *miles per hour*
Western speed horse (330 yards)	35 *miles per hour*
Thoroughbred racer	30 *miles per hour plus*
Barrel racer	16 *miles per hour* (average start to finish)

WHY ONE HORSE IS FASTER
THAN ANOTHER

If the ground provides the push, or frictional force, necessary for forward motion, then why can one horse run faster than another over the same surface? And how can this occur if both horses weigh the same, and are ridden by riders of similar weights and abilities? Some possible answers are:

1. One horse may tire more easily than another, for any number of reasons.
2. Different horses have different forward ranges of movement in both the femur (thigh bone) and scapula (shoulder blade).
3. One horse may possess better natural balance and agility than another, perhaps because of an inherited characteristic of the inner ear (responsible for balance) or of the nerve conduction paths from the inner ear to the brain (where the state of balance is actually interpreted).
4. Different horses may have different mental attitudes toward actually achieving very fast forward speeds. One horse may actually dislike the necessary rapid loss of balance which must always accompany very rapid speed.
5. At the gallop, longer and shorter periods of suspension, when no leg is in contact with the ground, can be measured for different horses.
6. Different horses inherit different bone lengths, and slightly different patterns of muscling.

You and I could probably think of fifty more reasons why one horse might be faster than another despite similar frictional forces, anatomical arrangements of the horse's body, weight distribution, efficient loss of balance to the front, and rider's position astride the horse.

Do not become concerned at this point that you do not know all of the specific areas in which this chapter's information might be applied. I will tell you where and how to apply this information as you continue to read. If you will only mentally file away this chapter's contents, or at least remember where to look up these ideas again, specific applications will be discussed soon enough in the following chapters.

Perhaps at several points within this chapter, you have asked yourself: "Well, all of this is his *opinion,* but how do I know if any of it is actually true?" Let me state my own case for my opinions. They are based in part on:

1. Observing hundreds of riding, schooling, and teaching sessions. (Actually, *thousands* would be more correct.)
2. A considerable amount of research dealing with the mechanics of motion of the horse. A sizable portion of this has been original investigation rather than reliance upon existing opinion right or wrong.
3. The close study of hundreds of photographs and films of moving horses.
4. Appreciating, as a veterinarian, what was likely to be occurring within each horse as he moved forward.
5. A very strong background in the physical sciences and mathematics, as well as veterinary training relating to the musculo-skeletal system of the horse.
6. Hundreds of hours of riding and schooling specifically to bear out or disprove what I felt was probably occurring beneath me as I rode, and as I observed others riding.

I believe that the information I can offer you will be of very practical value if you wish to be better at whatever you do with horses. If you do not understand the mechanics of motion of the horse, you will only be truly successful in the show ring providing that your competition remains equally uninformed. In other words, you can be much better at what you do whenever you begin to apply a knowledge of how and why the horse moves to your riding, schooling or teaching.

Do not excuse yourself from applying this information to your riding because you are too young or too old, too short or too tall, an amateur and not a professional, or for any other reason. Be bold enough to observe the physical nature of motion and to apply what you learn to the problems of the horses you ride, school, show or teach from. Solve your riding or schooling problems based upon your knowledge of the known properties of motion of the horse. Your knowledge will be enhanced as you read about position in Chapter 2 and control in Chapter 3.

Chapter 2

POSITION

This chapter describes the rider's position astride the horse: first, in terms of a correct design of position (how the rider arranges his or her anatomy while mounted) and second, in terms of a good functional position (how to obtain the best performance from a horse by allowing the rider's position to work efficiently in coordination with the horse's efforts).

Position is vitally important for anyone who wishes to ride well; for anyone already riding well, position is the key to riding even better. In order to school horses or to show successfully in classes requiring more than just slow, passive gaits along the rail, you **must** ride very well. The level to which you can **finally** school any horse is a direct reflection of your riding ability, and the lack of a good working position will hinder your ability to ride at the highest level to which you may aspire. Successful teaching begins when an instructor can effectively teach the elements of a good functional position to each student and explain to the student why each element of this position is important to improved riding.

A good position is just as important to the experienced rider as it is to the beginner. Much of the fixing often requested by experienced riders requires rearranging their position (which has deteriorated or been lost over many years of riding, schooling and showing) in order to make it not only pretty again, but also to make it more functional. For the experienced rider, increased success in the show ring most frequently means improving one's position astride the horse, rather than merely trying to acquire bigger, faster or more highly bred horses.

If you cannot ride effectively, you cannot possibly school the green horse correctly or efficiently. I believe that a good working position is the base of all correct and efficient schooling, along with experience in schooling many different horses. There is no design of position just for the beginning rider, or one just for the more advanced rider. There exists one correct position design for every rider in each situation. The beginner tries to learn it, and the more experienced rider simply tries to maintain and refine it.

Whenever we speak of a rider as having a good working position, we are really talking about *all* of the elements which comprise this good position. There is much more involved than merely the way in which the rider arranges or designs his anatomy while astride the horse. In this case we are talking about all of the *physical characteristics of a good working position:*

1. correct design of position
2. correct weight distribution
3. balance
4. rhythm
5. spring
6. grip
7. relaxation

These seven characteristics of a good position were first identified and formally taught by V. S. Littauer, who later wrote about them in his *Commonsense Horsemanship.* This book deals with English riders and riding, but don't be misled. It is really only the rider's design of position astride the horse (point 1) which is different for western and English riders; the remaining physical characteristics of a good position—balance, rhythm, spring, relaxation and so forth—are just as applicable to one as they are to the other. When the western rider begins competing in high performance events and the English rider ceases to ride cross-country and begins to concentrate on schooling horses on the flat, the two different designs of position begin to become quite similar, more so than either rider might be readily inclined to admit.

WHAT IS STOCK SEAT?

Very often you will find people referring to position design as the rider's "seat." Too much emphasis is placed upon this term; riding involves schooling, showing and teaching. The seat is only a part of all of this. There are many names given to the various seats: forward seat, balanced seat, dressage seat, stock seat and so forth. The name is of little importance as long as the rider and his horse can remain in balance with each other and the task at hand can be completed efficiently, with the best performance possible from horse and rider. The balanced seat, for example, does not imply that the other seats are out of balance; nor does the forward seat imply that the rider always leans forward. Similarly, the stock or western seat is not appropriate only to one type of horse. The seat to be used depends upon how the horse moves forward.

When we look at the western or stock seat, we find not one, but two different seats. The use of one over the other really depends upon how the horse is required to move: in western pleasure classes as opposed to barrel racing, for example. The better western pleasure riders use a seat very similar to that of the better dressage riders. The stirrup is long (below the rider's anklebone), and the rider's lower leg is under the body while the torso is carried erect and near the vertical. These riders are effectively in balance with their horses and with the forward rate of speed. On the other hand, the performance horse rider, a barrel racer for instance, generally adopts a more forward seat because the horse is being asked to move at fast forward speeds as a forward-balanced horse. In this case, the rider's upper body is inclined forward to more efficiently assist the horse in losing his balance to the front, and this inclination varies continually as the horse necessarily increases and decreases his own forward speed. Also, the rider's lower leg is underneath his body, not shoved forward or allowed to drift backward, so that his weight is best supported and that his leg can most effectively aid the horse in his efforts to beat the clock. Additionally, the stirrup is usually raised to about the level of the anklebone in order to increase the spring in the rider's legs. You can tell which riders haven't shortened their stirrups: they're the ones bouncing the highest out of the

saddle as they halt their horses just over the finish line.

A combination of the two western seats produces the most efficient performance in some classes. Consider the position of the rider on a reining horse or a horse worked on cattle as a good illustration of this combination of seats. The specific points relating to the correct design of position for both of the seats employed by western riders are described below.

CORRECT DESIGN OF POSITION

Shoulder, Hip, Heel Line

At the halt or at the very slow forward gaits, one should be able to pass an imaginary line straight down along the rider's body in such a way that it passes through the shoulder, hip and back of the heel. If this line is not straight and vertical, something is wrong with the rider's best design of position. He or she may have the torso inclined too far back, may be sitting too far back in the saddle with a rounded lower back or may have legs either pushed forward or pulled back toward the saddle cantle. A straight line from shoulder to hip to heel is the ideal at the halt and at the slow forward gaits. This ideal is illustrated for you in Pictures 24, 25, 26 and 27: at the halt, walk, jog trot and lope.

At the faster gaits, the shoulder-hip-heel line no longer applies in order for the rider to maintain a correct design of position. At these faster forward speeds, the rider must necessarily incline his or her upper body forward in order to remain in balance with the horse. Pictures 28, 29, 30 and 31 illustrate the rider's correct design of position at each of these gaits. As you look at these pictures, please note that in each case the rider's leg is situated underneath the upper body in order that the rider can support his or her weight without gripping and without struggling to maintain the proper upper body position.

Head and Eyes

The rider should carry his head and chin up and look ahead. There are two basic reasons for this. First, the average human head is heavy enough to have a considerable influence over the balance of the rider's torso. Whenever the rider drops the chin or looks down (as opposed to merely glancing

Picture 24. Rider's position at the halt.

Picture 25. Rider's position at the walk.

Picture 26. Rider's position at the jog trot.

Picture 27. Rider's position at the lope. *After the leading leg touches down, the next leg of the horse to be advanced and grounded will be the right rear. Then the left rear and right front will begin to advance simultaneously as a diagonal pair of legs. At this point the rider will be sitting even deeper in the saddle.*

Picture 28. Rider's position at the ordinary trot. *The rider's leg has drifted a little too far back, because she has allowed some of the weight to come out of her heels.*

Picture 29. Rider's position at the fast trot. *Although this rider can very capably sit the extended trot, she is appropriately in the standing position. This is a true extended trot: the horse has lengthened his stride without measurably increasing his forward speed over that for the ordinary trot (shown in Picture 28).*

Picture 30. Rider's position at the ordinary canter. *Note the very good depth in her heels. The rider's arm is relaxed and thus capable of smoothly following the balancing gestures of the horse's head and neck.*

Picture 31. Rider's position at the gallop. *The rider is in the standing position; the forward inclination of her torso permits her to be in balance with horse's forward motion.*

down with the eyes), the shoulders tend to become rounded making the upper body fall forward.

Also, when the rider looks in the direction the horse is being asked to move, circles and turns become more precise and accurate. Looking ahead in conjunction with leg and weight aids encourages the horse to move on the line. This applies to working the horse in a straight line, as well as on circles or variations of them. For example, when barrels or poles are run, performances will be improved and times will be faster if the rider looks where he or she is headed.

Shoulders and Torso

The rider's torso should be carried vertically while the horse is at a standstill, or when he is moving at the walk, jog or lope. At the faster speeds of the trot and canter, as well as at the gallop, the rider's body must be inclined forward to whatever degree is required to remain in balance with the horse. Generally, the faster the speed, the more forward-balanced the horse and thus the greater the forward inclination of the rider's upper body. You may wish to again look at Pictures 24 through 31. The rider's lower back should remain slightly arched with the shoulders back and the chest out, regardless of whether the rider is seated vertically or has leaned forward. When you incline the torso forward, remember that in order for your lower leg to stay underneath your body where it belongs, you will have to push your seat toward the rear of the saddle. This movement is very much like that of a duck about to shake the water from its tail feathers. If you are in a standing position with your torso inclined forward, not only will you have to make a conscious effort to push your seat to the rear and arch your back, but you may also have to move your leg slightly forward. If you assume a standing position at the halt, you can determine the extent to which the lower leg must be moved forward to support the upper body as you lean progressively forward with your back arched and your eyes up.

Your shoulders should be square when you are riding in a straight line. One shoulder should not lead or be ahead of the other. On circles and turns, especially as these become small or tight, one of your shoulders will naturally lead the other as you turn the horse with your rein hand. You should, however, minimize this as much as possible. Each time that you lead with a shoulder, the horse perceives additional weighting of his back in the direction of the turn. To a point this is good—a perfectly logical and correct use of the rider's weight aid in encouraging the horse to prepare for a circle or turn. However, if you lead excessively with your rein hand and shoulder, too much weighting in the direction of the turn may result. The horse may fall too much to the inside of the circle with his forehand.

Arms and Hands

If you ride with one hand, using loose reins, your upper arm should rest comfortably just ahead of your chest. The forearm should be relaxed and extended toward the horse's head. The wrist should be straight and in the same line as the angle formed between the elbow and hand, except when it is cocked slightly upwards to check the horse's forward movement with the reins. The rein hand should be carried at about the same level as the horn and just in front of it. Look at the position of the arm and hand in Picture 27.

Whether riding with one hand or two, it is important to keep your hands relaxed as you ride. Whenever your fingers are tense, the wrists and muscles of the forearm also become tight. If the wrists are stiffened, neck reining becomes less precise. For example, to turn right using neck reins, the rider moves his wrist and forearm to the right. If the wrist is stiff, it simply will not bend easily. The movement of the wrist will either be jerky or too slow in giving a definite aid to the horse with the rein. In addition, with the muscles of the forearm stiffened, the elbow and shoulder are affected, and the arms cannot follow the balancing gestures of the horse's head and neck whenever this is necessary. So you see that stiffening the fingers alone causes widespread side effects in the use of the reins. You may, in fact, squeeze with the thumb as hard as you wish in order to maintain a firm hold on the reins. Squeezing hard with the thumb only does not create nearly as much tension as does tightening all four fingers. Light, non-squeezing fingers produce the softest rein aids as well as more efficient following with the hands and arms. The thumbs are primarily used to provide security in holding the reins, to prevent dropping or losing them.

Following the Balancing Gestures with One Hand

As you will recall from Chapter 1, one way in which a horse balances himself is by moving his head and neck up and down. There are many different circumstances in which a rider likes to allow the horse to use his head and neck freely as a balancer and to do this, the rider must understand how and when to *follow*. The rider should follow the balancing gestures at the walk and canter by extending the forearm forward (opening the elbow joint) as the horse's head and neck are moved downward. As the head and neck are raised, the rider's arm retreats back, toward his body (closing the elbow joint). In order to follow softly and efficiently, the elbow and shoulder must be relaxed enough to move freely. If the arm is relaxed and the rider is following in rhythm with the horse's head and neck movements, constant bumping of the horse's mouth can be avoided (especially necessary when the rider must hold the reins quite short).

If the rider's arm and hand are placed correctly in front of him and the rein length is very long, following will not be necessary in order to prevent abusing the horse's mouth. However, for performance events that call for speed, the balancing gestures of the horse must be preserved in order for him to gain the best balance, speed and agility. The rider must therefore follow the balancing gestures. The reins in this case, even though technically they may still be viewed as loose, must be short enough to permit the rider to exercise quick and definite control over the horse. The rider must follow in order not to resist the horse's efforts to move forward, and to avoid unintentional abuse of the horse's mouth or nose (if a hackamore or bosal is used). If in competing in speed events you ride with reins so long that following is unnecessary, I would say your reins are suicide length, and of course, your control of the horse will suffer considerably.

For most western pleasure horses, following is not necessary. The Texas-style horse is ridden on *very* loose reins; there is little chance that he will be bumped in the mouth. The California-style horse, on the other hand, is ridden on very short reins, literally on contact (see Chapter 3 for a discussion of contact), but following is not done in this case either. The California-style horse is schooled to move in a semicollected manner in the show ring, and in this situation the horse has very

minimal balancing gestures. When outside the show ring and not riding at the semicollected gaits, the California-style rider should follow the balancing gestures of the *ordinary gaits* whenever the reins are short.

Riding and Following with Two Hands

When riding with two hands, which occurs most often outside the show ring, or when using the snaffle bit or bosal, the rein length is generally shorter. This shorter length ranges from semiloose to riding on contact with a constant feel of the horse's mouth (see Chapter 3). Because the reins are shorter, or because the horse is on contact, following arms and hands become most necessary. Many green colts are ridden on short reins or on very strong contact at times, due to control problems. If you wish to avoid head tossing and head problems in general, it will be necessary for you to learn to follow effectively. You will also win more consistently in the English pleasure classes.

Many riders when riding with two hands lower their hands down beside or below the swells of the saddle. They believe that by doing this, the horse will be encouraged to lower his head or flex at the poll. Quite the opposite is true for two reasons. First, most horses will resist a downward pull on the bit by raising their heads. (Have you ever jerked a horse while standing on the ground and had his head come down?) Second, with the hands in a lowered position, the elbow joint is almost straight. This arm position makes fluid following of the horse's head impossible. Therefore, when riding with two hands, try to carry your hands at a level that allows your arms to follow the balancing gestures of the horse freely.

The Free Hand

When riding with one hand, either in the show ring or when schooling, what should you do with the free hand? When showing, you should carry the free hand in one of three ways. Whichever position you choose, however; the free arm or hand should not move back and forth from your side.

1. The arm may hang naturally at the rider's side. The fingers may be closed softly—not in a tight fist. The whole arm should be relaxed.

2. The upper arm may be carried naturally along the rider's side. The elbow is bent at almost a ninety-degree angle, and the forearm is carried in front of the rider's waist. The palm is carried inward toward the rider's belt with the fingers slightly closed.

3. For junior riders, the free hand may be used to hold the end of the rommel (romal). In this case, the free hand is resting lightly on the upper one-third of the thigh. The hand holding the rommel should not be clenched, nor should the forearm be stiff. The free hand should look soft and natural.

When schooling with one hand, the free hand should be carried in a manner most conducive to the particular schooling situation. If a crop or the end of the reins are to be used as a supplementary aid, the free hand should carry either of these.

Pictures 32, 33 and 34 illustrate the standard ways to carry the free hand in the show ring. By show ring convention, the free hand is the working hand: if the rider is right-handed, the reins are held in the left hand, and vice versa for the left-handed rider. The roper, polo player, working stockman and others hold the reins in the non-working hand just as the show ring rider does.

Seat and Thighs

How the rider positions his or her seat in the saddle influences the position of the upper body. It also affects the way the rider can use weight aids. It is important to sit squarely (side to side) with the crotch and two seat bones in the center (front to back) of the saddle whenever you are not actively using your weight from side to side as an influence on the horse's movements. If you sit only on the crotch, your back will most likely be too arched, causing stiffness. This will hinder your ability to sit deeply and softly on a horse. On the other hand, if you sit back on the fleshy part of the buttocks, the lower back becomes rounded;

Picture 32. Free hand carried down. *This is one method of carrying the free arm when riding with one hand. The free hand does not touch the body, saddle or horse. You will see some senior riders using this method.*

Picture 33. Free hand carried up. *This popular way of carrying the free arm when riding with one hand assists the rider in balancing the upper body when faster speeds, turns, circles and prompt halts are required.*

then your use of the back and seat are not nearly as effective.

When making circles and turns, it is generally appropriate to weight the seat bone on the side in which the turn is being made, as an aid to the horse. Care must be taken, however, not to let either hip collapse. This causes the spine to become crooked and a shoulder to drop, which keeps other aids (legs in particular) from being applied efficiently. Other ways of using the rider's weight from side to side are described in Chapter 3.

The thigh should lie as flat as possible on the saddle because this is an important area of frictional grip (see the section on Grip later in this chapter). Excessive muscular grip with the thigh will decrease security by pushing the seat up out of the saddle. (Think of squeezing a plastic bottle with the cork fitted loosely in the top.) If you have a heavy thigh, try to do two things. First, as you sit in the saddle, pull the back and underside of the thigh away from the saddle with your hand. This will help the thigh to lie flatter on the saddle, as well as increase the area for frictional grip. You may have to do this several times an hour at first, until you have "reshaped" your thigh. Second, lose weight. Overweight riders are less secure and therefore more abusive on a horse and less able to use their aids efficiently.

Calf Position

The well-schooled horse cannot put in his best performance without the rider's efficient use of leg aids. This efficiency simply is not possible

Picture 34. Free hand carrying a romal. *This method is appropriate for junior riders. The romal hand is held in a relaxed position over the upper one-third of the rider's thigh.*

when your lower leg is not where it should be. Poor lower leg position also delays results in schooling and may produce upset, stiff and resistive horses. The timing of your leg aids suffers if you must always be adjusting your leg because it has moved out of position. The whole matter of unsteady lower leg position becomes more critical when good timing is required in higher-level exercises, such as the flying change of leads. The horse cannot comply quickly and efficiently to a rider's request to turn, halt or depart on the line at a new gait without relying on the rider to provide him with efficient, on-time signals with the lower leg. Additionally, if your leg slips back inadvertently and asks for the canter while your hands may be asking the horse to maintain the trot, you have a confusing and abusive situation

for the horse. Horses you school should accept a light feel (not a squeeze) of your lower leg without becoming nervous, confused or erratic in their pace.

The rider's inner upper calf should rest against the horse's side in nearly every instance. This feel enables the rider to use his leg quickly and efficiently, and gives greater security by keeping the lower leg from swinging. Depending upon the particular horse and his conformation (thin-sided or round-barreled), the amount of the rider's lower leg in contact with the horse's sides will vary. The length of the rider's legs will also determine to what extent the lower leg rests against the horse's sides. A good fit between horse and rider is important, because it determines how quickly the rider's leg, hanging naturally, will de-

Picture 35. Forward position of the rider's leg. *The rider is in the standing position, his lower leg moved slightly forward to support the forward inclination of his body. His back is correctly arched and his seat pushed toward the back of the saddle.*

part from the normal curvature of the horse's sides.

The rider's leg should remain underneath the upper body in nearly every instance, falling vertically beneath the body with the toe at the cinch. It is not only a matter of good position design, but also one of security for the rider. The only time the rider should not have his leg positioned as just described is when he or she stands in his stirrups and inclines the upper body forward. In this case, the rider should be able to support the upper body without gripping the saddle excessively with the thighs, pinching with the knees, or gripping the horse's sides with the calves. To avoid these things, the leg must be physically moved forward, perhaps only an inch or two, under the rider's center of balance in order to support the rider's torso weight in the stirrups. The farther forward the upper body, the farther forward the leg must move to support this adjustment. The back must also be

arched and the seat pushed toward the back of the saddle. Picture 35 illustrates this forward position of the leg.

If your leg tends to swing backward or forward as the horse makes rapid increases and decreases in pace, your lower leg position is unsteady. You may well be pinching the saddle with your knees to the point that your weight simply cannot drop into your heels. In this case, your heels may be down and your upper body position may be correct, but your weight distribution will nevertheless suffer as long as you continue to pinch the saddle with your knees. The fact that you can still manage to keep a leg on each side of the saddle even though your lower leg swings is not the point.

Foot Placement in the Stirrup

To allow the weight of the body to fall more efficiently into the heels, the ball of the rider's foot should rest on the stirrup. When you view the stirrup from the front, the inside of the boot should rest near the inside of the stirrup. Also, and this is very important, the inside edge of the boot sole should be lower than the outside edge. In other words, the sole of the boot should slant slightly upwards as you go from the inside margin of the sole to the outside margin. The rider's toes should point slightly outwards, not straight ahead. This arrangement of the foot in the stirrup is shown by Pictures 36 and 37. The purposes of this arrangement are:

1. Greater frictional grip between the rider's leg, saddle fender and horse's side in the areas of the rider's upper inner calf, knee and lower thigh—those portions of the leg providing correct frictional grip to steady the rider's leg.
2. Closer contact between the upper calf and the horse's side, enhancing the rider's most effective use of frictional grip. The entire lower leg remains steadier.
3. A more stable base of support for the soles of the boots themselves. The rider is less likely to lose a stirrup or to lose his weight in the stirrups.

This arrangement of the rider's feet in the stirrups is desirable for an adult western pleasure class, and is in fact necessary for the most effective use of the rider's legs in all other performance classes, particularly where fast forward speeds,

Picture 36. Placement of the foot in the stirrup, front view.

Picture 37. Placement of the foot in the stirrup, side view.

sharp turns or rapid halts are necessary. It provides security for the rider; the more demanding the performance, the greater the practicality of this arrangement.

If you teach, you should emphasize these points to your students. Such an arrangement of the feet in the stirrups is desirable for them. If you deal with beginners, they will find their overall security is increased; learning proceeds faster when the rider feels greater security and, hence, relaxation.

This arrangement of the feet in the stirrups is not used by many young riders. They roll their thighs inward, point their toes straight ahead, carry the outside margin of the boot level with the inside margin, and ride with a maximum length of leg (Pictures 38 and 39). My technical objections to this position are:

1. The upper calf is removed from the horse's side, providing less frictional grip (Picture 39).
2. Mechanical pinching of the saddle with the rider's knee occurs in most cases. The rider's weight tends to stop at the knees, and one of the three principal shock absorbers, the ankle, is lost. Of course, the knee itself is also stiffened and its flexibility as a shock absorber is similarly impaired.
3. The stirrups must necessarily be quite long, and the rider must pull the toes up (rather than let his or her weight drop into the heels) to give the impression that the heels are down.
4. There is no real weight in the stirrup. The steadiness of the rider's whole leg depends upon the muscular grip of the thighs and knees.

From a practical standpoint, this position will probably survive for some time to come for junior riders in the show ring. Great security is not required by a rider on a steady equitation horse. The slowness of the gaits, coupled with their rhythm, make few demands on the rider's security. Equitation classes are a test of the rider, and yet, unfortunately, riders must employ a position which

Picture 38. Youth horsemanship position, side view. *The leg is so long that the knee has been lost as an effective shock absorber. The rider has pulled her toes up rather than let her weight fall into her heels.*

Picture 39. Youth horsemanship position, front view. *The rider has no leg on the horse. The thighs are rolled inward, and she is pinching with her knees. The ankles and knees are ineffective as shock absorbers. The toes point straight ahead.*

is neither a good working position nor one which is functional in any other circumstances. That some riding instructors insist upon such a position for beginners who have not even caught their balance seems particularly incongruous; the shape of the rider's profile is given priority over security and function.

The horsemanship position is functional for the tasks required of junior riders. It will be necessary to rearrange this position, however, when the rider begins schooling green horses or competing in high performance events.

Heels

The rider's heels should be down with the heel lower than the toe. When the heels are down, the greatest security of position is provided. Although you can raise your heels and still remain astride the horse during fast turns and quick stops, this does not justify the flaw in position. The heels down position provides added security by helping you keep the lower leg where it belongs—underneath you. The heel position also helps you maintain your balance. In order to have your heels really down, your toes are not simply pulled upward. Instead, it is easier, and more efficient, to let the weight of your body push your heels down. By relaxing your knee grip enough to let the weight flow down to the heels, the whole process becomes very passive but very effective.

As a test (if you are over 21 and well insured), find an understanding friend who has an English saddle and a horse that jumps quietly. No high swells or cantle to help you here. Mount the horse and canter over any obstacle not more than 2′3″ high. Not very high, right? Feel free to grab some mane.

Raise your heels as you jump the fence, and you will find that your lower leg flies backward. You may also notice that you had to pinch with your knees to stay on—a common result of having the heels raised. Jump the fence again, but this time relax your knee enough to allow your weight to sink into your heels—before, during and after the jump. You will have a steadier lower leg and a greater feeling of security.

If you are interested in riding only made horses around the rail of the ring, you will do all right with your heels level, or even raised. But if you plan to school green horses or compete in performance events where fast turns or fast speeds are required, you will find that you do much better with your heels down. Your leg will be where it needs to be in order to provide prompt aids to your horse; your whole position will be improved, more secure, and your horses will perform better.

A last point: when the heels are pressed down, the muscles in the calf are pulled tight. Likewise, when the heels are raised, the calf muscles become loose and flabby. Leg aids are stronger (and less work) when the tight muscle of the calf contacts the horse's side. A loose calf muscle makes less of an impression on the horse than a tight one, regardless of how hard you squeeze.

These then, are the basics regarding the rider's correct design of position. Later, more will be said about position as it relates to different phases of schooling the horse. More will be said, too, about position as you continue reading this chapter about the remaining six physical characteristics of a good working position. No book can give a perfect description of the rider's correct design of position. The anatomical shapes of horses and riders vary so that a rigid set of rules concerning exactly how every rider must sit cannot be devised. However, if you can remember, and practice, each of the points made so far, I believe that both your riding and schooling will improve. Also, remember that whenever you change your position, even for the better, you will first be a little uncomfortable and even slightly unbalanced or insecure. This is quite normal, but I would encourage you to improve your basic design of position anyway. It will be worth it in the long haul. Look for greater

security, more efficient use of your aids and perhaps less inadvertent abuse of the horses you ride.

If you are a professional, periodically ask some other professional in your area to check your position. You ride, while the other person remains on the ground to assist you in fixing your overall position design. Do the same for the other person whenever he or she feels his or her own position design may be slipping. You are fooling yourself if you think that you can ride for many years, and still retain the same good position design you once had especially if you school green horses. Every good rider needs an occasional critique from the ground. If you teach, you will never stop emphasizing correct design of position. A good riding instructor continues to teach correct position design, as well as the other six characteristics of a good position, irrespective of what the main objective of the day's lesson might be.

CORRECT DISTRIBUTION OF WEIGHT

One of the keys to correct weight distribution is the ability of the rider to allow his or her weight to drop or sink down into the heels. The rider lets gravity do the work, and does not forcefully push the heels down or pull the toes up, since this tends to stiffen the whole position. If you allow your weight to sink into your heels, your lower leg will be steadier and your entire position astride the horse more relaxed. Your position will also be more secure because you will be able to absorb the shock of riding and at the same time be better able to support the weight of your upper body and maintain your balance. Keeping your center of balance over your lower leg helps gravity to do its work. Also, by not gripping excessively with the thighs or knees, your weight can fall better into your heels. If you do grip tightly with either the thighs or knees, your weight cannot possibly fall into your heels as it should.

A very quick way to check your weight distribution is to think about what happens to your body as you ride. If you often lose the balance of your upper body (back and forth) or lose a stirrup when turning or circling, or if your leg swings back and forth, your weight distribution is not correct. A more methodical means of putting your weight distribution to a test is this: assume the standing position at any gait. If your leg slips forward or backward, or your upper body collapses forward or falls back, then your weight distribution probably is not correct (I say probably because lack of spring or balance could also be at fault).

If you must squeeze very hard with your legs, or touch the horse's neck with your hands to maintain your balance, then similarly, your weight distribution may not be correct. If you do these things as a test, and find that your position is unstable, lean on the neck until you can adjust your lower leg underneath you to effectively support your weight without pinching with your knees or thighs.

Standing Position

Now, if you did not completely grasp the points just made, perhaps you do not really understand the standing position. *Standing position* is also called *galloping position*. Its explanation follows.

Generally, the standing position is used for forward movement of the horse at the fast speeds of the trot and canter, at the gallop and during schooling. The standing position is used during schooling to remove the rider's weight from the horse's back for purposes of relaxation of both rider and horse. Whenever you assume the standing position, you must stand in the stirrups; the seat bones and crotch do not touch the saddle. English riders often call this a two-point position, because only the rider's two legs support his weight; three-point position means sitting (two legs plus the rider's seat). The key to the standing position is to lift the seat slightly out of the saddle while balancing the entire body over the stirrups alone; riding with the heels down will be a considerable help.

Pictures 29, 31 and 35 illustrate riders in standing position. The heels are down, the crotch is low to the saddle but not touching it. The rider's legs, with the heels down, are underneath the body's center of gravity, providing a stable platform over which the upper body may be balanced without falling forward or backward. Beginning riders, or those who are not accustomed to the standing position, often find it necessary to rest their hands on either the mane or the swells of the saddle, in order to maintain their balance. This is fine, and is certainly preferable to inadvertently falling backward and perhaps hitting the horse in the mouth with the bit. Standing position helps any rider to develop correct weight distribution, balance and

spring. Briefly assuming the standing position can also provide a rider with a quick check of the correctness of his leg position for subsequently sitting at each of the gaits. When sitting, if the rider feels that his leg may be a little too far forward or back, he or she has only to assume the standing position momentarily, make the necessary adjustments of the lower legs to improve balance and then slowly sit down again, without letting the leg move.

BALANCE

This is an important quality of a good position, but one that does not require much commentary. Beginning riders do not have it because their position designs and weight distribution are not good. Experienced riders, on the other hand, possess this quality to varying degrees, depending upon just how good their designs of position and weight distribution are.

Aside from improved position design and weight distribution, balance is simply the learned ability of the rider to regulate and adjust the upper body, while keeping the lower leg underneath the body's center of balance as the position of the upper body changes. Riders make these upper body adjustments in response to the horse's increases and decreases in speed so as not to be ahead or behind the motion of the horse.

For the beginner, balance requires a conscious effort. For the better and more experienced rider, balance becomes automatic. The time when balance no longer requires a conscious effort on the rider's part is the time when a conscious effort is no longer needed to maintain a correct design of position and good weight distribution. Again, the rider's balance can best be demonstrated by the ability to maintain a good design of position while riding in the standing position at the walk, trot and canter—without gripping excessively with calves, knees or thighs.

RHYTHM

This is the quality of movement in the rider's own muscular efforts which permits him to stay in balance with the horse during forward movement at any gait or at any speed. It is also the quality in the rider which permits him to effectively use his aids in conjunction, or rhythm, with the horse's efforts. For example, if you wish to increase the speed of any gait, rather than a kick or tap on the horse's side, a series of mild squeezes in rhythm with the horse's efforts to establish a new cadence at the faster speed is appropriate. If you wish to increase the length of stride at the walk, you squeeze with your left leg as the horse's right foreleg begins to move forward, and with your right leg as his left foreleg begins to move forward. You do this in rhythm with the sequence of the horse's legs until the desired forward-moving walk is obtained.

Sitting the jog trot promotes the rhythm in the rider, as does sitting the canter (really sitting, not perching slightly in the saddle). At the canter you sit the deepest and push your pelvis toward the front as the horse begins advancing the diagonal pair of legs. You develop a rhythm based upon this motion so that you begin to feel that you are rhythmically pushing the diagonal pair of legs forward with your own pelvis once at each full stride of the canter.

SPRING

Three principal springs, or points of flexibility, exist in the rider's body when his design of position is correct. They are the hip joint, the knee joint and the ankle joint.

Good spring simply means a good ability of the rider to absorb the concussion sent upward through the rider's body from the stirrup. The rider must effectively absorb this concussion progressively upward through the angles of the ankle, knee and hip joints, in that order. A lot of spring in the joints is required in events such as poles and barrels and in the jumping classes.

If any of the angular shock absorbers in the rider's position are stiff because the stirrup length is too long and the rider's leg straight, the result is a rigid position—one which tends to lift the rider out of the saddle for both increases and decreases in speed, as well as when halting quickly. If you jump up and down on the floor with your knees locked and straight you will see what I mean. The same thing applies if you lock your hip or jump up and down with your ankles locked so that you land flat footed on the floor. In order to absorb the concussion effectively, comfortably and without jarring and a loss of balance, each of the three principal joints must have an angle to them; they must each remain bent as you ride (see Picture 30).

It is for these reasons that I object to a rider's

position design in which the leg is so long that the knees are straight and the heels cannot fall below the level of the stirrup. In this case, both the knee and ankle are locked into place; the joints are straight and have no angulation.

A long leg looks pretty on a horse, I agree, but the leg can be stretched downward so far as to make the absorption of concussion an impossibility. Looking pretty on a horse is important to some extent, but on the other hand, I believe that a correct design of position, one that allows the correct distribution of weight for purposes of function and security, is also pretty. A long leg with no angulation to the joints may be fine for riding very made horses traveling at very slow forward speeds; but if you ride a variety of horses, some highly schooled and others quite green, I believe you will quickly find that looks are no substitute for the function and security provided by correct weight distribution. Maintaining some degree of bending in the hip, knee and ankle is the most important facet of the rider's correct weight distribution.

The posting trot, provided that you post from the ankle and not the knee, tends to develop the characteristic of spring in your overall position. Standing position at the trot and canter also tends to develop this aspect of your position. In standing position, not only must the ankles absorb a good deal of the shock, but the knees and hips must also make their contribution to spring. Learn to relax your hip joints in particular; let your hips just float above the saddle when you are in the standing position. Low jumping is an excellent means of developing spring in your position; the obstacles you jump need be no higher than those found in any trail class.

SELECTING A STIRRUP LENGTH

A stirrup length appropriate for the type of riding you do is an important factor in how well you can incorporate good weight distribution and spring into your overall working position. Generally, the stirrup that falls about two inches below the center of the inside anklebone is a good all-purpose length. This length allows for good depth in the heels whenever you allow your weight to fall downward through the knee and lower leg.

If you barrel race, rope, run poles or ride in similar performance events, you may find a shorter stirrup length more functional. This is particularly true whenever the majority of your riding is done in the standing position. Greater heel depth, and hence better weight distribution and spring, is afforded by a slightly shorter stirrup length for these events.

On the other hand, you may choose a length slightly longer than the all-purpose length if you only ride at slow gaits along the rail. In this case, you give your leg a longer appearance for purposes of showing in the western pleasure classes. I suppose that there is nothing wrong with this, but in the final analysis I always hate to see a senior rider detract from the function of his position for the sake of show ring aesthetics. The recommended stirrup lengths are:

1. Just below the bottom of the anklebone: used to increase spring for high speed events, rapid turns or whenever a great deal of riding or competing must be done in the standing position.
2. About two inches below the center of the anklebone: an all-purpose length for most types of riding and schooling. High-speed events and riding in standing position are roughly workable from this length, also.
3. Lower than the all-purpose length: used when riding at the slow gaits on stabilized horses. It can be used if the standing position is not required.

These stirrup lengths are guidelines. A rider with unusual proportions—very long thighs for example or a very short torso—may find that some adjustment of stirrup length is necessary to best achieve good spring and correct weight distribution. By all means, make the modifications which will best enhance your correct weight distribution, balance and spring.

GRIP

There are two types of grip which may be employed by the rider's legs: *frictional grip* and *muscular grip*.

First of all, do not confuse grip with squeezing the horse's sides with your legs. Squeezing is something that you do in order to tell the horse to go faster, to move over, to engage his rear legs, to take a specific lead and so forth. Grip is just the property of stabilizing the rider's leg; it may or

may not be accompanied by squeezing to signal the horse to perform a certain movement or task. Frictional grip simply implies relaxed riding with the rider's leg contacting the horse's side. The frictional drag between the two surfaces (the horse's side and the rider's inner upper calf, inner knee and lower thigh) steadies the rider's lower leg position. Frictional grip helps keep the rider's lower leg from swinging back and forth on the horse's side at any gait. Frictional grip is a passive process; it only requires that the rider position the lower leg underneath him or her, in contact with the horse's side, and maintain correct weight distribution in the lower leg and heels. Any horse should be schooled to accept the rider's leg resting against his side. Frictional grip requires no exceptional mental or physical effort on the part of the rider.

Muscular grip is not often used for general riding activities. It is primarily used in emergency situations such as shying, rearing, stumbling or bucking, and it requires that the rider grip very strongly with all portions of the legs in order to stay mounted. For competitive situations, however, those primarily involving very rapid increases and decreases in speed, muscular grip is frequently used, and very correctly so. To rope a calf in ten seconds or to run the poles in twenty without the use of muscular grip would be ideal, but from a practical standpoint, you will not be able to avoid this type of gripping. In these cases, remember that whenever you do employ muscular grip, your entire position will stiffen. Obviously, the least amount of muscular grip which will also enable you to get the job done without getting hurt is the best amount to use.

RELAXATION

Relaxation includes both the mental and physical relaxation of the rider. Mental relaxation requires confidence in the security of your own position and your ability to control the horse in any circumstance.

Physical relaxation is really best reflected by the quality of spring in your position. Stiff joints may result from a lack of mental relaxation, or their stiffness may be due to physical causes such as a poor design of position. Physical relaxation can be prompted by riding without stirrups at all gaits, using only frictional grip, or by riding bareback.

FOUR FUNDAMENTALS OF A WORKING POSITION

The seven physical characteristics of a rider's position just discussed afford the rider a workable base from which to ride and school horses. In a somewhat broader sense, all of these seven physical characteristics contribute to four fundamental riding properties:

1. *Security of the rider.* This is the ability of the rider to remain astride the horse with a minimum of conscious effort. This fundamental results when all seven of the physical characteristics of a good working position are well developed.

2. *Adjustability of the rider's position.* This means that the rider is synchronized with the horse in such a way that he or she is neither ahead of nor behind the movements of the horse. Most often, this means that the rider must adjust the upper body forward as the pace of the horse increases, and back as the pace of the horse decreases. Correct design of position, balance and rhythm are the characteristics which primarily influence adjustability. Pictures 40 and 41 illustrate riders ahead of the motion and behind the motion.

3. *Correct use of aids.* This means that the rider has a working position sufficient to allow him to ''push the right buttons'' on a well-schooled horse and to obtain a good performance. The phrase *correct and efficient use of aids* carries a considerably different connotation. In this case, not only are the correct aids applied, but they are applied in coordination with the horse's efforts in order to obtain perhaps a superb performance. At the heart of the correct use of aids is a good working position, balance and rhythm. These same characteristics, plus experience in schooling horses and an understanding of the mechanics of the gaits, are necessary for the correct and efficient use of aids by the rider.

4. *Nonabuse of the horse.* Nonabuse is an important concept and one that, surprisingly, does not have humane treatment as its

Picture 40. Rider ahead of the motion. *This rider is overleaning to the front. He is effectively ''out of balance'' with his horse's slow forward speed.*

Picture 41. Rider behind the motion. *For this rider's position, the shoulder-hip-heel line is gone, by about one foot. You cannot rationalize this kind of position as one that is helpful in teaching slow, steady forward speeds to the horse. The rider is not really using his weight as an aid; he has only been left behind as the horse moves forward.*

primary consideration. Abuse of the horse by the rider is usually quite unintentional. Abuse includes such things as the rider's swinging leg irritating the horse's side, improper use of rein aids (Chapter 3), and the inability of a rider to sit quietly and softly on a horse's back.

There is a distinct difference between abuse, punishment and cruelty. Punishment is the rider's logical and justifiable response to a horse's willing disobedience of a request that he already understands: appropriate punishment should occur within seconds of the horse's disobedience. When the horse disobeys your hands, punish him with your hands; when he does not respond to your legs, punish him with your legs, spurs or crop.

Cruelty, on the other hand, is the willful abuse of the horse, and is not related to punishments for disobedience. Cruelty is

also the overpunishment of the horse.

Each of these four fundamentals provides a rider with quick feedback on how well his or her position is actually working. If there is a momentary loss of balance, difficulty in maintaining a steady lower leg or perhaps a frequent loss of one stirrup or the other, there is a fundamental lack of security in the rider's position. If the upper body falls forward or is thrown backwards behind the vertical, of course, the rider's position is not as adjustable as it should be to accommodate rapid decreases and increases in the horse's forward pace. If the rider cannot use his aids and coordinate these in order to teach a new exercise or perform one already known to the horse, the correct and efficient use of the rider's aids is in question. Inadvertently jerking the horse in the mouth or hanging on the reins to maintain or recover his balance is abusive riding; security and adjustability are lacking.

If any of these things occur as you ride, one or

more of the seven physical characteristics of your good position are lacking. In this sense, the four fundamentals are really nothing more than a quick check on each of these seven characteristics. At this point you will want to review and correct the exact nature of the problem. Is the problem position design, weight distribution, balance, rhythm, spring, grip or relaxation?

Chapter 3

CONTROL

In order for almost any type of good riding and effective schooling to occur, two things are essential. They are the rider's *position* astride the horse and his *control* techniques. Both are not just fundamental to good riding on made horses; they are fundamental to schooling any green horse or the reclaiming of a spoiled or rank horse.

The previous chapter focused on the rider's position. This chapter focuses on the rider's control techniques, and the whole subject of control really begins with the ways in which the rider may correctly employ his four *natural aids:*

1. Hands (the use of reins)
2. Legs (the actions of the rider's legs against the horse's sides)
3. Voice
4. Weight (sitting or standing, and shifted from side to side at higher levels of riding and schooling)

This chapter will define for you the ways in which the rider can most effectively use these four natural aids to achieve control of the horse. Before you begin reading and thinking about each of these control techniques, let me point out that the terms used in this chapter are universal. The vocabulary of this chapter is generally equally at home among educated riders in Stillwell, Kansas; Charlottesville, Virginia; or Aachen, Germany.

If you teach, I would encourage you to adopt the terms used in this chapter. Besides being in wide use, this vocabulary is equally applicable to the western horse and to the English horse. In other words, the terms used in this chapter are general riding terms. They are not restricted in their use to any particular breed or type of horse nor to any particular riding activity.

THE USE OF THE HANDS AND REINS

The western rider can employ six standard rein aids in riding and schooling. Each has a specific purpose, and each one very definitely influences the way in which the horse is capable of moving forward. The six standard rein aids are:

1. Neck reins (bearing reins or western reins are terms preferred by some riders)
2. Two direct reins of opposition
3. Leading rein (opening rein means the same thing)
4. One direct rein of opposition
5. One indirect rein of opposition used in front of the saddle horn
6. One indirect rein of opposition used behind the saddle horn

In the show ring, the first two rein aids, neck reins and two direct reins, are used exclusively in the western classes. If you ride in English hack classes, you will use one direct rein, rather than neck reins, for turning.

All six rein aids are generally required outside the show ring for schooling and teaching horses new or increasingly difficult lessons. Of the six rein aids, one indirect rein used behind the horn, is used the least for schooling.

Neck Reins

The action of this rein aid is to turn the horse. The use of neck reins to produce both a left and right turn, and the action of this rein aid upon the horse himself, is shown by Picture 42.

Neck reins may be employed with both reins held in only one of the rider's hands (as shown in Picture 43). The rider may also correctly choose to neck rein the horse with both of his hands: that is,

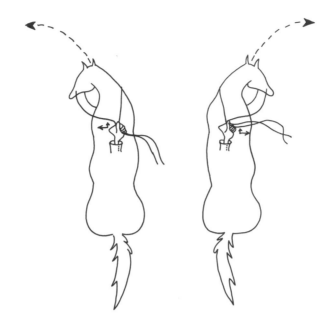

Picture 42. Neck reins (bearing reins). *Use a right bearing rein for the left turn. Use a left bearing rein for a turn to the right. Neck reins are, by definition, loose reins.*

Picture 43. Neck reining. *The rider is holding the reins in one hand and is applying a right bearing rein in order to turn left. I would like to see just a little more slack in both reins here—and I believe this very green filly would agree, since she has her mouth slightly open.*

with split reins bridged between his two hands (Picture 44), or with both hands holding closed reins (racing reins or an English type of closed reins). Reining with two hands is primarily reserved for schooling, while riding with one hand applies to a variety of situations including show ring riding, recreational riding and actual working or sporting situations where the rider must maintain a free hand much of the time.

Regardless of whether the rider holds the reins in one or both hands, the action of neck reining has the following sequence. In order to turn the horse to the left, for example, the rider moves his hand (or hands) to the left, thus bringing the right-hand rein to bear across the top half of the right side of the horse's neck. To turn the horse to the right, the rider moves his hand (or hands) to the right, thus bringing the left rein to bear upon the top half of the left side of the horse's neck. In either case, the action of the rein aid is to induce the horse to turn *away* from the pressure of the bearing rein as it is applied to the upper portion of

his neck (the top half or mane portion of his neck). Picture 45 illustrates neck reining from the rider's view. Picture 46 illustrates neck reining from a ground view.

Neck reining is a quick, light means of turning a horse schooled to obey this rein aid, but by itself it is also a rather crude way of turning the horse. Precision in turning with neck reins is generally possible only when the rider also employs his legs and weight.

The horse schooled to this rein aid obeys the pressure across the upper portion of his neck, regardless of how far forward or back the reins are carried on his neck. A more finished horse responds with the reins carried far back, toward the base of the neck. The young, unschooled horse responds more quickly with the reins initially maintained in a forward position on the neck.

Remember that for correct neck reining, the reins must be *loose*. There should be a definite loop or slack in each of the reins, and the reins should be of similar length. The rider should in no

Picture 44. Neck reining. *The rider is holding split reins bridged between his two hands. He is beginning to ask for a left turn by applying a right bearing rein. This horse is a green horse unaccustomed to neck reining. Therefore, the rider is using his bearing rein rather far forward on the neck in order to elicit a more prompt response from the horse in turning.*

Picture 45. Neck reining, rider's view. *A left bearing rein is just being applied to the horse's neck. In the next instant this well-schooled horse will begin to move his head and neck to the right. Note the loose reins and the rider's apparently soft hands.*

way have a hold on the horse's mouth. Nearly any rider should be capable of perceiving tension changes in loose reins as the horse moves his head and neck.

When the rider forgets that the neck reins are to be used as loose reins and that this looseness is to be preserved to some extent as he moves his hands to the side to cause the horse to turn, a certain defect in the rein begins to appear. If the reins are not slack enough, or the rider moves his hands too far across the withers and to the side, the bearing rein tightens considerably (becoming an indirect rein, which will be discussed shortly). The horse must then turn his neck in one direction while turning his head in the opposite direction in order to relieve the discomfort in his mouth from the rein which has been brought to bear tightly upon his neck. This defect—turning the horse in one

direction while forcing him to look or tilt his head in the opposite direction—is illustrated by Picture 47.

Neck reining is not the sole province of the western rider. Whippers-in in fox hunting use neck reining extensively; George Morris, a premier hunter seat equitation instructor recommends teaching open jumpers this rein aid. Neck reining was in wide use several centuries ago in Europe and Asia. Polo players rely heavily upon this same rein aid in competition today.

Two Direct Reins of Opposition

This rein aid is used:

1. To slow the horse's forward speed
2. To halt the horse
3. To back the horse

Picture 46. Neck reining, ground view. *A very soft use of a right bearing rein to begin a pivot to the left.*

In this rein aid, the reins are held either in two hands or, more commonly, in one hand. The direction of the rein tension is straight toward the rear as illustrated in Picture 48. When holding the reins in two hands, the rider should draw back his elbows to create tension on the reins. If the reins are being held in one hand, a slight upward movement of the wrist or a backward movement of the elbow can be used to put pressure on the bit. Obviously, the rider's reins should be of equal length if the horse's head and neck are to stay straight.

To slow the horse's forward speed, the rider simply places increased tension on the reins. The tension should not be constant if the horse is being ridden on loose reins or if any type of curb bit is being used. To slow the forward speed, a series of *check-and-release* movements are made with the reins; the rider moves his elbow back (the check) and then forward again (the release). The check applies tension rearward on the reins and asks the horse to slow down. The release permits the horse time to begin slowing and to obey the original

rearward tension on the reins. The release is also a reward of sorts for obedience to the check.

The young or very inexperienced horse generally requires several check-releases with the reins, but it is important that the rider not forget or minimize the releases. The check should be a quick movement lasting only a second or two, and the release should be slightly longer than the check. A very slight check-release with the rider's wrist (when holding the reins with one hand) should be all that is necessary to slow the more finished horse. The check is made with two direct reins and the release is simply a return to loose reins.

To halt a green horse that may be unwilling to obey your hands at first, or one that does not understand their meaning, the tension of the check may be increased to help accomplish the halt. Looseness should be restored to the reins as soon as possible to avoid resistance and to maintain cooperation. Repeat the check-release sequence along with your other aids (weight and voice) until the horse halts. Older, more experienced horses should halt with only a small check and release of

Picture 47. Improper use of neck reins. *The horse in this picture is looking in one direction while turning in another. This defect is seen when the reins are held too short, when the rider moves his hand too far across the withers or when the reins are used to produce a turn or circle too severe or too rapid for the horse's level of schooling. The same defect can be seen even in older, well-schooled horses, whenever the rider uses his reins correctly but forgets to employ his outside leg to assist the horse in turning.*

the reins in conjunction with the rider's use of weight and/or voice.

To back the horse, the rider increases the rearward tension on the reins until the horse begins to take a step backward, and then releases as the horse complies. In order to obtain a smooth rein back, the rider should release the rein tension as the horse's diagonal pair of legs are in the air and check again as they touch the ground, to activate the second pair of legs. Repeat this action until the desired number of steps have been taken. You will find that coordinating checks and releases with the

efforts of the horse will encourage him to back more willingly and fluidly. Picture 49 shows a rider using two direct reins in one hand to ask the horse to back. In the next instant following this picture, the rider released the reins before asking the horse for a second step.

Picture 50 shows the use of two direct reins with two hands, as the rider would view it. Note that in this picture the horse has his ears pinned: a prolonged check was used without a prompt release for the purpose of obtaining an acceptable photograph. There is a message for you here if you

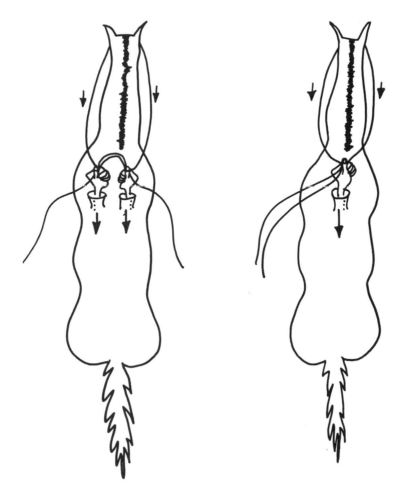

Picture 48. Two direct reins of opposition. *The rider applies direct rearward tension evenly on both reins for the purpose of slowing, halting or backing the horse. When this tension is of a short duration, it is termed a check. Subsequently, relaxation in rein tension in response to the horse's obedience is termed a release. Check and release is an important technique for effective, nonabusive riding and schooling.*

doubt the validity of the check-release technique and its relationship to good riding and cooperative horses.

The Leading Rein

This rein aid is extremely useful in the very early schooling of any horse. It is used to literally lead the horse's head or nose around a turn or along the arc of any fairly large circle. The leading rein has broad application in the schooling of any green horse who has not yet learned to make turns and circles under the new weight of the rider and in response to the use of neck reins.

The method of using the leading rein is diagrammed in Picture 51. Two versions are shown: closed reins held individually in the rider's hands, and split reins bridged (rather widely) between the rider's hands. Pictures 52 and 53 are further illustrations showing the actual use of this rein aid as you would view it both from astride the horse and from the ground as an observer.

To employ the leading rein to make a right turn, for example, the rider moves his or her right hand to the side and away from the horse's neck, leading or gently pulling the horse's nose to the right. To perform a left-hand circle or turn, the rider

Picture 49. Two direct reins of opposition, ground view. *The horse is being asked to back. In the next instant following this picture the rider released her rein tension before asking for a second step back. It would be preferable to see the horse's mouth closed.*

moves the left hand out to the side. Again, the action is to lead the horse's nose to the left.

When moving the leading rein hand to the side, the rider should be sure that the active hand is not raised above the level of the horn or pulled down below the horn toward the rider's knee. The leading rein must be carried straight out to the side, in a movement parallel with the ground.

Regardless of whether you employ the leading rein aid to turn or circle to the left or right, as the horse begins to turn his head and neck in the direction indicated by the leading rein, the opposite rein (the nonleading rein) will begin to tighten. Thus, it is imperative that you fall into the habit of always *giving forward* slightly with your nonleading rein hand as any circle or turn is developed.

This is very important. This giving forward with your nonleading rein hand is especially important if you are schooling green horses with your reins held especially short because of early control problems.

The leading rein is a marvelous aid in teaching the young horse to turn and circle. As you will see in Chapter 6, the leading rein also has broad application as the forerunner of teaching the horse to neck rein. The leading rein is a very unabusive aid; if the horse is bitted correctly, it can be used in the form of a rather strong, steady pull to the side to teach the horse what is required of him for purposes of turns and circles.

Any plain snaffle bit is quite acceptable for use in conjunction with the leading rein action. Shank bits, provided the shanks swivel to the sides easily, are also acceptable for use with this rein aid. One such bit is shown in Picture 54. Bits with frozen shanks or those which do not easily swivel to the side are *not* appropriate for leading reins. Too often a nutcracker effect is produced on the horse's tongue or the bars of his mouth. Insure that the horse is bitted correctly so that his head and nose can be led unabusively in the direction you wish. Never inflict pain as the horse's reward for obedience to your leading rein aid.

Aside from its simplicity of use and its effectiveness in teaching all types of circles and turns to the inexperienced horse, the leading rein has other advantages. For example, its use does not appreciably affect the horse's forward speed during turns and circles. This is important since very green horses are highly inclined to vary their speed when first asked to turn or circle, and especially when asked to circle for the first time under the new weight of a rider. The use of a leading rein will help the green horse to maintain an even pace when first learning turns and circles. The horse will be less likely to slow down or break to a

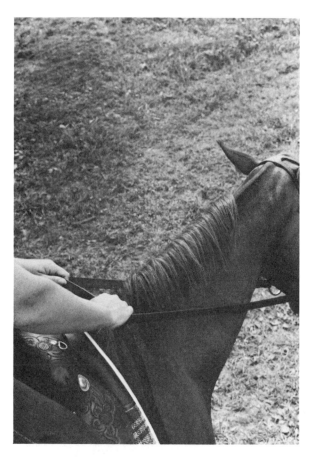

Picture 50. Two direct reins of opposition, rider's view. *The rider is holding the reins in two hands and is applying even rearward tension on both reins. The rider's elbows are sticking out to the side because her hands are being held in a flat position. She should turn her thumbs upward.*

slower gait. Because the leading rein does not slow the horse's forward speed, you will see many barrel racers riding with two hands in order to employ both a leading rein and a bearing rein as they make tight turns at high speed. This same rein aid can be used to discipline the older, well-schooled horse that for some reason has momentarily forgotten how to turn in response to a bearing rein. In this case, a sharp jerk with a leading rein is in order, whether or not the shanks of your bit swivel easily to the side.

Generally, green horses come to rely rather heavily upon your leading rein action to perform most circles and turns. This reliance is no problem when you are ready to move on in your schooling and teach neck reining or turning in response to one direct rein. You simply wean the young horse away from his reliance upon the leading rein by progressively decreasing the angle at which the rein is opened away from the neck for any given turn or circle. Also, by this time the horse has probably come to rely heavily upon leg and weight signals for most turns and circles, so weaning the horse from the leading rein is easy.

The leading rein works by the rider's opening of the angle between the rein and the horse's neck. Hence the common synonym *opening rein.*

One Direct Rein of Opposition

For convenience I will just call this aid *one direct rein.* I suggest you do the same in your conversations with other riders and your students.

This is quite a good rein aid for teaching a relatively inexperienced horse how to negotiate sharp turns or very tight circles. It also serves as an

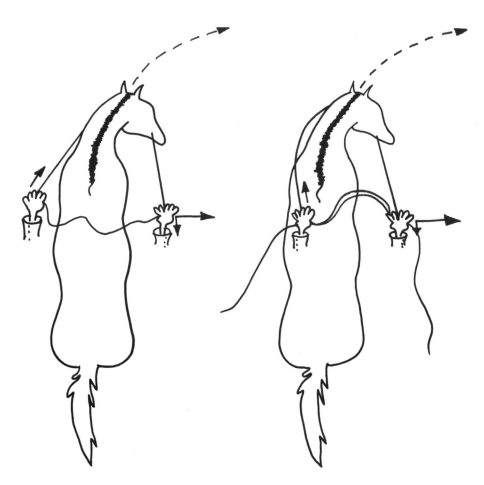

Picture 51. Leading rein. *Rein tension is directed outward to the side and slightly back. This rein aid is used to turn green horses along large circles or turns and before they have learned to neck rein.*

excellent disciplinary aid for the horse that disobeys either the leading rein or the bearing rein.

A snaffle bit with no curb chain is preferred when teaching the horse obedience to the direct rein.

The application of the direct rein is diagrammed for you in Picture 55. In particular, note that the rider's outside hand must give slightly as he or she takes with the inside hand, the direct rein hand. For certain schooling problems, you may wish to couple the direct rein of opposition with a slight opening of this same rein. All in all, you achieve a slightly milder effect.

The rider initiates the use of one direct rein by applying tension on the rein rearward and toward the point of his or her own hipbone. Pictures 56 and 57 illustrate the rein aid as you would view its use from the saddle and from beside the horse.

In some instances even though the outside rein (the rein opposite the active, direct rein) begins to develop some tension, you may not choose to give so liberally with your outside hand. Instead, you may wish to control or support the degree of turning with this outside hand in order to regulate the size of the circle or turn and control the attitude of the horse's head and neck—to force him softly to look exactly in the direction in which he is turning. In most circumstances, however, not giving with the outside hand during turns and circles is a flaw in riding technique.

Picture 52. Leading rein, rider's view. *The rider is using a right-hand leading rein to begin to lead the horse's head and neck to the right. However, the hand is being carried too low. If the rider's elbow were not so straight, her hand would be correctly carried at the level of the withers as she moves her leading rein to the side.*

One Indirect Rein of Opposition Used in Front of the Saddle Horn

The use of this rein aid is shown by the diagram in Picture 58. As you look at this diagram, please note that the effect of this rein aid is not only to turn the horse, but also to displace the horse's shoulder away from the pressure of the rein aid itself.

Because of this, the indirect rein used in front of the horn is most useful for three purposes. It assists the horse in performing precise circles and turns; it assists the rider in keeping the horse's forehand (head, neck and shoulder) on the rail when traveling along the sides of any arena; and it assists the rider in keeping the horse deep within any of the four corners of a rectangular arena, or deep within any turn for that matter.

For standard applications of the indirect rein in front of the horn, both of the rider's hands are active. The rider's indirect rein hand applies tension on the rein to the rear and *toward the horn* at the same time. This active hand should not, however, cross in front of the horn to the opposite side of the horse. This is important. Also, the rider's opposite hand moves slightly forward in order to give as the indirect rein hand takes. This allows the horse to yield his head and neck in the direction of the indirect rein.

Pictures 59 and 60 illustrate the application of the indirect rein from both a rider's and observer's viewpoint. In Picture 60 the indirect rein is being used to perform a half turn on the haunches from the halt—a pivot.

In certain instances the neck rein can act (incorrectly) as an indirect rein used in front of the

Picture 53. Leading rein, ground view. *The rider is using a leading rein to teach a young horse how to circle. He is correctly using his right leg also to assist the horse in moving to the left. While this rider's elbow is carried too far from his body, his hand is nevertheless at the correct level—neither too high nor too low.*

horn. For this to occur, the neck reins are either being held too short or the rider, despite ample rein length, has moved his reining hand too far across the mane in the direction of the turn. Remember that when a right bearing rein is applied correctly, the horse should turn to the left; when a right *indirect* rein is used in front of the horn, the horse should turn to the right. You can understand the confusion created for the horse if a right bearing rein inadvertently becomes a right indirect rein through a flaw in the rider's technique.

Three points of caution apply to the use of this rein aid. Because it is very effective, riders tend to overuse it to the point of forgetting both to use their inside leg effectively and to use their weight to the outside of turns and circles if the horse is being asked to move to the outside. This is especially true for riders with little or no experience schooling horses.

The second point concerns the use of the indirect rein on older horses and those who are highly tuned to the bearing rein. In order to work, the indirect rein must touch the neck; these horses may, at first, try to turn away from the indirect rein as if it were a bearing rein, rather than bend the head and neck and displace the outside shoulder in the direction indicated by the indirect rein.

Point number three is that this rein aid is really only to be used in schooling, and more by English than by western riders. Nevertheless, it has wide application for schooling the stock horse, particularly before the young horse has been taught to neck rein. Overuse of the indirect rein, even in a snaffle, can cause a considerable amount of resistance by the horse: he may cock his head and open his mouth. In such cases, a return to a direct rein and the more active use of the other natural aids (leg and weight) may achieve the desired results with much less resistance.

One Indirect Rein of Opposition Used Behind the Saddle Horn

This rein aid is unique because it affects the entire horse. The application of this rein aid not only

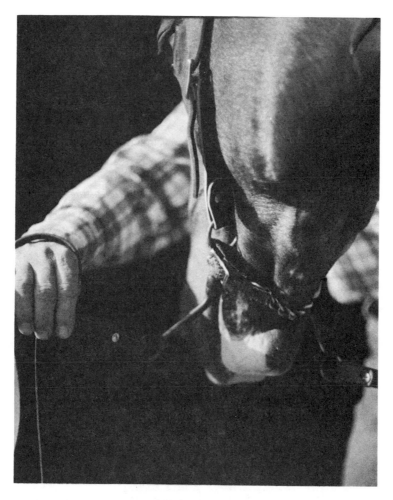

Picture 54. Bitting. *If you use a bit with a shank for early schooling (when you are often employing a leading rein for teaching turns and circles), the shank should be one that swivels easily to the side.*

acts to turn the horse's head and neck (you already have four rein aids which do this), but it also acts to displace the horse's shoulder *and haunches* away from the direction in which he is turning. This displacing action upon the haunches sets this rein aid apart from any of the rein aids previously discussed.

The application and action of the indirect rein used behind the horn is diagrammed for you in Picture 61. Its application is also illustrated from mounted and ground levels by Pictures 62 and 63. As you can see, if you were to apply this rein aid with your right hand, the rein tension would be directed toward your left hipbone and with your hand moving to a position behind the saddle horn.

Your left hand would give forward enough to allow the horse to bend his head and neck to the right.

Although this rein aid may be used to prevent the horse's entire body, forehand and haunches, from falling inward on circles and turns, its primary use is in two particular schooling problems. The first is to discourage the horse from traveling with his haunches inward as he moves in a straight line along the rail. The second is to promote straight backing at slow or moderate speeds. Generally, the rider's active legs would be expected to control either of these problems, but what might normally be expected and what actually occurs during a particular schooling session

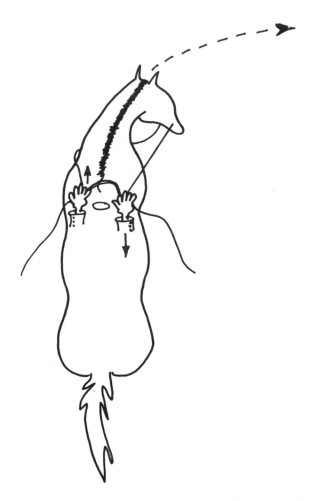

Picture 55. One direct rein of opposition. *Rein tension is applied toward the rider's hip on the side of the active (right) rein. The rein aid is used to turn green horses along sharp turns. This rein aid can also be used as a disciplinary aid for horses that disobey the rider's hands in performing turns or circles of any type.*

are sometimes two entirely different matters.

Use the indirect rein behind the horn for exceptional resistance to your leg; use it when the horse virtually refuses to range his hindquarters in response to your active displacing leg (discussed later in this chapter). Use it sparingly during schooling and with a plain snaffle bit whenever possible; its use is harsh enough even with such a mild bit.

Like the leading rein, the indirect rein in front of the horn and the single direct rein (for other than hunt seat riding), this rein aid is a schooling rein. It is not at all intended for show ring use.

THE USE OF THE RIDER'S LEGS

The rider should employ three standard leg aids when riding and schooling. These same leg aids are used in the show ring. Some riders define the three standard leg aids by describing the position of the rider's legs on the horse's sides: at the cinch, behind the cinch and far behind the cinch. While these are indeed legitimate terms, they merely define the position or placement of the rider's legs. An aid concerns an action, not just a position. Thus, the three standard leg aids are best called:

1. Urging leg or legs

Picture 56. One direct rein of opposition, rider's view. *A good example of the use of a direct rein. The rider's right hand is taking as the left hand is giving. The rider's active hand, directed rearward toward her right hip, asks the horse for a turn to the right.*

Picture 57. One direct rein of opposition, ground view. *An excellent picture of the application of a left direct rein.*

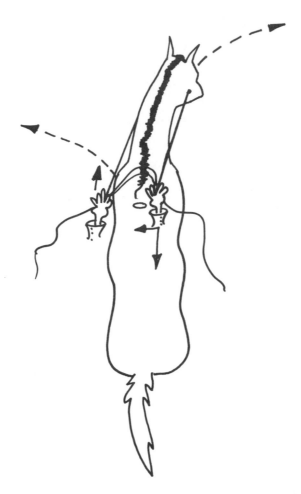

Picture 58. One indirect rein of opposition used in front of the saddle horn. *Rein tension is applied toward the rider's belt buckle, but the rider should take care not to carry the active rein hand to the opposite side of the saddle horn. This rein aid is used to turn the horse in the direction of the active rein and to displace some of the horse's weight to his opposite shoulder.*

2. Holding leg
3. Displacing leg

For *each* of these leg aids, the rider may use his leg to tap the horse's sides, kick the horse's sides, or squeeze the horse's sides. In other words, there are actually a total of nine ways in which the rider may use these three standard leg aids. A tapping leg is used for early schooling. A kicking leg is used as a disciplinary measure, or possibly to teach a new lesson. The squeezing leg is the most sophisticated action and is used on schooled horses or for lessons which even the green horse already understands. A squeezing action of the

rider's leg, regardless of whether an urging, holding or displacing leg is being used, enables the rider to obtain a smoother, more precise response from the horse. The definite but crude responses of the horse to the rider's tapping or kicking legs should be primarily reserved for early schooling and the teaching of new lessons.

The actual positions the rider's leg occupies on the horse's side while tapping, kicking or squeezing are shown by Picture 64 (urging leg), Picture 65 (holding leg) and Picture 66 (displacing leg). As you look at these pictures, realize that some variation in the position of the rider's leg will be necessary for each of the three leg aids. The variation

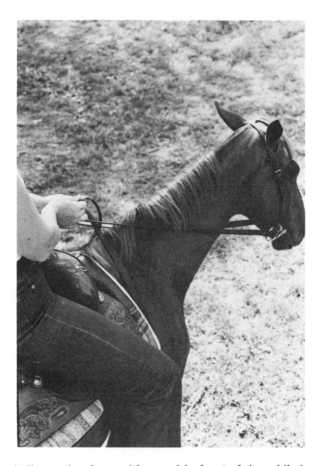

Picture 59. One indirect rein of opposition used in front of the saddle horn, rider's view.
This is an excellent example of how the rider employs the indirect rein. She has correctly carried her active rein hand to, but not across, the horn.

will depend upon the horse's forward speed and the particular exercise or movement being taught. For example, when the rider assumes the standing position, his or her legs must move forward in order to support the upper body. In this case the leg aid is still urging legs, but the leg position is correctly and necessarily moved slightly forward from that illustrated by Picture 64.

Urging Leg or Legs

Three situations affect the use of the urging leg aid:

1. The rider may use both of his legs actively at the cinch (by tapping, kicking or squeezing) in order to urge the horse forward; for example, to move from the halt to the walk or from the walk to the trot.

2. The rider may use only one leg actively at the cinch in order to urge the horse forward, while the opposite leg is busy with another task. The nonurging leg may be acting as a holding or displacing leg.

3. The rider may use only one leg actively at the cinch in order to encourage the horse to advance one of his hind limbs farther forward than another (more about this in the later schooling chapters).

I have used the term *at the cinch* to denote the approximate position of the rider's leg—the position at which the rider's urging legs are most effectively applied to the horse's sides. Do not take this phrase literally. Look again at Picture 64. Speaking about the rider's leg being at the cinch simply means that the leg occupies a position that supports the particular incline of the rider's upper body.

Picture 60. One indirect rein of opposition used in front of the saddle horn, ground view.
The indirect rein is being used in this instance to generate a turn on the haunches to the right. The rider's left hand has crossed over the horn a bit too much, but note the good use of the rider's left holding leg. The left indirect rein is being used to displace the horse's shoulders to the right, while a right leading rein (which you cannot see) is being used to assist the horse in looking in the direction of the movement being performed.

As you ride or observe others riding, you will note that the entire leg is not literally positioned at the cinch. Rather, you will note that the rider's toe is literally at the cinch, while the back of the calf and the heel of the boot actually fall behind the cinch. You will also observe that a rider who really does have his or her entire leg positioned at the cinch for slow or ordinary gaits in fact has pushed the lower leg too far forward—a poor design of position.

Holding Leg

The rider may employ a holding leg in the following situations:

1. The rider may use a holding leg to prevent the horse from falling inward or outward along the arc of a circle or turn.

2. The rider may use a holding leg to prevent the horse from cutting corners in a square or rectangular arena. In this instance, the leg aid can also be called a *supporting leg.*

3. The rider may often use a holding leg to assist the horse in remaining on the rail, straight head to tail, as he travels around the sides of an arena or riding ring.

4. The rider may use a holding leg on one side of the horse, using a displacing leg on the other, in order to control the horse's

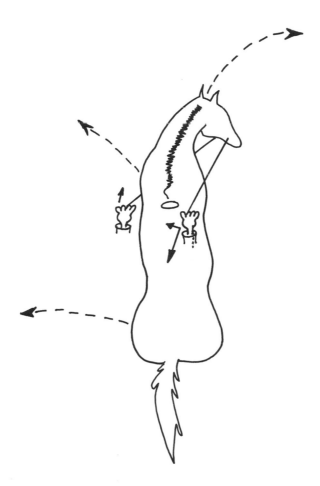

Picture 61. One indirect rein of opposition used behind the saddle horn. *Rein tension is applied toward the rider's opposite hip. This rein aid is used to turn the horse's head and neck and to displace the entire body (shoulders and haunches) away from the direction of the active rein. Because this rein aid is unique in its ability to displace the haunches to the side, it may be used to supplement the rider's use of legs, or to serve as a corrective measure for horses resistive to the use of the rider's displacing leg action.*

haunches and forehand.

5. The rider may use a holding leg to assist the horse in performing straight canter departures. In this case, the rider employs an inside holding leg and then an outside displacing leg in order to ask for the upward transition to the canter, assuming that the inside lead is that which is required.

The rider's holding leg does not necessarily occupy some fixed distance rearward of the cinch. The actual position of the holding leg behind the cinch is dictated by whatever is required in order

to discourage the horse from drifting sideways and against the action of the holding leg. If you will compare Pictures 64 and 65, you will see there is very little difference between the urging and holding leg positions as they have been photographed. Look at the amount of white between the back border of the cinch and the front of the rider's lower leg. To do its job effectively, the holding leg can actually occupy quite a range of positions behind the cinch, but its purpose always remains to prevent sideways movement of the horse's body, particularly the forehand. If the rider's holding leg moves so far rearward that the action

Picture 62. One indirect rein of opposition used behind the saddle horn, rider's view. *An excellent example of how to use the indirect rein behind the saddle horn. Note that as the rider's right hand is taking, her left hand is giving softly to the front.*

begins to become that of ranging the horse's hindquarters, one can no longer talk about a holding leg. In this case, the rider's leg becomes a displacing leg—the next topic.

Displacing Leg

The rider may employ a displacing leg aid in the following situations:

1. The rider's displacing leg is applied to the horse's side relatively far behind the cinch in order to displace the horse's hindquarters, to range the haunches away from the rider's active displacing leg.
2. A displacing leg aid is used in order to teach the horse the movement called the *turn on the forehand.* This movement is begun from the halt, and the rider uses his leg to displace the horse's haunches in an arc or circle around a relatively stationary forehand. This is the standard "gate opening and closing" movement taught in western classes.
3. A displacing leg is used to ask the horse to canter. Its standard use is on the outside of the horse, assuming an inside lead is desired. Of course, the displacing leg aid can be used either in a tapping or squeezing

manner, depending upon the level of the horse's schooling and his willingness to lope or canter forward.

One last point before leaving the three standard leg aids. Whenever a rider's leg is moved to the rear of the position normally occupied by an urging leg, the rider's heel will rise. This elevation of the heel is natural and cannot be prevented during the course of normal riding and schooling. This is not a flaw in the rider's position, and does not indicate poor weight distribution on the part of the rider.

THE USE OF THE RIDER'S VOICE

The use of voice constitutes a very effective aid for schooling and controlling nearly every horse. Along with hands, legs and weight, voice is one of the four natural aids which should be employed by the rider.

The primary use of the rider's voice is in schooling activities for the young or very inexperienced horse. Over months of schooling, and as the horse's level of schooling is continually improved, the rider will tend to use the voice aid less and less.

Picture 63. One indirect rein of opposition used behind the saddle horn, ground view.

There are six voice commands every horse should know. They are:

1. *Whoa, Ho, Hey* or any other word you choose which means *halt*
2. *Walk*
3. *Trot*
4. *Canter* or *Lope*
5. *Slow* or *Easy*
6. Any sound, such as clucking, which indicates that a faster forward speed is required. Whatever sound you choose, remember that this voice aid is no substitute for the effective use of your urging legs.

The green horse, the unbroken horse, when first mounted has no magic buttons which say to him *walk, trot, canter, halt, go slower* or *go faster*. He does not understand that when you sit deeply and then tap six inches behind the cinch with your outside leg, this means to canter. He does not understand that when you apply two direct reins, this may mean slow down, halt or even back. In this respect, the use of the rider's voice can greatly simplify schooling by reducing the need for punishment during all early riding on the green horse.

When you start a green horse, four to five days of longeing (lunging), while using your voice, will usually be adequate to get the horse started on voice aids. Of course, you may also choose to simply begin teaching the voice commands from the saddle the first time the horse is mounted *Whoa* and *Walk* will be your first priorities.

Picture 64. Rider's urging leg. *The leg is used in this position to urge the horse forward, whether to move from the halt to the walk or to increase speed at any gait. How quickly or how fast the horse moves forward is directly proportional to how actively the rider applies this particular leg aid. The rider's urging leg may be used singly, or both legs may be used at the cinch to urge the horse forward.*

Most horses, if not all, will quickly learn to associate the rider's hand and leg actions with a particular voice command, especially when the rider consistently uses the appropriate voice command slightly in advance of his reins or legs. The use of voice hastens the progress of schooling and permits the rider to be less abusive during all the horse's early schooling.

Horses are creatures of habit, so it is important to use your voice in a consistent manner. Use your voice commands in advance of your other aids. Say what you mean, and more importantly, say it in a tone of voice that helps your horse understand your request. For instance, the commands *Walk* and *Trot* have two appropriate tones of voice in which they may be used. For upward transitions, the rider's voice should be authoritative and the

pitch should rise at the end of the spoken word (*taaaROT!*) Similarly, for downward transitions, the voice should be soothing, and the command spoken slowly and in a drawn-out manner *(trrrot)*.

The use of voice in the normal course of schooling has other important ramifications. For example, horses that have been schooled to the use of voice in conjunction with the other three natural aids make excellent lesson horses in any teaching situation. The beginning rider can always use his voice effectively even though he may not yet be proficient in using weight, hands or legs. While the new rider may not be able to obtain a canter with the use of his ineffective leg, the canter can nevertheless be obtained by the use of his ineffective leg plus the use of the command *Canter!*

Voice, for horses schooled to its use, allows

Picture 65. Rider's holding leg. *The leg is used in this position (or slightly further to the rear) to move the horse to the side away from the active leg or to prevent the horse from moving to the side, toward the active leg. This same leg aid is termed a supporting leg by some riders when the purpose is to prevent the horse from moving sideways toward the supporting leg.*

control of any riding class from the center of the ring; it allows the instructor to control the lesson horses being used by each student. This is useful to the instructor in emergency situations. Suppose the beginner, one who is really not ready to canter, allows his leg to slip a little too far backward and the horse begins obediently to canter. The instructor can avoid a potentially nasty situation from the center of the ring by saying "Cochise, Whoa!" or "Cochise, SLowwww." He can then instruct the rider to sit up, move his leg forward, check and release, and so forth.

Voice constitutes a very effective natural aid. It should be used liberally in conjunction with all early schooling of the horse. It is invaluable to the riding instructor.

THE USE OF THE RIDER'S WEIGHT

Don't relegate the use of weight to a place of least importance simply because it is the last to be discussed. If you school green horses or attempt to improve the precision and accuracy of various movements for older, more experienced horses, the use of weight constitutes an especially important aid. If you teach, all of your students, and especially your higher-level students, will require instruction concerning the correct use of weight as an aid.

Basically there are two ways in which a rider may employ weight as an effective aid:

1. Vertically, with the weight centered equally

Picture 66. Rider's displacing leg. *Here the leg is used to range the horse's haunches to the side away from the active leg. The same leg aid is used to indicate an upward transition from the halt, walk or trot to the canter or lope. The rider's heel naturally elevates somewhat whenever a displacing leg aid is used.*

over the midline of the horse's back (Picture 67)

2. Laterally, with weight partially displaced to one side or the other and away from the midline of the horse's back (Picture 68)

Vertical Use of Weight

The vertical use of weight requires that the rider maintain his or her own center of gravity over the midline of the horse's back. This may involve sitting deeply in rhythm with the horse's efforts at any gait, assuming the standing position or posting in rhythm with the horse's efforts at the trot. Regardless of which of these things the rider might be doing, the vertical use of weight requires that the rider maintain *equal weight* in each stirrup. The rider's center of gravity must remain over the midline of the horse's back and the rider should not lean or shift weight from one side or the other in an effort to influence the horse.

The primary purpose of the vertical use of weight lies in achieving a steady forward pace, fast or slow. The rider's efficient vertical use of weight gives a steady rhythm to each of the gaits, especially the trot (jog) and canter (lope).

Probably no facet of the rider's vertical use of weight is more important than the ability to sit well at the trot and canter. Sitting in rhythm with the horse's own efforts contributes to calm, steady forward speeds. In conjunction with this, the rider's legs and hands help eliminate erratic forward speeds and unexpected changes of pace. Later in this chapter, after lateral uses of weight have been discussed, you will find a short discussion of sitting the trot and the canter. Read it carefully if

Picture 67. Vertical use of weight. *This rider is using his weight vertically to assist a young horse in learning to halt promptly. The rider's weight is divided equally between his two stirrups, and his upper body and seat remain centered in the saddle. If this rider were not able to sit so well in rhythm with the horse's efforts during a rapid decrease in pace, the whole process of learning to halt promptly would have been a rather abusive one for the horse.*

you are dissatisfied with your ability to sit these two gaits as well as you think you might.

Inclining the upper body forward or backward constitutes another use of vertical weight. Its purpose is to signal the horse to increase or decrease his speed. These inclinations of the rider's upper body can be made from either the sitting or standing position. In the standing position the usual purpose is to promote very fast speeds such as the gallop or the hand gallop, occasionally required in the show ring.

In the sitting position, the rider can obtain smooth and balanced downward transitions with almost invisible rein aids by the effective use of weight. To use weight effectively, the rider must be sure his or her torso is on the vertical and then brace the back by tucking the seat bones farther underneath the torso. This action presses the seat bones more firmly into the saddle, and the give in the lower back will momentarily diminish.

Museler, in his book *Riding Logic,* compares this action to pushing a swing higher with one's back or to facing a table which has a book protruding slightly over the edge and pushing the book onto the table, using just a forward thrust of the pelvis. When mastered by the rider, this action is a very effective way of slowing or stopping the horse (see Picture 69). At higher levels of schooling, bracing the back assists the horse in beginning to stop with his hindlegs well engaged, up underneath his body.

Posting is a desirable means of schooling any horse at speeds of the trot faster than the jog. Posting is not simply an up-and-down movement of the rider's upper body and seat. It originates in the rider's flexible ankles; it is not accomplished by squeezing with the knees in order to elevate the rider's seat out of the saddle momentarily. When posting, the rider's hips and pelvis should be softly thrust forward as the seat rises out of the saddle. Like it or not, posting is sexy. It does not simply

Picture 68. Lateral use of weight. *This rider is sitting well vertically, but he is also using his weight laterally (to one side) to encourage the horse to move a little closer to the fence of the riding ring. Lateral uses of the rider's weight are extremely difficult to see in a photograph so I will describe his actions. He has simply sat a little harder on his right seat bone and stepped down in the right stirrup a little harder. If you could compare his legs, you would see his left leg has quite naturally traveled slightly up on the horse's side. Lateral uses of weight are seldom used by themselves to move a horse to the side. The rider here is also employing a left holding leg actively, and he is using a left indirect rein to displace the horse's shoulders toward the fence. He is glancing slightly in the direction in which he wishes the horse to move.*

involve rising and sitting again in a straight up and down fashion. Also, the rider's pelvis should be moved toward the front of the saddle each time the horse's outside front leg is advanced forward for posting on the correct diagonal (Picture 70).

Posting higher, lower, faster or slower can help regulate the speed of the trot. If you wish to push the horse forward, thrust your hips toward the front more energetically as you post. With posting in combination with two urging legs used each time you sit, the horse should lengthen or at least quicken his trot without breaking to the canter. If you wish to slow or steady the horse's trot, post very low, barely rising out of the saddle. If you can sit in the saddle just slightly longer than you feel like you should (without missing a beat) most horses will try to synchronize their pace with the slower rhythm of your posting.

Picture 69. Bracing the back. *For demonstration purposes, this rider has exaggerated the bracing of her back to illustrate the slowing or stopping of any horse while maintaining good engagement of the horse's rear legs as the forward pace decreases. Her upper body would not normally fall this far behind the vertical. Bracing the back is a demanding but unabusive, clear signal to the horse to begin slowing, or to halt promptly if the appropriate aids are also supplied by the rider. Bracing of the rider's back encourages the horse to retain good qualities in his movement as forward speed is decreased—not to become strung out or to collapse forward on the forehand as a halt is achieved.*

Lateral Use of Weight

The lateral use of weight means that the rider moves at least a portion of his weight to one side or the other of the midline of the horse's back. It does not mean that the rider leans his upper body to one side or the other. Instead, either the hips alone move to one side or the other, or one stirrup is weighted more than the other or both of these actions are performed together.

Leaning to the side with your upper body badly unbalances the horse, and is particularly unsuited for a green horse that is already rather unbalanced simply by virtue of carrying the rider's entire weight for the first time. Leaning to the side in any form is appropriate only on experienced or well-schooled horses. Even on these horses, riders should lean to the side only for sharp or very tight turns at high speeds. In this case, the rider leans *with* the horse to the inside of the turn, but does not overlean. With respect to the ground, both the horse and rider are leaning to the inside, but with respect to the horse, the rider still remains centered over the saddle. He does not lean farther to the inside than the horse himself.

I can think of no legitimate reason for the rider to ever lean to the outside of a circle or turn, no matter what the speed nor how close the horse may appear to be passing by a barrel or pole. Use your inside holding leg and your reins instead.

Western polo players, Appaloosa steer daubers and rope race competitors, rodeo steer wrestlers and precious few others can be excused from these restrictions on leaning.

Picture 70. Posting the trot on the correct diagonal. *To post on the correct diagonal (meaning diagonal pair of legs), the rider rises out of the saddle and moves his pelvis toward the front of the saddle as the horse advances the outside front limb. The rider then sits again as the horse's outside front leg moves rearward. While the rider in this picture is posting quite high out of the saddle for illustrative purposes, exaggerated posting like this has a practical side—it encourages the horse to increase his speed at the trot. Conversely, lower posting encourages any horse to control, or slow, the speed of the trot. A rider may choose to post at any speed of the trot that is faster than the jog, but not the jog itself.*

If a rider does not lean to the side under practically any circumstances, how does he use his weight laterally in order to obtain a better performance from his horse? To begin with, there are some basic reasons for using your weight from side to side:

1. To move the horse closer to the rail or wall as he travels straight along the side of a riding ring or arena.
2. To prevent the horse from cutting corners in a rectangular ring or arena
3. To assist the horse in improving his accuracy and precision when performing almost any type of turn, circle or circular ring figure
4. To assist the horse in understanding how to perform new exercises which you may introduce to him, such as sidepassing, flying change of leads, pivots and spins

The primary purpose of the lateral use of weight is to improve the horse's accuracy and precision when turning or circling. Of course, this weight use may also be employed to move the horse to the side for practically any reason. In any case, the lateral use of weight is a subtle aid, usually supplementing the use of the rider's leg and use of the reins.

Faults in the horse's movement which can be corrected or improved by the rider's lateral use of weight are a tendency to drift to the inside as the horse travels along the rail and a tendency to cut corners or fall slightly to the inside on circles and turns. For these problems the rider should use his or her weight to the *outside*.

Picture 71. Lateral use of weight. *The point here is to move the horse to the right, toward the fence. The rider's lateral use of weight in this picture includes sitting harder on the right seat bone than on the left, and stepping down a little harder in the right stirrup. The rider's left leg will naturally rise slightly on the horse's side as he shifts his weight to the right. The arrows show the direction of the weight shift.*

This can be done in two ways. First, the rider may simply shift his or her weight predominantly into the outside seat bone, and step down slightly in the outside stirrup (Picture 71). The second way in which he or she may use lateral weight is by sitting firmly on the inside seat bone and pushing this seat bone toward the center of the saddle—by directing the weight on the inside seat bone toward the outside (Picture 72). In either case, the total effect is to shift the weight of the rider's hips to the outside and to move the horse to the outside.

In the first case, where the rider sits firmly on the outside seat bone, the effect is to unbalance the horse slightly; he finds the rider's weight no longer in the center of the saddle and he generally moves to the outside in order to rebalance himself—to put the rider back in the center of the saddle. In the second case, sitting rather hard on the inside seat bone, at the same time pushing this seat

bone toward the center of the saddle, has the effect of saying "move over, move away from the direction of the pressure on your back." Also, because the rider's hips are ultimately displaced toward the outside, the movement encourages the horse to move over under the rider's weight. This second method demands somewhat more of the horse's attention than simply sitting more firmly on the outside seat bone or dropping your hip to the outside.

Whenever you move your hips to the outside in either manner you will normally lose some weight in your inside stirrup, and your inside leg will move slightly upward on the horse's side. This is a normal occurrence and not a position problem.

What about the use of weight to move the horse to the side when the rider is in the standing position? In this case, the rider's only options are to use weight while remaining in the standing posi-

Picture 72. Lateral use of weight. *Again, the aim here is to move the horse to the right, toward the fence. In this case the rider sits harder on the left seat bone but subsequently (almost as one motion) pushes this seat bone toward the center of the saddle. He pushes it to the right. At the same time he also steps a little harder in the right stirrup. His left leg naturally rises slightly on the horse's side.*

tion or to briefly sit and use weight in either of the two manners just described.

In order to use your weight while remaining in the standing position, simply move your hips to the side. This displacement of the hips does not have to be drastic; you still have your hands and legs to assist you in controlling the lateral movement of the horse. As you move your hips to the left and step down slightly in your left stirrup, the horse should follow this use of weight by moving to the left. You can supplement your weight with a right holding or supporting leg as circumstances warrant.

There are some special cases of lateral use of weight in which the horse does not respond as you might expect. For example, if you choose to move the horse closer to the rail using your weight softly, you simply sit a little harder on your outside

hip—drop your hip, so to speak—and step down on your outside stirrup. This is correct, but you will find some horses will tend to move quickly away from this type of weight use; in effect they will mildly shy to the inside of the ring, and they will do this despite the correct use of your weight to the outside. For these cases, the alternate and rather more forceful method of sitting on the inside seat bone and then pushing this seat bone toward the center of the saddle may be the better method of moving the horse to the outside.

If you still do not obtain good results through the use of your weight, use your leg (kicking inside holding leg) and hand (inside indirect rein) forcefully. If you keep using your weight correctly to the outside with these other aids, the horse will generally begin to respond cooperatively by moving to the outside.

Most horses with problems of moving crookedly tend to drift inward off the rail, to fall to the inside of circles and turns or to cut corners at the ends of rectangular arenas. However, you may also rarely encounter a horse that has problems in quite the opposite direction; he tends to drift to the outside rather than to the inside. In this case just reverse the weight use that I have described. Use your weight to the inside rather than outside. Sit a little harder on your inside seat bone, drop your hip somewhat to the inside and step down a little harder on your inside stirrup, or push your outside seat bone toward the center of the saddle.

As you practice using your weight laterally to move a horse to one side or the other, you will notice that some horses respond to the uses of the rider's weight better than others. You will also notice that some horses move to the outside a little better if you use your outside seat bone and stirrup, and others will respond better if you use your inside seat bone moved toward the outside. Probably all of this depends upon the horse himself, his mental attitude and his particular stage in schooling. Finding what works best is simply a matter of riding well; it is a matter of educated riding and your correct and efficient use of aids.

Sitting the Trot and Canter

The correct and efficient use of weight, vertically and laterally, really depends upon how well (and in most instances, how quietly) a rider can sit the gaits of the trot and canter at their various speeds. If you cannot sit both of these gaits rather well, the whole discussion of weight use becomes academic. You should be capable of sitting different speeds of the trot and canter quietly, without bouncing or finding it necessary to perch above the saddle. You should be capable of sitting quietly, *in rhythm with the horse's efforts,* in order to effectively use your weight as a clear signal to the horse.

What follows is an outline for learning to sit more effectively at both the trot and the canter. If you have problems in either of these two areas, read carefully and follow this reading with some actual practice. Trying to describe rather than actually demonstrate the essence of sitting well is like trying to describe the shape of a waffle to someone who has never seen one. It's a difficult proposition, but here goes.

Sitting the Trot

1. Pick a quiet steady horse, not a schooling project. Borrow one if necessary. Warm the horse up. Do a lot of quiet transitions in order to get him to listen to all of your aids (walk-halt, lope-walk, jog-halt, etc.).

2. When ready, gently ask him, with both legs at the cinch, to move smoothly from the walk to the jog trot. When the jog trot is steady, then sit, on both of your seat bones. Sit up very straight but not stiff. Simply keep your upper body close to the vertical and keep your shoulders back; arch your back toward the front *slightly*. Relax your lower back; relax it even more. Reverse your direction and do all of this again.

3. Next, ask the horse to increase his speed at the trot. Do everything as you did before, except this time at a faster trot. Finally, select a forward speed at which you begin to be a little uncomfortable, one at which you begin to bounce in the saddle slightly. At this point make a concentrated effort to relax, especially your lower back and your hip joints. As you do so, remember to remain upright with your upper body; don't slouch. Keep your shoulders back and your head up. Look ahead of your horse. Look where you are going.

4. Now, if you are still bouncing slightly, take both reins in one hand (if you are not already riding with one hand) and raise your free arm straight up and over your head—like when you were in fourth grade and you knew the answer for sure. Straighten your elbow joint and stretch your arm upward as far as it will go. You should now be sitting much better. Get the feel of this, and practice. Ride with your arms in a normal position, but when you feel yourself slipping back into the old bouncing habit, momentarily raise your arm above your head and make a conscious effort to relax your lower back.

5. Repeat all of these steps for increasingly faster speeds of the trot until you are well satisfied with your ability to sit almost anything at the trot. Practice on different horses. Also, when first learning to sit speeds of the trot faster than the jog, do not be particularly concerned about your lower leg position (unless your legs are slipping so far back that they are encouraging the horse to trot faster than you are currently prepared to cope with).

6. Watch others ride. Watch those who can really sit a trot. Watch their belt buckles. You will see that the buckle rises and falls as each of the horse's diagonal pairs of legs strike the ground. At faster speeds, the rider's belt buckle will rise and fall rather rapidly, and this action of the rider's stomach muscles somewhat resembles belly dancing. Sitting well at faster speeds of the trot is not a passive process. It takes mental and physical effort on the rider's part to absorb the concussion of a fast trot by moving the stomach up, slightly inward and then downward again, all the while leaving the lower back very relaxed, the shoulders back and the head and chin up, looking ahead of the horse.

Sitting the Canter

Sitting the canter is not at all like sitting the trot. The motion is quite different. Until your back has become supple enough to sit well at the trot, sitting the canter will probably not work out for you as well as it should.

1. First of all, sit down. Do not avoid the issue by perching in your saddle. Sit up straight, shoulders back, head up, and put a slight arch in your back. Ask the horse for either lead and obtain a steady canter. Then, as the horse's leading leg is advanced, make an effort to sit very deeply. Try to get the feeling that you are *beginning* to tuck your seat a little farther underneath you and slightly forward. Then, as the *diagonal pair* of legs is just beginning to be advanced, you should be the deepest in the saddle. At this time your crotch should be moving very definitely forward toward the front of the saddle, and your seat should be tucked underneath you, still trying to move down and forward.

2. The rhythm of your downward and forward movements of the seat and pelvis should coincide with the horse's initial effort in advancing the diagonal pair of legs. You should get the feeling that if you do not literally push these legs forward with your seat and crotch at each stride, the horse will stop in his tracks or break to the trot. Make a conscious effort to wear out the seat of your pants by pushing down and forward each time the horse begins to advance the diagonal pair of legs. Do not get so involved in sitting and pushing that your shoulders start to move. They should remain quiet. The motion is in your hips.

3. As you do this, you will notice that the horse will tend to slow his forward speed. If you have never really been able to sit deeply before (and have previously just perched in the saddle), your horse may actually break to the trot as you begin to sit deeply. This should illustrate to you that weight is a very effective aid. It is essential in producing a slow, steady, calm canter in any horse.

4. Practice sitting the canter in both directions of the ring. Very likely you will have a little more trouble sitting well in one direction. This is a reflection of the fact that most horses travel more smoothly in one direction than the other.

5. There are two exercises that work well for learning to sit both the trot and the canter. The first requires that the rider lean slightly behind the vertical while practicing. This helps to direct the rider's weight more easily down into the saddle. The second exercise is riding without stirrups. It is important to do this without gripping excessively with your knees and thighs. Gripping only aids in pushing the rider's seat out of the saddle, quite the opposite of what the exercise is trying to accomplish.

Almost uniformly I have found that advanced beginners can do nothing more beneficial for their riding than learning to sit correctly. Along the same line, a surprising number of experienced riders, even those who school quite a few horses, often sit rather poorly at speeds of the trot above a jog and speeds of the canter above the lope. Many of these riders simply choose to perch in the saddle (especially at the canter) rather than learning to use their weight as an effective aid.

On green horses that tend to raise their heads as they break from canter to the trot or walk, *do* perch momentarily if you must. Even the very best of riders cannot sit well for this type of erratic downward transition, so fake it for a moment: perch slightly to avoid bouncing and then sit.

Remember that your lower leg position will tend to deteriorate while you are putting your mental efforts into learning to sit. Learn to sit well first and then repair your leg position. Do not worry about losing a stirrup now and then while you are practicing. When first learning to sit well you will have to lighten the weight in your stirrups; this is the only time when you may correctly pull your toe up rather than push your heel down.

In regard to sitting well, let me make a final comment—a comment I feel may be important to some of you, especially those who have high goals but limited experience.

Books on riding always seem to be notoriously deficient in assisting the reader in learning to sit well. Still photographs, diagrams and drawings do not seem to help very much. The rider's use of weight and sitting well are very important facets of good riding but difficult to describe. Narrative and illustrations simply cannot replace the personal attention of a well-qualified instructor. So, if you have carefully read and practiced what I have written, but sitting well at either gait seems to remain a problem, you need some personal attention. If you still cannot sit well, you need a riding lesson—with you on a steady school horse and a qualified instructor on the ground. Return to this book for review after you have had some actual riding time with a qualified instructor.

Chapter 4

SELECTING HOW THE PERFORMANCE HORSE SHOULD MOVE

Why would you want to select the ways in which a particular horse is required to move? The answers, of course, are quite simple. But at the same time, there is a complex aspect to these same simple answers. That is what this chapter is about.

Suppose your interests happen to be in pole bending horses. In this case you would like your horse to be very quick leaving the starting line, agile and well balanced while running, capable of fast and accurate turns at each end of the line of poles, well schooled to flying changes of leads and very fast in the context of arena speed.

In other words, to school and compete with this horse successfully, you must emphasize certain types of movement. To be successful you will have to actively produce the kind of movement required for competition. You cannot just rely on the horse's raw speed and merely sit astride while the horse himself chooses the type of movement which best suits his mental state at the moment.

Now, the complex part to the question is this. While it is one thing to recognize that you require accurate fast turns or reliable flying changes of leads to be successful in certain events, it is quite another to recognize that in order to teach these things, you must also teach the horse lateral agility, movement on the line, engagement, impulse, and perhaps even semicollected movement.

This chapter will discuss the various desirable qualities of movement in the horse: those qualities which are the very basis for a high standard of performance in any competitive event. Certainly, if you do not know what these desirable qualities of movement are, the horse will have a very rough time figuring them out for himself.

First, I want you to learn about the overall qualities of movement of any well-schooled horse. Depending upon the type of western horse that you ride, and the events in which he competes, some of these qualities will be more important than others. For a few horses some of these qualities will appear naturally; for most, they will have to be learned. The qualities of movement you should always have in mind as you ride and school are:

1. Stabilization
2. Moving on the line
3. Engagement
4. Impulsion
5. Longitudinal agility
6. Lateral agility

Later in this chapter I will explain the importance of the relationship of the horse's head and neck to the bit, so that you will understand:

1. The natural carriage of the horse's head and neck
2. The elevated carriage of the horse's head and neck
3. Direct flexions of the horse's head and neck
4. Lateral flexions of the horse's head and neck

Finally, I will discuss the balance of the horse. In most western classes (pleasure horses are excluded here), horses are required to make rapid adjustments in their centers of balance (the roping horse as the catch is made, for example, and the reining horse as the sliding stop is begun). The two types of balance you will learn about are:

1. Forward balance
2. Central balance

My purpose in this chapter is limited to describing and defining these various important terms for you, and then drawing a few pertinent examples of each quality of movement. Later in this book, I will tell you which of these qualities of movement have priority for certain types of performance horses and how to teach these various qualities of movement to the horse.

STABILIZATION

This characteristic of the horse's movement requires that he move forward at whatever speed is indicated by the rider and that he continue to move forward at this speed, no faster or slower, unless the rider indicates a change. The stabilized horse moves forward at the speed indicated by the rider and maintains consistency at this pace while being ridden on loose reins. In essence, the western pleasure classes are one formal test of the horse's stabilization at each of three gaits.

Stabilization is a goal which should be achieved early in the schooling of any horse, regardless of what types of performance events or work the rider ultimately has in mind. In order to produce stabilized gaits, the horse must first obey the rider's hands, legs, voice and weight. This is the very essence of schooling for any horse. Without first teaching stabilization, higher levels of schooling become very difficult—in most instances, nearly impossible for the average rider.

If you have ever watched hunters show, you have probably noticed that these horses are ridden on contact, with two direct reins. The riders use following arms to maintain a constant light feel of the horse's mouth. Constant tension is maintained in both reins. Whenever you watch any horse being ridden on contact this way, at any gait, you cannot really determine his state of stabilization. The rider may in fact be containing and regulating the horse's forward speed with the reins, following a little more here and not so much there with varying rein tensions to achieve the appearance of a steady forward pace by the horse. Only if the horse ridden on contact can also be placed on loose reins, and subsequently maintain consistency in his forward pace, can we say that he is

stabilized. The maintenance of a steady forward speed on loose reins is the test of true stabilization. At any gait you choose, even the well stabilized horse will occasionally require a light check and release with the reins, a light squeeze with your legs or perhaps a soft word or two in place of brief uses of the reins, legs or weight. There is nothing wrong with this.

Also, there are degrees of stabilization. For example, we would be hard pressed to deny that the winning senior pleasure horse in practically any show is stabilized. But outside of the show ring we might find that this same horse possesses even better stabilization than we had originally suspected. We might well find that he is not only stabilized at the jog trot, but that he is also stabilized at ordinary speeds of the trot, or perhaps even at the very fast trot.

He might also be stabilized at ordinary speeds of the canter in addition to the slower speed of the lope. Stabilization then, while usually not expressed in degrees (the horse is either stabilized, or he is not), can certainly be taken to a point above the three standard western gaits. And indeed it should be, if your riding and schooling goals are high.

Aside from success in competition, or even just pleasant recreational riding, the stabilized horse has important uses. It is the stabilized horse that is the backbone of any professional establishment which concerns itself with teaching riding, in particular whenever beginners, or rank beginners, are being taught. The stabilized lesson horse permits the beginner to ride entirely on loose reins so that he or she can concentrate on balance and position, just steering occasionally. Mounted on a stabilized horse, the beginner does not have to worry about controlling the horse's forward speed or using a variety of rein and leg aids to cope with erratic changes in the horse's forward pace.

So long as he is not harshly or continually abused, the stabilized horse will continue to perform whatever gait is required of him, not speeding up or slowing down unless requested to do so. The beginner may catch his balance at the gait being taught by holding the saddle horn, swells or even the mane. Because the horse can be ridden solely on loose reins at a steady forward speed, there is no need for the beginner to balance himself on the horse's mouth using the reins.

Instructors who use only stabilized horses for beginners and low-level riders of all types find that these horses generally remain very cooperative in lesson situations over long periods of time. The abuse of lesson horses often associated with new riders does not exist or at least is held to a minimum. Because these stabilized horses travel on loose reins at consistent forward speeds for each gait, potentially abusive riding by the beginner who is inclined to hang on the reins for balance can be stopped almost as soon as it starts. The mane, saddle horn, saddle swells or even a neck strap (an old English stirrup leather or a lead shank) can be used by any badly unbalanced beginner. Also, the unabusive technique of check and release is easily taught to even rank beginners once they have initially caught their balance (see Chapter 3, Two Direct Reins of Opposition).

In addition, stabilization is without a doubt the basic ingredient for a winning trip around the arena for any pleasure horse. In the western pleasure classes, stabilization should be faultless. Beyond the western pleasure classes, stabilization of the horse must be achieved if higher levels of schooling are to be successful and if you plan to school the horse to a level where he may compete successfuly in several very different types of performance events.

Teaching stabilization is discussed in Chapter 6, on schooling at the elementary level. Simply described, teaching stabilization is a matter of teaching the horse obedience and prompt responses to your hands, legs, voice and weight. On top of this, lots of circles in both directions at the

Picture 73. Moving on the line on a straightaway. *The horse that moves on the line along a straightaway travels forward with a straight head and neck; he does not let his shoulders drift to either the inside or outside, and the haunches remain straight, neither drifting inward nor outward. The horse is straight head-to-tail, and he looks ahead in the direction he is moving.*

various gaits while encouraging a natural carriage of the horse's head and neck during all early schooling will be your key to achieving a stabilized horse.

I did not include any illustrations of stabilized horses in this discussion since nearly any horse will appear stabilized in a still photograph. Movie film would be required to capture the qualities of stabilization during steady forward motion.

MOVING ON THE LINE

Teaching movement on the line is basic to the schooling of any horse. Very simply, it involves teaching the horse to look in the direction in which he is moving. He must carry his forehead and haunches along this same line (Pictures 73 and 74).

On a Straightaway

If you wish the horse to move on the line while riding along a straightaway, these simple principles apply:

The horse's head and neck should be straight. He should be looking ahead, not to one side or the other, along the straight line in which he is moving. His inside back foot should follow the same line described by the inside front foot, and his outside back foot should follow the same line described by the outside front foot. In other words, the horse must not travel forward with his haunches to either the inside or outside, nor may he drop a shoulder to either the inside or outside.

On a Turn

If you want the horse to move on the line while riding along the arc of a turn or while performing a circle, these ideas apply:

First, his head and neck should be bent along the turn he is describing. He should be looking ahead along the circular path. He should not, for

Picture 74. Moving on the line while turning. *The horse that moves on the line while turning or circling follows the arc of the turn with his entire body. His head and neck are bent to the inside along the arc in which he is turning. He does not cut corners by popping a shoulder to the inside or allow his haunches to drift to the outside or inside of the arc being described. His head and neck follow the turn or circle being executed. His front feet follow his head and neck; his back feet follow in the tracks of the front feet.*

instance, be moving along a circular path to the left while having his nose tilted out to the right. Also, his back feet should be following the same line being described by the front feet. In other words, if you were to dismount after completing a circle and connect all of the shoe prints of the outside front foot by trailing a stick between them in the arena floor, and then did the same thing for all of the shoe prints of the inside front foot, you would have drawn two circles which would be separated by the approximate width of the horse himself. If the horse had actually been moving on the line as he circled, you would find that the prints of the outside *hindfoot* were also on the first line that you drew in the arena floor, and those of the inside *hindfoot* were likewise on the second line. Thus, the tracks made by the back feet would be on top of the tracks made by the corresponding front feet. Look at Picture 75 for an illustration of how the back feet follow the front for movement on the line while turning or circling.

Horses most commonly avoid moving on the line by:

- turning the head to the outside or the inside during upward transitions, particularly when beginning the canter from any slower gait (Picture 76).

- allowing the haunches to move off the line, usually by moving them to the inside during upward transitions, particularly when beginning the canter from any lower gait (Picture 77).

- moving the haunches away from the rail during halting, frequently seen for green or relatively unschooled horses (Picture 78).

- circling with the haunches skidding to the outside of the circle.

- cutting the corner of a circle or by making egg-shaped or D-shaped circles, instead of the intended round figures. In this case, it is the horse's forehand which moves off the line; the forehand falls inward toward the center of the intended circle.

- traveling along the rail with the head cocked to either the inside or outside, with the rest of the body remaining reasonably well on the line (Picture 79).

- cutting the corners at the ends of a rectangular riding ring, or arena—diving inward, so to speak, while beginning to negotiate a corner of the ring or arena

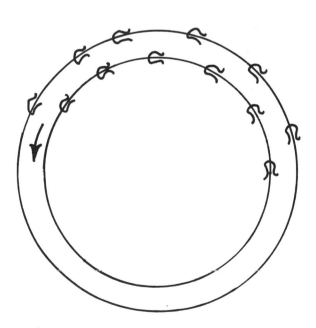

Picture 75. On the line around a circle. *This horse is moving on the line along a circle, assuming that his head and neck are also following the circle being described.*

Picture 76. Movement off the line with the head and neck. *The horse's head and neck are not following the arc of the circle being described. He should be looking in the direction of the turn being performed—very much as his rider is doing at this moment.*

Moving on the line is something that should be taught to every horse, and the defects just mentioned should be scrupulously avoided. The value of schooling a horse to move forward with movement on the line is threefold:

1. When moving on the line, the horse is in a position to respond to the rider's aids more quickly and efficiently.
2. When moving on the line, the horse does not have the upper hand in resisting the rider's aids when being taught new lessons.
3. Because the horse cannot literally bend his back to any useful degree, movement on the line permits the greatest accuracy in performing lateral movements such as circles,

serpentines, figures of eight, barrel and pole patterns.

How to teach movement on the line is a topic of Chapter 6. Primarily, teaching movement on the line involves the active use of the rider's holding and displacing legs; some use of weight, generally to the outside; and the use of one indirect rein of opposition, or a leading rein for the very green horse which has not yet learned to neck rein or for a horse that does not neck rein responsively.

Is there ever a time when movement on the line should not be required of the horse?

There are a few such instances; they occur while the horse is performing certain higher-level exercises. They are not examples of normal riding or

Picture 77. Movement off the line with the haunches as the canter is begun. *The horse's haunches have drifted inward here just as the canter is being initiated.*

showing. For example, the shoulder-in exercise is one where being *off* the line is in fact demanded as a test of the horse's obedience to the rider's aids.

Except for a few special schooling exercises (Picture 80), always think in terms of producing movement on the line. It is an extremely important quality to engrain in the horse's movement.

ENGAGEMENT

Stabilization and movement on the line are basic to the schooling of any horse. Whether you have heard these specific terms before or not, the substance of what I had to say is common knowledge.

Engagement may be less familiar. The substance of this is not always such common knowledge; it is not always something assumed for the schooling of any horse. An understanding of schooling for engagement as a desirable quality in the horse's movement often separates the good rider from the average and the average from the poor.

The term *engagement* denotes the forward swing of the horse's rear limbs. *Disengagement* refers to the corresponding rearward swing of these same limbs. Picture 81 shows a horse moving forward at the trot: the left rear limb is engaged, the right rear limb is disengaged. Quite obviously, any horse must engage and disengage the rear limbs in succession if he is to move forward at all. Of course, the front limbs must also engage and disengage for forward movement to be produced, but this is not the consideration here. When riders

Picture 78. Movement off the line during halting. *While this horse did halt promptly, he allowed his haunches to fall inward as the halt was obtained.*

speak of engagements, they mean that of the rear limbs.

Engagement as a general term denotes the distance or length of the forward swing of the hind limb ahead of the vertical—ahead of the position that would normally be occupied by the rear limb if the horse were standing still, squarely halted. Correspondingly, disengagement denotes the distance behind the vertical that the limb travels during its backward swing as the horse moves forward (Picture 82).

The relevance of engagement to schooling, and later to the horse's performance in the show ring, is simply this. Whenever the engagement of the rear limbs is *less* than the corresponding disengaged distance, the horse is said to be *strung out* (Picture 83). On the other hand, if the horse en-

gages his rear limbs more or as much as he disengages them, his forward movement can be termed engaged (Picture 84). This is good forward movement.

Engagement is an important positive quality in the horse's forward movement. True, no one ever says "My, isn't that marvelous, your horse is traveling with nice engagement," but on the other hand, if your horse travels in a strung-out manner, people will comment on the poor quality of forward movement. Knowledgeable riders and judges alike will generally note this particular defect in the overall quality of your horse's forward movement.

Different types of western horses move in different ways; the quality of the stride for the reining horse is necessarily different from that of

Picture 79. Another form of movement off the line. *The head is tipped to the outside.*

the pleasure horse for their respective events—a longer stride versus a shorter one. The qualities of engagement for these two types of horse also differ, but neither horse should travel forward in a strung-out manner. Hence, we really need a way in which to recognize different qualities in the same good trait of engagement for different kinds of horses and for the tasks they perform. One such way is to modify the word engagement—to make it more precise.

Horizontal Engagement

Horizontal engagement is really no more than has already been discussed. The horse moves forward with a swing of hind limbs toward the front at least equal to, and perhaps even greater than, the distance covered by the rearward flight of these same limbs. In one instance a horse might be asked to engage his rear limbs two feet ahead of the vertical, while making the rearward flight of these same limbs no more than two feet. In another instance, this same horse might be asked to engage his hind limbs even more—perhaps four feet ahead of the vertical while their rearward

flight covers a distance less than four feet. In either case the horse is engaged horizontally: a minimal engagement in the first instance, and greater engagement in the second.

Minimal horizontal engagement is correctly associated with the slow forward speeds of the jog and lope. Greater horizontal engagement is associated with faster speeds of the trot and canter—the ordinary trot and canter. Pictures 85 and 86 illustrate these points.

Vertical Engagement

Vertical engagement can be applied to any horse whose schooling is at a point where he can begin to learn something of *collection,* where he begins to carry more of his weight on his haunches at slow speeds of the trot and canter. However, its most frequent application is to the schooling of better western pleasure horses. It secures a good quality movement at the very slow speeds of the trot and canter—in other words, at a jog trot and lope which possess very good impulse while remaining quite slow in forward speed.

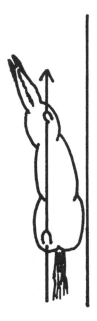

Picture 80. The shoulder-in exercise. *This horse is being purposely asked to move off the line as a matter of schooling for increased lateral flexibility. Such exercises are fine, provided the horse has already been schooled to move on the line.*

Vertical engagement implies a definite shortening of the stride of the rear limbs, but it necessarily requires a more animated up-and-down movement of the hocks; some of the energy normally expended in moving the limb forward now begins to travel up and down the leg as well (Picture 87).

Later, I will talk about shifting the horse's weight back toward the hind limbs as an aspect of collection at the trot and canter. If you have an interest in collection, teaching good vertical engagement is for you, and your primary use of vertical engagement will probably be to improve the appearance of your western pleasure horses in the show ring. Greater impulsion can be maintained for each of the gaits, but without necessarily increasing the horse's forward speed. The horse can move forward slowly and steadily while maintaining the appearance of being very pulled together, not strung out.

Good vertical engagement involves shifting the horse's weight to the rear, good flexion of the head and slow but energetic forward speeds. However, if a measure of horizontal engagement is not present in the forward stride, the quality of the horse's movement will not be good. It makes no difference that the forward swing of the vertically engaged limb might only be one foot ahead of the vertical and the corresponding disengagement no

greater than one foot. No matter how great the vertical engagement, if the horse is strung out horizontally, good forward movement suffers. Strung out is simply strung out, even at desirable slow forward speeds with vertical engagement. Look at Picture 87 again. Not only is this horse well engaged vertically but horizontal engagement is also present. Even though the stride here has been considerably shortened, the forward swing of each rear leg still is greater than the corresponding disengagement.

While good vertical engagement is not intended to permit fast forward speeds, it does permit any horse to become handier, or lighter in your hands. Schooling for good vertical engagement at the slower speeds of the jog and lope can benefit any horse, regardless of whether he might ever be shown in western pleasure classes. The ability of any performance horse to switch back and forth between these two types of engagement, for rapid increases and decreases in speed or for purposes of smoothly lengthening and shortening his stride, allows him to remain in a frame to respond promptly to the rider's aids all the time.

If you cross-enter some of the English classes, you will of course be performing the ordinary trot and canter. Long, low strides with good horizontal engagement will be what you are after.

Picture 81. Engagement and disengagement of the rear limbs. *The left rear leg of this horse is engaged. The right rear leg is disengaged.*

Schooling the same horse for good vertical engagement at the slower speeds of the trot and canter at home may well pay off in your English classes—downward transitions in English classes will probably be smoother.

Vertical engagement has no place in schooling for a good walk. The emphasis here for any type of horse is a forward-moving walk, one with good horizontal engagement and a long stride. The only exception is for the trail horse, for which walking over obstacles, sometimes quite closely spaced, is required in most classes.

The horse that does not move forward with engagement of either type is in a poor position to perform quickly any movement which might be required of him. Rollbacks, rapid halts and rapid starts, sliding stops, quick increases and decreases in pace and other movements simply are not possible without the presence of engagement in one form or the other in the overall quality of the horse's forward movement. Without engagement of the forward stride, the horse's rear legs are simply not up under him and he will not be able to

perform any of these movements either quickly or precisely. Whenever the horse remains strung out during forward movement at any gait, his entire performance suffers.

Experienced riders often refer to a certain horse as being an athlete or to another as being without much athletic ability. If you observe these athletic horses, you will find being an athlete is largely a matter of being engaged.

Teaching the horse, particularly the young horse, to engage his rear limbs in practically any acceptable fashion at each of the three gaits is not always an easy task. Teaching engagement not only requires certain techniques on the part of the rider, but some normal physical limitations of the horse himself often come into play.

For example, the horse normally possesses a limited range of movement in the long bone of the hind limb called the femur. (This is the long bone between the hip joint and the stifle. It is labeled in Picture 19, Chapter 1.) In order to travel forward with good horizontal engagement, the young horse must be willing to move the femur farther

Picture 82. Engagement ahead of the vertical. *The distance which this horse's leg is engaged ahead of the vertical is shown by the arrow labeled E. The corresponding distance of disengagement is shown by the arrow labeled D. The dotted line defines the vertical—the normal position of the horse's rear legs if he were halted squarely.*

forward than he might normally be expected to do if left strictly to his own devices. This requires a little more work on the part of the horse. In fact, I believe that a very large percentage of all horses would be quite content to travel strung out all of their lives, unless their riders demanded that they do otherwise.

IMPULSION OR IMPULSE FORWARD

The term *impulsion, impulse forward* or simply *impulse* is gaining wider use among professional riding circles, educated riders and judges today. It is an important term with practical value in schooling and later in showing. Littauer, in *Commonsense Horsemanship,* defines impulse in part as

> quick, energetic but quiet response to the rider's legs. . . . Don't confuse impulse with speed. Impulse is keenness, alertness, energy of movement, willingness to go forward; it may or may not be transformed into speed.

It may at first seem to you that this term might be of interest to armchair theoreticians, but has little practical value. Not so.

Concerning the practicality of impulse in the horse's movement, suppose that I were to say to you, in a quiet and unassuming way, "Could you come over here for a moment?" Now suppose I were to say to you, "HEY YOU, COME HERE!" Well, quite a difference for two requests that really mean the same thing!

In the first instance, you probably would just amble my way to see what I wanted. In the second instance, however, though you might not walk toward me any faster than in the first instance, your whole bearing in making your approach would be quite different. Perhaps you would be moving no faster, but something about the way in which you were moving would be different. An appearance of a *reserve of energy.* This is impulsion or impulse forward. The appearance of a reserve of energy, alertness and presence improves the show ring appearance of any horse.

Picture 83. Traveling forward in a strung-out manner. *This mare's engagement is not as great as her disengagement. Look at the hocks in relation to their distance ahead of and behind the vertical. The attitude of this horse's head and neck alone would lead you to believe that she is strung out.*

Most of you will probably agree that impulse is a worthwhile quality which you might add to the movement of practically any horse. After all, what show ring rider doesn't want his horse to appear keen and alert, and to respond quickly and energetically to his leg aids whenever necessary—in other words, to have impulse forward. What may bother you about this term impulse and its practice is that it concerns the appearance of the horse. After all, how does one define keenness or the appearance of a reserve of energy? Perhaps the following will clarify matters:

1. Impulse is a mental attitude of the horse. Its key points are alertness, keenness and the appearance of a reserve of energy to each of the gaits.
2. Impulse requires a certain physical state of the horse. The key points are a) during all early schooling, a natural carriage of the head and neck, coupled with engagement of the rear limbs and mental attitude specified by 1 above, and b) during more advanced schooling, a head brought back toward the vertical while engagement of the rear limbs is maintained.
3. In any case, impulse forward almost always comes from the rider's soft use of urging legs. Forward speed, if it needs to be contained for your particular event, is contained by the rider's definite use of weight, vertically, and the soft use of hands.
4. Impulse not produced by the rider's legs is the mark of a very nervous and upset horse or one that has been startled or is being ridden in new surroundings for the first time.

Impulse is not to be confused with fast forward speed. An extreme example will illustrate the difference. Most barrel and pole horses have a lot of impulse. You will see many of them actually trotting in place as they wait to run. In fact, you may see some of them actually cantering in place

Picture 84. The engaged horse. *The engagement phase of the rear limbs is greater than their disengagement phase.*

as they prepare to run. This is a maximum impulse situation, yet forward speed is very nearly 0 mph.

Another point. Engagement in and of itself does not necessarily guarantee that the horse will travel with impulse at any gait. Any horse may be traveling with engagement or be engaged rather well, but still not have the appearance of energy or keenness about him. If this is the case, during schooling you need to wake him up a little. Use your legs or your voice. Then, if necessary, contain his forward speed with your hands to prevent an increase in pace or an erratic pace.

While the presence of engagement does not necessarily guarantee the quality of impulse forward, the lack of engagement makes impulse forward impossible. Impulse without engagement of any type simply is not possible.

As you will see later, it takes a little technique on the rider's part to teach impulse forward; this is especially true whenever slow forward speeds on loose reins are required by a western pleasure class. Teaching impulse for the pleasure horse requires finesse and common sense on the part of the rider.

If you teach, I would offer this suggestion. First, inform your interested students about impulse as part of educated riding. Very likely, if they are serious students, they will run across this term at some point in the future anyway. During the routine business of teaching, simply use the term energy, or energy forward, as a substitute for the term impulse. Energy is easily understood by practically everyone, and the word conveys the same basic idea as impulse forward.

Photographing impulse is not an easy task. Engagement comes across fine in a photograph, but the horse's mental state is almost impossible to capture in a still picture. Astride the horse, you can easily perceive the alertness and keenness of impulse, but in a photo these things are difficult to perceive.

Most of the horses in this book were photographed moving forward with impulse—the horse in the position illustrations (Chapter 2) is just one example. However, the most dramatic illustration of the difference a little impulse can make in how a horse moves can be gleaned from two photos early in Chapter 1. In Picture 3 the

Picture 85. Horizontal engagement at the jog. *While this mare is moving at the jog with quite a short stride, she nevertheless remains engaged. The forward swing of the hind limbs still remains greater than the corresponding rearward swing of these same limbs. The degree of engagement shown is entirely appropriate for the type of forward movement being required by the rider.*

horse completely lacks impulse, but in Picture 4 the same horse has begun to move forward with impulse. Of course, the horse is grass green, but if you had been riding him in both pictures, you would have a better feeling about the quality of his forward movement in Picture 4.

LONGITUDINAL AGILITY

This term refers to the agility of the horse along his length: the ability to lengthen or shorten his entire frame and to regulate his forward speed and length of stride, as well as the ability to shift his center of balance forward or backward. Every one of these attributes is part of the horse's *longitudinal agility*. You could also use the term *longitudinal flexibility* to describe these same attributes.

More specifically, longitudinal agility is the ability of the horse, through schooling, to do the following, listed in their approximate order of difficulty:

1. To increase his forward speed at any gait without breaking to a higher gait. In other words, to increase his speed at the walk without breaking to the trot, or to increase the speed of the trot without breaking to the canter.

2. To decrease his forward speed at any gait without breaking to a slower gait. In other words, to execute a slow canter without breaking to the trot, or a slow jog trot without breaking to the walk.

3. To lower his head and neck in response to a release of the rider's aids: decreased tension on the reins, a decrease of leg pressure by the rider or both. In this case, the horse stretches his overall length from head to tail, and this acts to shift his center of balance forward. Depending on how a horse

Picture 86. Horizontal engagement at the ordinary trot. *The horse shown here is well engaged at the ordinary trot. While the engagement phase of this horse's stride is indeed much greater than that for the horse shown in Picture 85, it is not in itself better. The engagement of this horse is appropriate for the type of movement being required—a very forward-moving trot with good speed.*

has been schooled, decreased rein tension and a steady increase in leg pressure may act to extend the horse's head and neck. At the same time, they may also act to lengthen his stride.

4. To elevate his head and neck in response to the rider's aids: increased rein tension, active urging legs or both. In this case the horse shortens his overall length from head to tail, shifting his center of balance rearward. Willing flexion of the head is also a part of longitudinal agility; flexion of the head tends to shorten the horse's frame even more.

5. To be capable of changing from a stride where the emphasis is on horizontal engagement to one where the emphasis is on vertical engagement. In other words, to compete in events such as barrel racing or English pleasure class (where substantial horizontal engagement is needed), and be capable of competing in a western pleasure class (where the emphasis is now on vertical engagement).

6. To be capable ultimately of rapidly shifting his balance from the front to the back, and vice versa. In other words, to perfect points 3 and 4 to a high degree.

7. To either lengthen or shorten his stride, but without measurably altering his forward speed. In other words, to increase or decrease his horizontal engagement in response to the rider's use of aids without measurably changing his overall forward speed. Technically, this is the essence of extending the trot, but too often judges and competitors alike view this as simply trotting faster.

Refer to Pictures 88 and 89. These two pictures visually summarize several of the points just made concerning longitudinal flexibility.

Picture 87. Vertical engagement. *Vertical engagement requires that the horse convert some of the energy of forward movement into a greater up-and-down movement of the rear legs. The hocks show greater bending and the forward swing of the legs becomes less. If you compare this photograph with Pictures 82 and 85, you will see a great difference in hock action as well as in length of stride. Vertical engagement is viewed as a dressage-type of engagement by many riders.*

The parts of the horse which should possess longitudinal agility are the head, neck and legs. The head and neck may either be raised or lowered; rearward flexion of the head at the poll may be present or absent. These actions, singly or in various combinations, tend to shift the horse's center of balance either back or forward. Elevation of the horse's head and neck tends to shift his balance back. Flexion of the head toward the vertical also enhances this rearward shifting of the horse's balance.

For example, elevation of the head and neck with flexion of the head is associated with slow forward speeds at the trot and canter and good vertical engagement of the hind legs. The extension or lowering of the head and neck, along with the absence of flexion at the poll, is associated with faster forward speeds at the trot and canter, *providing* the rider also demands good horizontal engagement of the rear limbs.

The horse's legs may act in three different ways to produce longitudinal agility. First, they may act by simply moving faster or slower to affect overall speed. Secondly, they may act by lengthening or shortening the distance of the stride, depending on whether the horse's center of balance is located forward or back toward the croup. This alteration in the length of the stride may or may not be accompanied by noticeable changes in the horse's forward speed.

For example, a shift in the center of balance slightly rearward with a simultaneous lengthening of stride tends to control forward speed; a lengthening of stride without a noticeable increase in speed is the result. A shift in the horse's center of balance to the front with a lengthening of the stride results in an increase of forward speed.

Third, the legs may demonstrate longitudinal agility by altering their type of engagement. The emphasis is on horizontal engagement for such

Picture 88. Longitudinal flexibility. *Compare this picture with Picture 89. The caption under Picture 89 explains the aspects of longitudinal agility in both of these pictures.*

classes as roping, English pleasure, reining and the speed events, while the emphasis is on vertical engagement for the western pleasure classes.

Probably the most common show ring test of whether the horse possesses longitudinal agility is the judge's call for an extended trot (a lengthening of the stride at the trot), or his call for a hand gallop (an increase in speed with the horse moving fast enough to develop a four-beat gait at the gallop). Contestants of their own accord also put their horses to the test of longitudinal agility by entering the western pleasure class and then cross-entering the English pleasure class, or by entering the western pleasure class and then entering a western riding class or perhaps even a hunter-over-fences class.

Chapter 7 discusses in detail how to teach longitudinal agility. Teaching longitudinal agility is really the prerequisite to teaching useful flexions of the horse's head. These flexions have absolutely no relationship to the artificial outline or attitude of the horse's head which is accomplished through head setting.

Useful flexions of the horse's head toward the vertical are produced by teaching the horse cooperation with the rider's hands, and to a lesser degree cooperation with the rider's weight and legs. Useful flexions of the head are the basis for excellent downward transitions and the efficient shifting of the horse's weight rearward for a variety of purposes: rapid halts without "falling on his nose," short fast turns and many, many others.

Teaching longitudinal agility is not really difficult. Teaching the horse two or three stabilized speeds at the walk, two at the trot, and two at the canter will automatically give any horse a head-start at longitudinal agility. For nearly every horse, you will also find that teaching different speeds at each of these gaits is a necessary prerequisite to developing useful flexions of the head toward the vertical, not just a useless, stylish head carriage designed to fool the judge in a single pleasure class.

Picture 89. Longitudinal flexibility. *In Picture 88 this filly has moved her center of balance forward, while here she has moved it rearward. In 88 she has extended the head and neck, while in 89 she has elevated the head and neck and flexed the head rearward. In 88 she is moving forward at a rather fast speed of the trot, while in 89 she has considerably slowed her pace at this gait. In 88 she has lengthened her stride, while in 89 she has shortened it. In 88 her engagement is more of a horizontal type, while in 89 there is a definite tendency toward vertical engagement.*

LATERAL AGILITY

Lateral agility, or *lateral flexibility*, describes the horse's ability to bend his head and neck to the side in cooperation with the rider's use of reins. It is also the ability of the horse to remain on the line with the head and neck during circles and turns. Lateral agility includes the ability of the horse to cooperate with the rider's use of hands, legs and weight in moving to the side—moving his forehand or shoulders to the side in some instances, and the haunches in others. Good lateral agility in cooperation with the rider's aids is best reflected by exercises and ring figures such as:

1. Accurate circles ranging from very large to relatively small diameters, perhaps as small as 25 feet. Needless to say, these circles are executed with movement on the line.

2. Serpentines and figures of eight (Chapter 7), as well as barrel and pole patterns. The barrel and pole patterns do not have to be performed in competition or at fast speeds when they are employed as schooling exercises for teaching lateral agility.

3. Half circles.

4. Accurate turns, on the line with even speeds.

5. Higher-level schooling exercises such as the pivot spin, counter-canter, and volté. Higher level performance events such as pole bending, western riding, reining and cutting.

The development of lateral agility in the horse is largely a matter of his obedience to your aids at first, and later, during higher levels of schooling,

Picture 90. Lateral flexibility. *While not illustrating a specific schooling exercise, this picture does demonstrate one aspect of lateral agility: the ability of the horse to cooperate with the rider's aids in moving the head and neck to the side.*

his cooperation with each of them. The development of lateral agility through schooling permits both accuracy and softness in performing all types of lateral movements which may be required of the western horse. One aspect of lateral agility, the cooperation of the horse with the rider's hands in moving the head and neck to the side, is shown by Picture 90.

SELECTING A BIT

The bit is one of four principal means by which the rider communicates with his horse; voice, weight and legs are of course the other three.

Few riders intend to be purposely abusive with the reins. However, heavy hands (which do not check and release, but only hang) or those that cannot efficiently follow the balancing gestures of the horse's head and neck can develop one of the following: a horse with an insensitive mouth, a horse that is hard to control, one that habitually moves off the line, or one that insists on moving forward while traveling either above or behind the bit.

When the primary issue is that of abusive riding, the selection of one bit over another is really of little consequence. But when riding is accomplished through correct and efficient use of aids, experience in riding and a good working position, then selection of the proper bit can assist the rider in accomplishing even more with the horses being ridden and schooled. The horse's education and quality of movement can be enhanced through the use of different types of suitable bits.

Bits are made from many different materials and come in countless designs. Most of these work on the bars of the mouth, corners of the lips, or tongue. Some, however, work principally on the chin groove, roof of the mouth, and even the poll. Bitless bridles (such as the bosal and hackamore) work on the cartilage and soft tissues above the nose and on the sides of the muzzle.

The *snaffle bit* has the reins attached directly to the mouthpiece via rings of various shapes; these are usually O- or D-shaped rings. The mouthpiece of the snaffle may be either solid or jointed in the middle. The solid snaffle, especially one with a rubber mouthpiece, is the mildest form of the snaffle. The mouthpieces of jointed snaffles come in several variations: smooth, twisted, twisted wire and even double-twisted wire. The twisted wire versions are the most severe form of this bit.

The solid snaffle principally affects the corners of the mouth and thus has quite a mild overall effect. The jointed snaffle, with either a smooth or twisted mouthpiece, is slightly more severe since its action is scissor-like and affects the tongue and bars of the mouth as well as the corners of the lips. The bars of the horse's mouth are located in the interdental space, which exists between the front teeth (incisors) and the cheek teeth (premolars and molars).

Twisted wire versions of the jointed snaffle can act as an extremely severe form of bit. Though persistent or dangerous control problems in the green horse may indicate the use of this type of bit, it should only be employed by a rider who possesses highly educated hands and a very secure position. For the rider who cannot check and release efficiently, or who cannot follow the balancing gestures of the horse's head and neck when riding on very short reins, the scissor-like effect of the twisted wire snaffle can quickly result in laceration of lips, tongue andbars. A horse with an insensitive mouth may be the result, and control problems may in fact worsen.

Curb bits come in a variety of designs. Although the mouthpieces may vary considerably from jointed to bar-type mouthpieces, curb bits have two consistent features: bit shanks (to which the reins are attached) and a curb chain or strap. Curb bits are considered typical western-type bits for most older schooled horses.

Shanks for the curb bits come in a variety of lengths. The longer the shank, the greater the leverage or pressure that can be applied to the horse's mouth, providing that the curb chain is adjusted properly.

Curb chains (metal) or curb straps (usually leather or nylon) should fit within the horse's chin groove, but not tightly. One or two fingers should fit comfortably between the curb chain and the chin groove. Whenever rearward tension is applied to the reins, the curb chain should remain centered under or within the chin groove and should not travel (far) rearward of this area.

Curb bits are available with a variety of mouthpiece types: bar, hinged or jointed mouthpieces, and mouthpieces with ports. (A port is simply an upward curve located in the middle of a bar-type mouthpiece.) Ports come in different heights which are generally described as low, medium or high ports. The higher the port, the more severe a rider can make the bit—if he so chooses. Some ports can be made high enough to affect even the roof of the mouth.

The spade bit is a special type of curb bit which can have an extremely severe action; it affects the roof of the mouth (hard palate) as well as other sensitive structures within the mouth cavity, principally the bars.

The so-called training snaffle (Picture 54) is also a special type of curb bit. It is a relatively mild form of the curb bit whose principal advantage is a bit shank that swivels easily to the side. The training snaffle allows the rider to continue using the leading rein unabusively, while at the same time retaining better control of the horse's forward pace and head carriage.

The mechanical hackamore is a type of bitless bridle; it is a favorite of many riders who enjoy the western speed events. This type of hackamore is fine for schooled horses and for horses that must make quick and definite responses to the rider's aids in order to be competitive. However, the mechanical hackamore is generally inappropriate for schooling the green horse; teaching all of the rein aids with this type of setup is nearly impossible. For schooling more experienced horses, where precision and smoothness are to be emphasized, the mechanical hackamore presents a similar disadvantage for both the horse and rider.

The bosal, or non-mechanical hackamore, is sometimes suitable for beginning the schooling of a green horse, but again, teaching all of the standard rein aids becomes a difficult proposition. Generally, a plain snaffle is more satisfactory for all early schooling.

You should bear in mind that AQHA horses must be shown in a bit from age five years. The mechanical hackamore, bosal and plain snaffle are not considered bits by the AQHA. However, for horses less than five years of age the snaffle bit reining classes, hackamore horses worked on cattle, and other bitless classes represent some of the best horse-and-rider combinations that can be seen in competition.

As a general rule, employ a snaffle for all early schooling. Use a standard O- or D-ring snaffle with either a bar-type or jointed mouthpiece. If you choose a jointed mouthpiece, use either the smooth or twisted type (but not twisted wire). The six standard rein aids are more easily taught using these types of snaffles. Teaching any new lesson at the elementary level will generally result in less abuse of the horse when this type of bit is employed by an educated rider. Better movement on the line will be possible, and avoiding horses that tend to travel above or behind the bit will be an easier matter.

Beyond the elementary level of schooling, consider moving to a more complicated bit such as the curb bit with a low or medium port. At this point, your primary rein aids will be two direct reins of opposition and the bearing rein; these two rein aids are ideally suited to the use of a curb bit. The curb bit increases the horse's tendency toward central balance and teaches willing soft flexion of the head rearward. (However, the bosal can also accomplish these goals, as can several other bits, including the snaffle.)

A brief summary of bits and bitting is all that I have provided in the preceding discussion. While I do not mean to minimize the role of proper bitting for all facets of riding and schooling, remain aware that selecting a new bit, using more severe bits, or frequently changing from one bit to another cannot remedy flaws in your basic riding technique or position design. Continually strive to achieve soft and sympathetic hands and a good working position. You must also have a basic understanding of how the horse moves, how schooling is accomplished systematically, and which methods are most easily understood by the horse.

If you require more information about bits and bitting, there are several good books on the subject that you can consult. Or, talk to a knowledgeable person in your local tack shop or saddlery; don't hesitate to seek advice from a professional you might know. You should also take advantage of current articles in popular horse magazines. If your riding is unabusive and your position is secure, do not be afraid to experiment with more complicated bits as your horse's level of schooling improves.

THE CARRIAGE OF THE HEAD AND NECK

Understanding how a performance horse should carry his head and neck is vital for good schooling and riding. The carriage of the head and neck is important for all western horses, not just the western pleasure horse.

The western pleasure horse is only one of several different types of western performance horses. He represents perhaps ten percent of all of the basic types of performance classes that can be found at any large national show and as little as two percent of all of the uses to which any western horse might conceivably be put. In fact, the western pleasure horse during his show ring performance is the only western horse which can compete successfully using only a show-type of head carriage, one that is not necessarily functional for the majority of tasks to which any well-schooled western horse might actually be put.

The sections that follow concern the head and neck carriage of any performance horse: reining horse, barrel horse, pole bender, trail horse, roping horse, cutting horse, western riding horse, stock horse and yes, the western pleasure horse and any others you might choose to ride. If you are to ride and school successfully, you should understand something of the relationship between the carriage of the horse's head and neck and the type of performance event for which you are schooling.

RELATIONSHIPS OF THE HEAD AND NECK TO THE BIT

Probably the first thing to consider about the role and importance of the horse's head and neck carriage is the relationship of the horse's head carriage to the bit. There are four universal ways in which this relationship can be described:

1. above the bit
2. behind the bit (also called over the bit)
3. accepting the bit (also called up in the bridle)
4. on the bit (also called very up in the bridle)

Above the Bit

The term *above the bit* (Picture 91) means that the horse carries his head about parallel to the ground, that he is high headed and may even point his nose upward at times. Traveling above the bit is an evasion technique used by the horse in response to the rider's use of the reins: the use of two direct reins of opposition to control the horse's forward speed, to halt or to back the horse. It is a common fault in young horses being ridden for the first time and a temporary fault in

Picture 91. Above the bit. *The horse above the bit is attempting to avoid the use of the rider's hands. Going above the bit is an evasion of the rider's aids.*

older horses being taught a new lesson for the first time. It can be a consistent defect in any horse ridden only by a heavy-handed or abusive rider, particularly when most of the riding is performed in a snaffle bit. For the rider with soft, sympathetic hands, a horse's traveling above the bit is usually only temporary. The head will come down as the horse begins to understand exactly what is required of him.

However, one often sees well-schooled barrel, pole and roping horses ridden by riders with soft, educated hands, and yet substantially above the bit as they prepare and wait for their event. They may also be above the bit at instants during the event. Depending upon how particular you might be, you may or may not consider most of these horses to be justifiably above the bit for their events. I believe that these horses are generally justified in their head carriage, for the following reason. I will use the barrel horse as the example.

As the barrel horse waits at the line to begin his run, he may move his head substantially above the bit. You will especially see this in Appaloosa shows where the horses not only run against the clock, but run horse against horse. To a great extent, moving above the bit is tied to the excitement of the event itself. But part of this movement above the bit is tied to the horse's efforts to shift his weight rearward by correctly elevating the head and neck—to become handier or more centrally balanced with greater weight on his hindquarters in order to respond quickly to the rider's aids in beginning his run. The ideal, of course, would be for the horse to raise his head and neck as I have described, but then to flex the head toward the vertical rather than remaining above the bit and possibly straining against a tie down. This would be the mark of a very well-schooled horse, one that could ignore the excitement of the event itself.

As the horse actually begins his run, he will no longer travel above the bit; he will lower the head and neck in order to achieve the fast forward speed required. However, as each barrel is encountered, you may again see a tendency to go above the bit. His purpose again is to lighten the forehand by raising the head and neck in order to transfer more weight to the rear, to become handy for smooth changes in speed, for the very tight turns required and for ease in performing a flying lead change after turning the first barrel.

The ideal would be to accompany this elevation of the head and neck with flexion of the head back

Picture 92. Behind the bit. *Moving behind the bit is another way a horse attempts to avoid the use of the rider's aids. It is another bit-evasion technique. A horse will frequently move behind the bit when a rider attempts to teach the horse flexions of the head before teaching him to move forward from the leg.*

toward the vertical, rather than merely raising the head and neck to the point of going above the bit for the purpose of shifting the center of balance rearward.

At any rate, barrel horses are not judged on their way of going—their quality of movement. Beating the clock is the criterion for this performance event. If elevating the head and neck and traveling slightly above the bit at times will accomplish this, fine. But if the horse were to raise the head and neck with flexion of the head at those times when greater weight must be carried on the haunches, this would constitute the better performance. This would permit the horse a slightly smoother regulation of his forward pace just before turning, and the flying change of leads would probably come off more smoothly, also.

In essence then, traveling above the bit is an unacceptable form of forward movement for any horse with the possible exception of speed horses or the roping horse in the box. These horses can be more or less excused on the basis of the excitement of the events.

I will comment briefly on two medical problems that may induce the horse to travel above the bit. The wolf teeth are technically the first premolars and are found on the upper dental arcade. A horse may acquire these two teeth as early as five months of age. They will pose no problem to head carriage until the horse is ridden with a bit, around the age of two years. Have them extracted if head problems remain in schooling despite good riding technique. It is a perfectly safe and simple procedure. Remember to give the horse a tetanus vaccination before extraction.

The canine teeth (not related to the wolf teeth) begin to appear around the age of four or five years. They are found in either the upper or lower dental arcade, or both. They occur in mares as well as geldings and stallions. While they are *not* to be extracted, the horse will often remain rather tender-mouthed until the teeth have substantially erupted through the soft tissue of the mouth. Try different bits, if you must ride the horse. Be especially soft with your hands. Use a bosal if you can during this period. If the horse is bitted, make sure your bit is adjusted properly; especially insure that it does not hang low in the mouth. (The canine teeth are located relatively close to the front of the horse's mouth, while the wolf teeth are located several inches to the rear of the canines.)

In any case, do not be too quick to blame the horse's teeth for any difficulty. Review your own riding technique first and the horse's previous schooling. He may have been started by a heavy-handed rider.

Behind the Bit

The term *behind the bit* (Picture 92) means that the horse travels with his head behind the vertical: he overflexes his head toward his chest. This is a bit-evasion technique. This overflexion has *absolutely no relationship* to collected movement,

which I will talk about later. A horse that travels behind the bit is just as undesirable as the horse that travels above the bit. There is no legitimate reason for the horse to ever travel behind the bit.

There are two instances in which traveling behind the bit becomes a problem. The first occurs with the western pleasure horse, although we are seeing less of this as riders are becoming more educated about schooling the young horse. In this case the rider has become so engrossed with producing flexion (to meet someone's idea of the perfect head carriage for the western pleasure horse) that he has actually taught the horse to drop behind the bit. Unclear goals in schooling are sometimes at fault: the rider has tried to produce flexion before the horse has been taught to move forward from the rider's legs. Sometimes heavy, uneducated hands are the problem; in other cases the premature use or overuse of draw reins and running martingales are at fault.

The second instance in which we see horses

Picture 93. Accepting the bit. *This horse is accepting the bit nicely and cooperating with the rider's hands by flexing her head and neck. She is not resisting the bit in any way. Her mouth is closed, and she is neither above nor behind the bit. If this rider were to close her legs on the horse's sides and give softly with her hands, the horse would be willing to extend her head slightly, softly take the bit and increase her forward speed while remaining engaged.*

traveling behind the bit results from hurry-up schooling or poor priorities in schooling. In either case, the horse is again encouraged to flex the head before he has even been taught to move forward from the rider's leg.

The simple fact is that the horse that travels behind the bit is not in the rider's hand. It is a serious fault in head carriage as well as in the quality of the horse's forward movement. The horse that evades the rider's hand by falling behind the bit cannot possibly have a good quality of forward movement; certainly there is no correlation between overflexion and the type of movement which some riders incorrectly term collected movement.

To avoid teaching the horse to move behind the bit, first recognize that you should not teach flexions in response to rein tension or use any sort of artificial gadgets until the horse will move forward willingly from your legs. Whenever a rider uses urging legs at the girth (with even an extremely mild urging leg action), the horse will naturally elevate the head and neck. The trick is to teach the horse to elevate the head and neck slightly, at the same time saying with the reins, "Don't go faster, just elevate the head and neck and extend the head to take hold gently of the bit and then bring the head back toward the vertical."

Producing soft flexion is a matter of obedience to the rider's mild use of the legs and cooperation with the rider's hands. Note that I refer to flexions of the head *toward* the vertical; only the most advanced horses can travel with the head flexed to a point where it lies exactly on the vertical while preserving all of the good qualities of movement: engagement, impulse, longitudinal agility, excellent movement on the line and lateral agility. In conjunction with the rider's mild use of legs and hands, the use of the rider's weight can assist in producing these flexions of the head toward the vertical.

Accepting the Bit

Accepting the bit (Picture 93) is a most useful term to the western rider. It is the desirable relationship of the horse's head carriage to the bit for purposes of schooling and showing. Accepting the bit means that the horse accepts the rider's hands—his use of reins. More specifically, accepting the bit means:

1. The horse is willing to extend the head slightly to take the bit softly in response to the rider's mild urging legs.
2. The horse is willing to regulate his forward speed by obeying rearward tension on the reins without trying to avoid the bit either by traveling above or behind the bit; or by opening his mouth.
3. The horse travels with engagement and impulse as he moves forward. The type of engagement may be horizontal or vertical, depending on the events for which you are schooling or on the classes in which you are showing.
4. As schooling advances, the horse will begin to cooperate with the rider's hands by flexing the head willingly to assist him in further fine regulation of his forward speed at slow and medium speeds, as well as to assist him in transferring some additional weight to the hindquarters and rear legs.

When I say that the horse is willing to extend the head somewhat to take the bit softly, I do not mean that he obviously stretches his head and neck forward, nor do I mean that he pokes his nose to the front. Instead the horse almost imperceptibly moves his head forward in order to gain a soft, consistent feel of the bit in his mouth—a sort of security blanket which allows the horse to maintain a very light, but consistent, feel of the bit as he moves forward, changes from one gait to the other and makes whatever changes in speed might be demanded by the rider.

Of course, the rider must make adjustments in rein tension or length at different points to best assist the horse in maintaining this consistent feel of the bit in his mouth: to shorten the reins slightly for slower speeds, or to lengthen them slightly or use following hands for the faster forward speeds.

Accepting the bit is also termed *up in the bridle* by some horsemen, especially when schooling has proceeded to the point where the horse will begin to willingly flex his head in response to increased rein tension: shorter reins, heavier reins or a more severe bit with longer shanks and hence a greater pressure, even on relatively loose reins.

I believe *up in the bridle* is more nebulous than *accepting the bit*; it is more difficult to define. Nevertheless, many of you may still prefer it. Accepting the bit is, however, more universally used.

If you turn back to Chapter 2 and look at the

horses pictured moving forward, you will see that all but one are accepting the bit.

On the Bit

On the bit is really an English riding term, but I would like to adopt it here for the western horse. The English horse moves forward on the bit *only when he is ridden on contact*—on two direct reins of opposition, with the rider using following arms to maintain a consistent feel of the horse's mouth. A loop or slackening the reins never appears. By contrast, the western horse is ridden on loose reins except for when he is cross-entered in some of the English riding or jumping classes.

For the western horse on loose reins, traveling on the bit represents something more than merely accepting the bit. Forward movement on the bit represents an even higher goal than accepting the bit. It is a mark of a very advanced horse *and* rider. Many horses, national champions included, compete very successfully by moving forward while only accepting the bit. Placing a horse on the bit, even for a talented horse with a very experi-

enced rider, simply is not generally required for success in competition.

Moving on the bit really entails everything entailed by accepting the bit and more. The horse that moves on the bit shows a greater willingness to cooperate with the rider's hands and legs. Not only will he flex the head *toward* the vertical, he will in fact move forward with the head literally on the vertical—perpendicular to the ground if asked to do so by the rider. This willingness to flex the head to the maximum without dropping behind the bit is a mark of the cooperation of the horse with the rider's hands and legs. The rider's legs prevent the horse from dropping behind the bit as his head approaches the vertical. There is no relationship between this willingness to flex the head and the use of severe bits or the overuse of mechanical gadgets, draw reins, running martingales and so forth. Merely creating a profile of the horse's head is not the point; it is the ability of the horse to create this flexed profile willingly through cooperation with the rider's hands and legs. This is a mark of advanced schooling.

Picture 94. On the bit. *This horse is moving forward on the bit while being ridden on contact. This Quarter mare is a second-level dressage horse originally started as a western horse. Picture 107 is a good example of a horse in western tack moving forward while on the bit.*

The horse that is on the bit, cooperating to the maximum with the rider's hands and legs, is also more engaged than the horse that is merely accepting the bit. As the horse begins to move on the bit, his overall engagement increases. A greater increase in vertical engagement for the pleasure classes and a more consistent head carriage result.

The horse on the bit will regulate his forward speed in relation to the rider's use of both hands and legs. He will do this to a greater extent than the horse that simply accepts the bit. In other words, the horse moving on the bit accepts the use of the rider's legs not only for speeding up or lengthening the stride; he also accepts the use of the rider's legs for slowing down, shortening his stride and shifting his center of balance to the rear.

For example, if the rider squeezes lightly with his legs, but maintains or lightens his rein tension, the horse should lengthen or quicken his stride without substantially altering his head flexion. However, if the rider squeezes lightly with his legs, but *increases* his rein tension, the horse should do several things: elevate his head and neck softly, increase the flexion of his head (providing this does not take him behind the bit), and increase his vertical engagement. Ultimately, this will result in a *slowing* or shortening of the horse's stride.

In one case, the rider uses his legs and hands to increase the pace or length of stride, and in the other he decreases the pace or shortens the stride. The horse on the bit really moves primarily from the rider's legs, and secondarily from his hands. Flexions are first produced by the legs, and secondarily by the rider's hands.

Along with increased cooperation, a horse on the bit demonstrates another quality: softness. The horse on the bit performs all transitions, gaits and movements with a soft, nonresistive response. The quality of movement is better in everything the horse does. The rider can *feel* the horse's increased cooperation. Not only does the horse respond quickly and with greater longitudinal agility, he also feels lighter in the rider's hands.

This increased softness and harmony between horse and rider can give the talented horse and advanced rider the edge in almost any class. Schooling the horse to move on the bit requires an above-average horse, mentally and physically. It requires an above-average rider—a well-educated rider, one with a good deal of experience, time and patience.

As stated earlier, the horse that accepts the bit is said by some to be up in the bridle. Likewise, the horse that travels consistently on the bit is sometimes said to be *very up in the bridle*. Now you are into degrees of something, which is one reason I didn't like the term *up in the bridle* in the first place.

Pictures 94 and 107 show two horses moving on the bit. The second picture is that of a California-style pleasure horse on the bit. The first picture is of a second-level dressage horse working on the bit as she is being schooled at the ordinary trot. This dressage horse is a quarter mare first started as a western horse, later converted to a hunter and even later to a dressage horse.

NATURAL CARRIAGE OF THE HEAD AND NECK

We have dealt so far with certain qualities which should be included in the schooling of any horse: stabilization, engagement, impulse, movement on the line, longitudinal and lateral agility. We have just looked at the various ways in which the horse may carry his head in relation to the bit. However, we have not yet looked at the ways the entire head and neck, the horse's balancer, affects each of these things—the ways in which the head and neck must be carried in order to best promote engagement, lateral agility, acceptance of the bit and so forth.

Natural carriage of the horse's head and neck means just what you would expect. It is the same carriage you see as the horse moves about freely in the pasture or a large paddock, or at any relaxed, but reasonably alert, gait. It is the same carriage you see as horses stand relaxed but attentive in practically any show ring line-up. The natural carriage of the horse's neck is the one most useful in early schooling and later in the show ring.

If you look again at the pictures in Chapter 2, at the horses and not the riders, you will notice that all of these horses show a natural carriage of the head and neck.

With the exception of the western pleasure horse, virtually every western performance horse relies on a natural carriage of the head and neck to successfully perform. I am not saying that the trail horse may not lower his head momentarily as he moves forward over a set of ground poles or that the barrel horse should not elevate the head and neck as he prepares to begin a sharp turn at the gallop around a barrel. In general, though, a natural carriage of the head and neck at the three standard gaits and the gallop signifies a relaxed but alert horse.

The upset horse, the one who is stiff and resistive, tends to travel with the head and neck elevated much of the time and even above the bit at times. On the other hand, the horse that has been "trained" (in the most negative sense) may travel with an exaggerated, low carriage of the head and neck. Such a horse has been trained to assume a nonfunctional carriage of the head and neck. He is not in the rider's hands because he invariably travels behind the bit, and he cannot be ridden with effective use of the rider's legs. His quality of forward movement is invariably strung out. He is

the product not of good riding or schooling, but rather of constant nagging by the rider or outright, consistent abuse.

When people talk about a horse that "really drops his head, and pleasures," they are essentially referring to a normal carriage of the head and neck. Probably the first thing they mean is that the horse is, in fact, well stabilized at the standard three western gaits. They are really saying that the horse does not raise his head and neck, that he moves forward in a relaxed, steady manner, with a normal carriage of the head and neck. He can remain attentive to the rider's hands, legs and weight without becoming stiff, resistive or excited.

A pleasure horse that can travel with his neck relaxed and in a normal position and also obey the

Picture 95. Elevation of the head and neck. *This horse is elevating the head and neck quite naturally in order to perform a pivot. He is not above the bit, nor is he attempting to evade the rider's aids; he is only raising his head and neck in order to lighten the forehand so that the exercise may be performed efficiently.*

rider's hands by flexing his head toward the vertical is the ideal. You would still consider this as a normal carriage of the head and neck, with the understanding that the horse has deviated somewhat from the norm simply by obeying the rider's hands. All of this is quite desirable so long as he maintains his engagement and impulse while producing these rearward flexions of the head.

You will see some outlandish examples of head and neck carriage in many pleasure classes—the horse with his nose on the ground, moving behind the bit, for example, but if you look at the total picture, and pay special attention to the winners of large national shows, you will find a consistent picture of the superior pleasure horse. You will find all the qualities of good forward movement: stabilization, engagement (vertical engagement for the pleasure horse), movement on the line, impulse, longitudinal and lateral agility, plus a natural carriage of the head and neck, slightly modified by flexion of the head in response to the rider's soft hands.

ELEVATED CARRIAGE OF THE HEAD AND NECK

It is a fact of life, a fact of mechanics and physical law, that a horse must elevate the head and neck in order to transfer more weight to the hindquarters (Picture 95). The more the head and neck are elevated, the shorter the horse's frame becomes as you measure him from head to tail.

As the head and neck are raised, the horse's center of balance also moves rearward; the forelegs bear progressively less weight, while the hind limbs bear more. The entire forehand lightens while the hindquarters bear a greater percentage of weight. Of course, if the head is flexed back toward vertical at the same time, the horse's overall frame is shortened even more; a greater lightening of the forehand occurs.

To place any horse in a collected frame, an elevation of the horse's head and neck is required—an elevation greater than that of the natural carriage. The head and neck must be raised to lighten

Picture 96. Mild direct flexion.

Picture 97. Direct flexion with the head approaching the vertical. *A filly this green should not be demonstrating flexion this good, but a good rider helped her to make the picture.*

the forehand so that the horse's center of gravity is shifted rearward. Flexions of the head without an accompanying elevation of the head and neck do tend to shorten the horse's frame from head to tail, but the effect is minor; substantial lightening of the forehand simply cannot be obtained by flexions of the head alone.

My point is that the elevation of the head and neck is allowable for many performance horses. To perform their events successfully, many horses must become very light in the rider's hands at certain points during their performance. Moving quickly from a halt or very slow speed to a very rapid forward speed requires this kind of preparatory lightness. Sliding stops, rollbacks at the canter, pivots and spins all require a collected frame. Of course, if some willing flexions of the head can be obtained in conjunction with the elevation of the head and neck, so much the better. This is not always possible, even on well-schooled horses, for events such as roping, speed events, the Appaloosa rope race and a few others.

DIRECT FLEXIONS OF THE HEAD AND NECK

Actually, we have already talked about this very thing many times. Direct flexions of the head and neck are flexions back toward the vertical. These may range from very mild responses to the rider's hands (Picture 96) to those which ultimately result in the horse carrying his head perpendicular to the ground or very nearly so (Picture 97). The purpose in either case is to shorten the horse's overall length, to "pull him together" by shifting a portion of his weight to the hindquarters. These direct flexions, when accompanied by a reasonable elevation of the head and neck, tend to lighten the horse's forehand considerably, making him quite handy and light in the rider's hands.

Direct flexions are also termed *longitudinal flexions* by many English riders. Nevertheless, these flexions are one of the requirements for placing a horse in a collected frame of movement. A little later in this chapter you will see that these

Picture 98. Flexion behind the vertical. *While you cannot deny that this green filly has flexed her head rearward to a maximum, flexions of this sort are useless. She has dropped behind the bit, evading rather than cooperating with the rider's hands. While flexing the head does transfer some of the horse's weight to the rear legs, this filly remains very heavy on the fore-hand as she prepares to back. In this case the low position of the head and neck more than offset any advantage gained by flexion of the head itself.*

direct flexions, coupled with an elevation of the head and neck and great longitudinal agility while maintaining impulse forward, are the basis of what you might term the semi-collected gaits (Pictures 106, 107 and 108).

Useful flexions of the head toward (but not behind) the vertical require that the horse be capable, through schooling (and not through abusive riding or reliance upon gadgets) of cooperating with the rider's hands during turns, moving forward in a straight line, backing and during the execution of downward transitions (Picture 98). This cooperation means coming back softly to the rider's use of hands—in other words, to cooperatively flex the head toward the vertical in response to rein tension. The characteristics of useful direct flexions of the head toward the vertical are:

1. Relaxing the poll—the junction of the base of the skull and neck—and retracting the head slightly toward the vertical in response to slight increases in rein tension, or in response to a check and release action of the reins; and subsequently relaxing the degree of flexion by extending the head and neck slightly in response to a release of rein tension (a lengthening of already loose reins).

2. Flexing softly, and repeatedly if necessary, during downward transitions in order to avoid rapid shifts in the horse's center of balance from the back to the front. The result is a very smooth downward transition with a minimum of disturbance to the rider's own balance. These same flexions provide smooth transitions from any gait to the halt; the more rapid the halt, the greater their value becomes (Picture 99).

3. Becoming attentive and better impulsed through a shortening of the horse's entire frame by elevating the head and neck and flexing the head softly in response to the rider's increased leg pressure at the girth in conjunction with increased rein tension, a shortening of the reins or an elevation of the

Picture 99. Flexions during downward transitions. *Excellent direct flexion of the head, softly and in cooperation with the rider's hands, is shown by this mare during a sliding stop. As she slides forward, she will use repeated direct flexions of the head in adding fine control and smoothness to this stop. She will use gradations in flexing her head repeatedly as she gradually comes to a complete halt—a little greater flexion here, a little less there. These same repeated flexions will allow her to finely regulate the slide so that it may be held for a relatively long period of time. In fact, you will notice she has even begun to walk in front as her forward speed has begun to slow. Elevation of the horse's head and neck and good engagement of the hindquarters are required to make flexions of the head a useful tool in riding. You cannot achieve greater collection by simply shifting a horse's weight rearward and flexing his head, while allowing a low carriage of the head and neck and strung-out movement.*

rider's hand—or even a cocking of the wrist to the rear in some cases.

The real value of direct flexions of the horse's head and neck lies in the ability of the horse and rider to produce good downward transitions, accurate regulation of forward pace, steady and accurate circles and turns and good movement on the line. Again, flexions of the head are generally worthless for these purposes unless engagement (either type) and impulse can be maintained.

The use of direct flexions permits *softness* and *fluidity* in downward transitions. Better movement on the line is possible and deviations of the horse off the rail during the upward transition from the walk to the canter is less likely.

Better backing is possible. Greater accuracy on turns and circles, along with a steadier forward pace can be achieved. In fact, greater precision in most movements and exercises is possible because the horse is capable of finely regulating the shift of his weight from front to back by flexing or regulating the subsequent shift of his weight forward by relaxing the flexion.

Providing that the rider maintains engagement and impulse at each of the gaits, soft flexions of the head and neck provide the most pleasing appearance for any western pleasure class. These same soft flexions enhance the performance of the western riding horse as well as the reining horse. For each of these horses a natural carriage of the head and neck should be the rule, perhaps with the exception of the California-style horse, which will travel with the head and neck more elevated and

Picture 100. Lateral flexion along a gradual turn. *This horse is willingly bending the head and neck to the side in order to follow the arc of a rather gradual turn. The horse is not only demonstrating good lateral flexion, but he is also showing some good direct flexion at the same time by flexing his head back toward the vertical.*

with the head flexed very near the vertical for his pleasure classes.

Direct flexions accompanied by increased engagement will often assist the horse in pulling himself together in preparation for a flying change of leads or a sharp, fast turn from the gallop.

The horse that willingly cooperates with the rider's hands in performing direct flexions invariably relaxes the lower jaw as he flexes the head rearward. This relaxation of the lower jaw has absolutely nothing to do with opening the mouth; the jaw is relaxed while the mouth remains closed.

Relaxation of the horse's lower jaw is a sign of cooperation between the horse and the rider's hands. This is why I keep emphasizing soft hands, or soft increases in rein tension. One of the things

you will notice if you recall the green filly shown in Picture 98 is that her lower jaw was not relaxed. Not only was she behind the bit with her mouth open, but her jaw was set rigidly.

LATERAL FLEXIONS OF THE HEAD AND NECK

This type of flexion is merely the ability of the horse to bend his head and neck to the side and subsequently look in the direction of the bend, the ability not to overbend or underbend the neck to the side, or to cock his head to the inside or to the outside during circles and turns. Lateral flexions of the head and neck permit good circles and

Picture 101. Lateral flexion along a sharp turn. *This horse is demonstrating very good lateral flexion of the head and neck as he turns sharply at the gallop. By comparing this picture with Picture 100, you can see that the sharper the turn, the greater the need for increased lateral flexion.*

turns, serpentines, figures of eight, zig-zags, rollbacks, pivots, turns on the haunches, spins and high-speed turns at the gallop. It is simply a matter of remaining on the line with the head and neck during all types of lateral movements. The nature of lateral flexion is shown by Picture 100.

English riding authors and those concerned with high levels of schooling for these types of horses interpret lateral flexions a little differently. They require that the horse turn his head in the direction of his circular movement while also maintaining very good direct flexions of the head. The problem here is that these English horses (and dressage horses) are ridden on contact (on two direct reins of opposition), while the western horse is ridden using loose reins—an entirely different matter. If you can insure that your horse remains on the line with his head, neck and rest of his body for the most difficult lateral exercises and movements on loose reins, this is really all that is required.

If he can do all of this, and still respond to your hands by way of direct flexions, this would repre-

sent a sort of pinnacle in schooling for both types of flexion on loose reins. But don't push the issue; a stiff and upset horse may be the rapid result of trying to achieve both types of flexion simultaneously, particularly where young horses are involved.

Remaining on the line with the head and neck around very wide turns or for large circles, while maintaining direct flexion of the head and neck, is not particularly difficult, however. If the horse understands the technique of direct flexions, he should be willing to do this without becoming stiff, upset or resistive. In fact it is done every day by pleasure horses on the rail of a large ring or arena.

It is the more demanding lateral movements, such as sharp turns, pivots and rollbacks, for which you may well have to sacrifice a degree of direct flexion in order to obtain cooperative lateral flexions of the head and neck. Pictures 101 and 102 are additional illustrations of lateral flexibility.

Picture 102. Lateral flexion for a turn in place. *Excellent lateral flexion of the horse's head and neck is demonstrated during this spin to the left.*

FORWARD BALANCE VERSUS CENTRAL BALANCE

Think of any western horse you might be trail-riding outdoors at a pleasant relaxed walk, and you will have a very good picture of a forward-balanced horse. Now, if you simply ask this same horse to trot forward or perhaps canter, but still in a relaxed way, you would still have a very good picture of the forward-balanced horse. It would really make no difference whether you chose a slow, passive type of forward movement or quite a brisk pace.

But suppose you were moving along this same trail, doing any of the things that I have just mentioned, and suddenly a large black bear jumps from the brush beside the trail, stands to his full height directly in front of you, and simultaneously

utters a deafening growl. Up goes your horse's head and neck, back toward his chest comes his head; he holds his head perpendicular to the ground with great flexion. His entire frame head to tail seems to have shortened immensely. He has never felt so light in your hands, and he seemingly canters in place for a few seconds, before turning to gallop in the opposite direction.

Well, at this brief instant, and while all of those things were happening underneath you, you were momentarily riding a centrally balanced horse—one that even gave you the feel of a fully collected canter for a split second. However, as the horse retreated in the opposite direction, he lowered and extended the head and neck and assumed long and efficient strides; you were suddenly riding a forward-balanced horse again.

If you were to tabulate the characteristics of forward balance for the western horse in motion versus those for the centrally balanced horse, your lists would look very much like the ones following.

How you want any horse to move forward, and with what type of balance, is a goal which you should have clearly in mind before you begin a program of schooling. Making this decision is equally important if you have lesson horses which you use for teaching all different levels of riders. Recognizing these two different types of balance is also important in order to ride effectively both horses which have had very little schooling and those which have undergone extensive schooling.

Forward balance requires the following:

1. A natural carriage of the head and neck, although for better-schooled horses the rider may ask for increased soft flexion of the head rearward, providing that the neck remains in a *naturally* extended position.
2. The ability to move forward at any speed, from very slow speeds and passive gaits to the fast forward speed of the gallop, while generally preserving the natural carriage of the head and neck. As the horse moves forward at increasingly faster speeds, head and neck extension will naturally increase. The horse's entire frame simply becomes longer from head to tail.
3. Literal forward balance. The forward-balanced horse bears approximately 3/5 of his total body weight on the front limbs and 2/5 of his total body weight on the rear limbs. The horse is *literally* balanced forward; it is not merely a figure of speech. The quality of movement for the forward-balanced horse may range from an undesirable, strung-out movement at any gait to very good engagement and impulse at any gait. It will be a function of the horse's schooling and the level of his rider.

Forward balance permits the horse to gallop when required; likewise, he may execute slow or medium speeds when required. By contrast, the centrally balanced horse may only execute slow forward speeds, and the very slow forward speeds of the collected gaits are often associated with this type of balance.

Central balance results from schooling, not just encountering a bear on the trails. The centrally balanced horse should be relaxed as he moves forward at the collected gaits. Teaching central balance takes a lot of time, patience, riding technique and tact on the part of the rider. For the horse, central balance requires:

1. A definite elevation of the horse's head and neck, along with flexion of the head back toward the vertical. For many of these horses, the head is carried literally on the vertical. Without elevation and flexion, the horse's weight just cannot be shifted rearward.
2. Very good vertical engagement and impulse forward consistently maintained.
3. Slow forward speeds. By definition, the fully collected gaits of the centrally balanced horse can only result in slow forward speeds, even with impulse being maintained at a maximum.
4. Increased animation in the front limbs. There is greater knee action, and the forward stride of these limbs becomes quite short. A purposeful inefficiency in the front legs assists the horse in maintaining the slow forward speeds of collected gaits, while maintaining good engagement and impulse in the rear legs at the same time.
5. That the horse's croup remain lowered for a longer period of time during each stride of the fully collected canter than at the ordinary gaits. This lowering of the croup, along with the elevation of the head and neck, flexion of the head and great vertical engagement and impulse, is typical of the very centrally balanced horse. The total result is to shift a good deal of the horse's weight to the rear.

Central balance may be obtained *without* flexion of the head as long as the head and neck are substantially elevated. However, central balance without flexion is often the mark of a nervous, upset or excited horse, and obviously, there would be little point in exhibiting a horse at the standard three gaits while he maintained central balance in this manner.

A state of central balance with little or no flexion of the head can be functional at certain times for a few types of performance horses. Recall the earlier discussion about speed and roping horses, which at times move justifiably above the

TABLE II
TYPES OF BALANCE RELATED TO PERFORMANCE CLASSES

CLASS OR EVENT	TYPE OF BALANCE	TYPE OF GAIT
barrel racing	forward balance	galloping
competitive trail and endurance	forward balance	ordinary gaits
English pleasure	forward balance	ordinary gaits, canter may be somewhat slow
open jumper	forward balance primarily, central balance on the approach to very big or "trappy" fences	ordinary gaits, semicollected canter in a few instances
pole bending	forward balance	galloping and fast speeds of the ordinary canter
racing	forward balance	galloping
reining	alternating between forward balance and central balance for the different movements required by a particular pattern or test	alternating between the ordinary gaits (medium and fast speeds), a semicollected canter often required
roping	forward balance prior to the catch	galloping and fast speeds of the ordinary canter
rope race (Appaloosa only)	forward balance	galloping and fast speeds of the ordinary canter
stock horse	alternating between forward and central balance	same as reining horse, plus the jog and lope
stock horse (hackamore)	alternating between forward and central balance	same as reining horse, slightly slower overall movements permitted; canter very pulled together but not necessarily semicollected
stock horse (snaffle bit)	alternating between forward and central balance	same as stock horse with bit, slightly slower overall movements permitted
trail	forward balance	ordinary walk, jog and lope
western pleasure (general)	forward balance, but soft flexion and some very pulled together horses are seen here	ordinary walk; semicollected trot often seen for the better horses; lope
western pleasure (California-style)	central balance	ordinary walk, semicollected trot, semicollected canter
western pleasure (Texas-style)	forward balance, often extreme	slow or ordinary walk, the jog and lope
western riding	forward balance, but a very pulled together lope or ordinary canter is seen for most of the better horses	ordinary walk, jog, a very pulled together lope or ordinary canter; canter verging on semicollection for some of the better horses
working hunter (over fences)	forward balance	ordinary gaits

bit while shifting their weight rearward.

Central balance may seem to be completely a matter of the anatomical shape of the horse. While central balance and collected gaits do depend upon the shape of the horse, shape is not an end in itself. Central balance and the collected gaits must also necessarily center around increased vertical engagement in addition to increased impulse. Without these, you only have a particular shape to the horse, not the quality of movement required to produce collected gaits or brief moments of collection. To say that your horse is collected simply because you can coax him to flex his head clear to the vertical is as ridiculous as say-

Picture 103. Forward balance at the walk. *This horse is exhibiting a nice forward balance. She shows a natural carriage of the head and neck, slightly modified by some soft flexion.*

ing that the same horse is a race horse merely because he can gallop in a straight line.

What is the usefulness or role of forward or central balance for the western performance horse? The remainder of this chapter discusses the advantages, disadvantages and some functional compromises for each of these two distinct types of balance.

You will see from Table II (Types of Balance Related to Performance Classes) that whenever medium or fast speed are required, forward balance is also required. On the other hand, whenever great longitudinal or lateral agility is required at slow forward speeds, central balance is preferred. You will also find that slow forward speeds are possible from either state of balance, but that the greatest handiness is possible when the horse maintains central balance at these same slow speeds.

Central Balance and Collection

There is often confusion about the relation between forward and central balance and the quality of the three gaits—the walk, trot and canter. Many riders, primarily dressage riders, insist that central balance and the fully collected gaits are inseparable. While this idea of true collection may be ideal for a Grand Prix dressage horse in international competition, it does not represent a realistic or desirable ideal for the western performance horse.

Western horses competing in high performance events do in fact need moments of central balance—moments of collection—to perform an excellent spin, to cut cattle or to shorten their frame in preparation for a sharp, fast turn. They must be capable of rapidly changing from forward balance to central balance in order to perform well at the many tasks required of western horses.

Teaching Central Balance

So, how do you help the horse learn to be centrally balanced—to be collected—without teaching the fully collected gaits?

Picture 104. Forward balance at the trot. *This horse shows ideal forward balance at an engaged trot with a very natural carriage of the head and neck.*

First, teach each of the three gaits in a forward-balanced frame. School for all of the good qualities of movement discussed in this chapter. You will find that forward balance does not really have to be taught; it must only be left undisturbed, and actually preserved by encouraging a natural carriage of the head and neck during the early schooling of the horse.

Later during schooling, if you choose to teach soft flexions of the head, this will not appreciably affect the horse's basic state of forward balance. True, you will have desirably shifted some of the horse's weight rearward. He will become lighter in your hand and his overall quality of movement will improve, but you will not have destroyed his basic preference for forward balance.

To begin to develop central balance, school for greater longitudinal and lateral agility. Begin to develop direct flexions of the head through continued schooling and the soft use of your hands. Teach the horse to shift his weight rapidly rearward by schooling for exercises such as prompt halts, good backing, pivots, spins and rollbacks.

Practice for events which demand prompt shifts in the horse's center of balance from front to back.

Fully Collected Movement

Fully collected movement (the type seen in the better dressage horses) does not come naturally to any horse. In nature you will see horses assume an extreme state of central balance only for brief instants when they are excited or suddenly startled. Even brief moments at the collected trot or canter will rarely be seen. Horses that do nothing but dressage, under very capable riders, require two to four years of schooling before they can maintain collected gaits for more than a stride or two here and there.

If you are schooling western horses for a variety of events, you probably will not have the time to school your horses for the true collected gaits. However, what you may have time and use for is a sort of middle ground between forward balance and the collected gaits—semicollection.

Picture 105. Forward balance at the canter. *A natural carriage of the head and neck is maintained as this horse canters forward.*

Semicollected Movement

Semicollection, even as only an exercise, can be useful in improving your horse's cooperation and agility. It is reasonable to expect any experienced rider who has a good position and who can use his aids effectively to be able to obtain some semicollection from horses that are already on an intermediate level of schooling. Brief moments of semicollection are a good way to tune and lighten any horse in advance of competition. A more consistent use of semicollected gaits can be functional for higher-level pleasure horses. In fact, these gaits are the movement of choice for California-style pleasure horses. You will see very good examples of consistent semicollection at all gaits for most of these California-style horses, although for some you will see only the shape and not the overall quality of movement required.

What is semicollected movement? It is almost everything that was described as collected or centrally balanced movement, but not quite so extreme. The elevation of the head and neck is not so great, and the horse's head is usually slightly in front of the vertical. Vertical engagement is always present, but the up-and-down movement of the joints in the rear leg is not so great. The front limbs are not greatly animated, because there is not as much weight on the hindquarters as in the fully collected gaits, but the stride does remain quite short. The croup is not lowered. Of course, the horse must still move with excellent impulse and should remain light in the rider's hand.

Forward speed at any of the semicollected gaits is slightly greater than at the fully collected gaits. Once you have taught a horse to move on the bit, you will not have far to go to produce semicollected movement or even consistent semicollected gaits. In fact, you may have already done so.

While the entire matter of forward balance and central balance did not pose any particular problem for me as I wrote this section, the introduction of the word *collection* did. That a western horse could be collected, but without the necessity of learning and practicing the "true collected gaits," was rather a revolutionary idea—or a distortion of

Picture 106. Semicollected walk. *The semicollected walk is not particularly spectacular. The stride is shortened, the horse maintains good impulse forward and the head is flexed toward the vertical. The real difference is seen if the rider suddenly changes to very loose reins. In this case, the horse would maintain the semicollected frame for several strides before extending the head and neck and lengthening the stride. The nature of the semicollected gaits is best understood by comparing an ordinary jog with the semicollected trot, or an ordinary lope with the semicollected canter.*

classical riding principles if you talked to almost any knowledgeable dressage rider. However, at the same time that these classical horse people insisted that no horse could be collected except when at work at the fully collected gaits, they had never

had the occasion to spin a western horse, perform a sliding stop, or rope a steer—all on loose reins.

Pictures 103, 104, 105, 106, 107, 108 and 109 will help you put forward balance, central balance and collection into perspective.

Picture 107. Semicollected trot. *The semicollected trot shows a very definite shifting of the horse's weight to the rear. The elevation of the head and neck coupled with very good flexion of the head tends to shift a good deal of weight to the hind quarters. The length of stride in front is shorter than the stride behind. The rear legs maintain very good vertical engagement and the horse moves forward with good impulse at a slow but energetic trot.*

Picture 108. Semicollected canter. *The semicollected canter exhibits a very profound shifting of the horse's weight to the hindquarters during most of the horse's forward stride. The horse almost appears to be going downhill. Again, the elevation of the head and neck coupled with good direct flexion of the head enables a good deal of the horse's weight to be transferred to the hindquarters. Substantial animation of the front limbs, good vertical engagement and impulse forward round out the entire picture of the semicollected canter. The horse here is on soft contact—necessary for achieving semicollected gaits in a relaxed frame. Note the sequence of legs which is developing: outside hind, diagonal pair, and then the (left) leading front leg. This was exactly the sequence of the original canter departure.*

Picture 109. Fully collected trot. *Fully collected movement is being demanded of this dressage horse. If you compare this picture with Picture 107, you will see some distinct differences between the fully collected and semicollected trot. A fully collected trot requires greater elevation of the head and neck, greater direct flexion of the head, a more animated and shortened stride in front, greater vertical engagement of the hind limbs and greater overall impulse forward. A more definite cadence at the trot is evident. In general, greater longitudinal agility coupled with increased impulse forward, but at a slower speed, separates the fully collected trot from the semicollected trot of Picture 107.*

Chapter 5

LEVELS OF SCHOOLING

To divide the schooling of the horse into a logical progression of steps and lessons only makes good sense. It is important to understand the purpose of schooling for the green horse versus that for the schooled horse. It is also important to understand how much quality of movement may be reasonably demanded from any horse at a particular stage in his schooling.

Virtually any good trainer understands the importance of these things as each horse is schooled to progressively higher stages of performance. The professional knows what to teach and when. He or she does not attempt to teach the canter before teaching the trot, or a flying change of leads before teaching a simple change of leads. Any good professional will tell you about the fallacy of skipping steps during the schooling of any performance horse.

I have chosen to divide the schooling of the western performance horse into three broad categories—three levels of schooling. Within each of these three levels are specific lessons which should be taught to each horse as he continues to improve and enters the next higher level of schooling. The three levels of schooling chosen are the elementary, the intermediate and the advanced.

At the elementary level the horse is taught the basics: those things he must know before schooling at higher levels can be successful. The intermediate level of schooling develops a horse that can compete successfully in the show ring at a variety of events ranging from trail classes to reining classes. The advanced level of schooling will not be for everyone, nor is it intended to be taught to every horse. A superior rider, as well as a superior horse, is required for advanced riding and schooling.

The three levels of schooling are outlined in Table III, which occupies most of this chapter. The lessons to be taught to each horse, beginning at the elementary level of schooling, are tabulated for you. As you review Table III, do not be concerned that you may not understand a serpentine, or how to produce a rollback, spin, sidepass or any other exercise. What is important is that you understand the sequence of schooling, the types of exercises and qualities of movement demanded by each of the three levels of schooling.

The "how to's" associated with each point in this table are contained in Chapter 6 (Schooling at the Elementary Level), Chapter 7 (Schooling at the Intermediate Level), Chapter 8 (Advanced Riding and Schooling).

After you become familiar with Table III, begin reading Chapters 6, 7 and 8. As you learn how to teach the walk, trot, canter, rein back, pivot, lead changes and so forth, refer back to Table III as frequently as you need to. Use it to keep a general perspective on good schooling: the purpose of schooling at a particular level and the quality of movement that should be demanded at each level.

TABLE III
LEVELS OF SCHOOLING

THE ELEMENTARY LEVEL

The Purpose of Schooling at the Elementary Level

1. To achieve *quick and definite responses* by the horse to the rider's aids and control techniques
2. To establish *obedience* to rein aids, leg aids and the use of weight and voice

The purpose of elementary schooling should be in the forefront of your mind as you ride and school at this level. Higher levels of schooling depend upon your keeping these purposes constantly in mind.

The Rider's Control Technique

The following use of aids are appropriate at the elementary level.

Reins:

1. Use two direct reins of opposition with a *check-release* for slowing forward speed, halting and backing.
2. Use a leading rein when first teaching turns and circles.
3. Teach neck reining when the horse clearly understands the use of two direct reins, the leading rein and the rider's use of urging, holding and displacing leg aids.

Remember, at the elementary level of schooling, loose reins are employed whenever possible. The exceptions are: when checking with a check-release; when using a very strong leading rein to first teach circles and turns; and when riding on contact, or with very short reins, is required for early control problems. Whenever other than loose reins are employed, return to loose reins as soon as possible.

Legs:

1. Urging legs or leg
2. Holding leg
3. Displacing leg

Remember to use your leg in a tapping manner at first to introduce the horse to the desired action for each of the three leg aids. Replace tapping leg actions with squeezing leg actions as soon as the horse understands what is required of him.

Use kicking legs as a punishment for disobedience to any of the three leg aids; use a kicking leg or legs to reinforce any particular leg aid which has been disobeyed. The crop, spur or ends of split reins may also be used in the place of a kicking leg to enforce any leg aid which the horse understands but disobeys or is slow to obey.

Weight:

1. Use your weight to assist the horse in learning what is required of him, in conjunction with the use of voice, rein and leg aids.
2. Weight is used vertically to control forward speed: Inclining the upper body forward or assuming the standing position should increase the horse's forward speed *within* any gait. However, *do not* use your weight in this manner to secure an upward transition from a slower gait to a faster one—the trot to the canter, for example.
   Sitting upright and in rhythm with the horse's efforts at any gait should assist in the control of forward speed, obtaining even speeds and stabilization at each gait.
3. Sitting upright and in rhythm with the horse's efforts should precede every upward transition: the halt to the walk, the walk to the trot and the trot to the canter.
4. Sitting upright and in rhythm with the horse's efforts, but with the lower back slightly braced, should precede each downward transition: canter to the trot, trot to the walk and walk to the halt.

Remember to use your weight in advance of your hands for decreases in forward speed and particularly for downward transitions. Use your weight (while sitting upright) in advance of your legs for upward transitions. Increases in forward speed within any gait can be obtained by the use of weight only or in conjunction with urging legs.

Voice:

1. Use the voice liberally at the elementary level of schooling.
2. Teach the following voice commands: *Walk, Trot, Canter* (or *Lope*), *Whoa* or an equivalent term, *Slow* or *Easy*, and *Back.*
3. Use the appropriate voice command in advance of using your legs or hands. In most instances, use your weight in advance of your voice.

The use of voice early in the elementary level assists the horse in learning the other aids.

It gives the horse warning in advance of the use of your hands or legs, and it verifies your use of weight aids, which precede the voice. The use of voice not only helps the horse to learn what is required of him, but also allows less abusive early schooling.

Voice is used gradually less as the elementary level of schooling proceeds. It should be largely unnecessary by the end of elementary schooling.

Forward Movement

The Walk:

1. Teach a stabilized walk.
2. Make the walk brisk—about 5 mph.

The Trot:

1. Teach a reasonably slow, stabilized trot with the horse's head and neck carried in a natural position. Teaching the jog trot, with flexion of the head and neck, is not necessary at this level of schooling. The overall quality of the trot will improve when circles and turns are taught.
2. The trot should be approximately 6–8 mph.

The Canter:

1. Teach a reasonably slow, stabilized canter. Allow the horse to employ balancing gestures of the head and neck freely.
2. The canter should be about 8–10 mph.

The Gallop:

1. Omit at this level of schooling.

Transitions

Upward Transitions:

1. Response should be quick and obedient from the halt to the walk and from the trot to the canter, and gradual and obedient from the walk to the trot, when a slow trot is first being learned.
2. If the horse is disobedient for any transition that has already been learned, be rough. Punish the disobedience with your legs (kicking). Reinforce leg aids with a crop, spur or ends of split reins for any continued disobedience.
3. Late in the elementary level of schooling, begin teaching better precision. Mentally select a point well ahead of you, and then perform the desired transition just as you reach this selected point. Prepare for these precise transitions well in advance.

Downward Transitions:

1. Response should be quick and obedient from the canter to the trot, trot to the walk, and walk to the halt—mouth closed, head and neck in natural position.
2. Also, teach quick and obedient transitions from the trot to halt, and from the canter to the walk or halt.
3. If the horse is disobedient for any transition, be rough. Punish the disobedience with your hands.
4. Late in the elementary level of schooling, begin teaching precision. Complete the desired transition exactly at some point ahead of you which you have mentally selected.

Avoid hanging on the horse's mouth to accomplish these more precise transitions. A sharp check is better, provided you have used your weight and voice appropriately in advance of your first check-release.

Halting:
1. Halts should be quick and definite—mouth closed, head and neck in a natural position.
2. Teach precision: halting at a preselected point.
3. Square halts are not required at this level of schooling; only some reasonable alignment of the horse's legs at the halt is necessary.
4. Make ample use of weight and voice in advance of rein use.

Other Movements

The Rein Back:
1. Reasonable cooperation in backing for short distances is required.
2. Straight backing is required, and this primarily entails obedience to the rider's holding and displacing legs.
3. Speed in backing, or backing for long distances, is not required at this level of schooling.
4. Cooperation with the rider's *soft hands* in backing is the beginning of the horse's education to *willing* flexions of the head and neck in response to the rider's soft use of reins.

Circles:
1. Teach large circles at an even speed with movement on the line.
2. Perform great numbers of circles at the trot with emphasis upon even speed and movement on the line.
3. Perform great numbers of circles at the canter with emphasis upon even speed and movement on the line.

Leads:
1. At the elementary level teach the *inside lead*—the left lead when traveling in a direction which will require left turns, and the right lead when traveling in a direction which will require right turns.
2. Begin to teach the inside lead for all canter departures after a quick and definite transition to the canter has been learned *and* when the horse can maintain a relatively even pace around the complete perimeter of the schooling area.
3. It is pointless to punish the horse for an incorrect lead before he has even learned to maintain his balance at the canter. When you teach the canter, the purpose is to afford the horse practice in learning to canter. Later, when you teach the inside lead, the purpose is to obtain a good canter departure on the inside lead.

   Simple Change of Leads: Omit at this level of schooling.
   Flying Change of Leads: Omit at this level of schooling.

Turn on the Forehand:
1. This exercise may be used to assist the rider in teaching the horse obedience to the displacing leg aid.
2. High quality in performing this movement is not required at the elementary level of schooling. Demand that the horse does not attempt to walk forward or back as the turn is performed.
3. Do not attempt to teach the turn on the forehand and the rein back during the same schooling session.

Turn on the Haunches:
1. Teach this movement from the halt.
2. Teach a quarter turn on the haunches to the left and to the right first. The turn should be gradual and unhurried—one step at a time.
3. When a quarter turn on the haunches from the halt can be reliably produced, teach the half turn on the haunches, from the halt.

4. High quality is not demanded, but the horse should not move forward, backward or to the side with his haunches. The turn on the haunches should not degenerate into a turn on the forehand, or into a turn on the middle at any point.

Pivot:
1. Omit at this level of schooling.

Rollback:
1. Omit at this level of schooling.

Spin:
1. Omit at this level of schooling.

Sidepass:
1. The sidepass is required for short distances with the horse remaining reasonably straight from head to tail.
2. High quality is not demanded, but if the horse crosses his back feet (one in front of the other) and the front feet (one in front of the other) as he moves to the side, so much the better.

Exercises to Be Practiced

1. Full circles (large circles—50 feet across) at all gaits
2. Half circle *and* reverse, at the walk and trot
3. Half circle *in* reverse, at the walk and trot
4. Turn on the forehand (optional)
5. Turn on the haunches—quarter and half turns from the halt
6. Sidepass
7. Straight rein back
8. Riding in company with quiet horses, both indoors and out

Quality of the Horse's Movement

1. Stabilization at the walk, trot and canter
2. Prompt upward and downward transitions; canter departures on the inside lead
3. Movement on the line when traveling straight along the rail, during upward and downward transitions and when turning and circling
4. Engagement at the walk and trot
5. Impulse forward at the walk, relaxed alertness at the trot
6. Canter not strung out

Showing

1. Junior western pleasure upon completing elementary schooling
2. Junior English pleasure upon completing elementary schooling
3. Junior Trail, for the exceptional horse, upon completing elementary schooling and practicing with obstacles normally found in the trail classes

Formal Testing Situations:
1. Pleasure classes in national breed shows.
2. Affiliated National Riding Commission rider rating examination (Western Section) at the Qualifying Ride level. This is a rider rating, but it requires a horse schooled to a *high* elementary level. (You will have to develop two speeds at the trot, the jog and ordinary trot. This slightly exceeds the requirements of the elementary level presented here.)

THE INTERMEDIATE LEVEL

The Purpose of Schooling at the Intermediate Level

1. To achieve *soft* but definite responses to each of the rider's aids
2. To achieve prompt and *precise* responses to each of the rider's aids
3. To develop *cooperation* with each of the rider's aids

4. To achieve a *better quality of movement* from the horse: better engagement, impulse, movement on the line, smoother and more precise transitions, softer halts and a greater *willingness* to flex the head and neck in response to *soft* increases in rein tension
5. To begin teaching the horse central balance for short periods

The Rider's Control Technique

The following uses of aids are appropriate at the intermediate level.

Reins:
1. Use two direct reins of opposition in a check-release manner for slowing forward speed, halting and backing. Softer and more precise check-releases should be employed at this level.
2. Use neck reins for turning and circling. Use neck reins to maintain better movement on the line of the horse's forehand.
3. Use the following rein aids when teaching a new lesson or when improving turns, circles and movement on the line: the leading rein, the indirect rein in front of the saddle horn, one direct rein of opposition, and (rarely) the indirect rein behind the saddle horn.

Legs:
1. Urging legs or leg, used in a squeezing manner
2. Holding leg, used in a squeezing manner
3. Displacing leg, used in a squeezing manner

Remember, tapping leg aids may be used when first teaching a new lesson or when reviewing an old one which seems to have been forgotten.

Weight:
1. The vertical use of the rider's weight is used in the same manner as in the elementary level.
2. The rider employs a greater use of lateral weight aids in achieving better movement on the line, for remaining on the rail when moving in a straight line, for more accurate turns and circles, and for any movement to the side which may be rendered more soft and precise through the lateral use of weight.

Voice:
1. The use of voice is discontinued.
2. Voice is used primarily as a form of punishment, or when teaching a new lesson.

Forward Movement

1. Engagement, impulse and movement on the line when moving forward, turning, circling
2. Prompt, but soft and precise downward transitions
3. Prompt, but smooth and precise upward transitions
4. Improved longitudinal agility, including the ability to perform more than one even speed at each gait and the ability willingly to flex the head toward the vertical in response to the rider's soft hands
5. Improved lateral agility, including the performance of extremely accurate circles and a variety of lateral movements (sidepass, pivot, spin and others) smoothly, precisely, and without undue resistance
6. Moving forward while accepting the bit

The Walk:
1. Teach two speeds at the walk: the ordinary walk and the fast or extended walk.
2. The ordinary walk has impulse forward and is no different than the one developed at the elementary level.
3. The fast (extended) walk is a schooling exercise designed to increase the cooperation of the horse with the rider's aids. The rider increases the length of stride beyond the ordinary walk; impulse, engagement and forward speed are increased.

The Trot:
1. Teach three speeds at the trot: the jog trot, the ordinary trot and the fast (extended) trot.
2. The jog trot should possess the following quality of movement:
   a. Vertical engagement of the hind limbs: an increased bending or animation of the hocks, as opposed to an increased forward reach of the whole limb
   b. Alertness of the horse, or impulse forward, coupled with a rhythm or cadence to the jog; greater knee as well as hock action
   c. A willingness of the horse to flex his head and neck softly toward the vertical.
Remember, the jog trot should *not* be a slow, lazy, passive gait with a strung-out movement.
3. The ordinary trot should possess good horizontal engagement and forward impulse at a medium speed (approximately 8 mph). The horse's head and neck are carried in a natural position.
4. The fast (extended) trot has as its principal features greater forward speed, impulse, engagement and length of stride. Greater extension of the horse's head and neck is permitted.

The Canter:
1. Teach two speeds at the canter: the lope and the ordinary canter.
2. The lope should be a relaxed gait with the following quality of movement:
   a. The forward speed of the lope is slow, but movement should not become strung out, nor should forward speed be decreased to the point that a four-beat gait develops.
   b. Some flexion of the head toward the vertical will assist the horse in maintaining a slow, steady forward speed.
   c. The balancing gestures of the head and neck are an important feature of maintaining a slow forward speed at the lope, but for a semicollected canter these balancing gestures should be largely absent.
3. The ordinary canter is a forward gait possessing good engagement and forward impulse. The speed is 10–12 mph. The horse's head and neck should be carried in a natural position with normal balancing gestures permitted.

The Gallop:
1. Utilize the standing position and urging legs to develop the gallop: a true four-beat gait.

Transitions

Upward Transitions:
1. Prompt, smooth and precise
2. Engagement and impulse maintained from the last stride of the slower gait, present again from very nearly the first stride of the new faster gait
3. Canter departure on the correct inside lead from the walk with no intervening strides at the trot
4. Movement on the line. If necessary to obtain the inside lead reliably, the canter may be begun with the haunches *slightly* to the inside, but this crutch should be eliminated as soon as possible.
5. Stabilization at the new gait present from its onset

Downward Transitions:
1. Prompt, soft and precise
2. Engagement maintained during downward transitions and present from nearly the first stride of the new slower gait
3. Use of willing direct flexions of the horse's head and neck to soften each downward transition, and to add precision without unbalancing the rider through rapid shifts in the horse's center of balance
4. The ability to perform *very* rapid and precise downward transitions if required for a particular event

Halting:
1. Prompt, soft and precise
2. Square halting

3. Willing to stand quietly, with alertness to the rider's request to move immediately to any other task
4. Willing flexions of the head, repeatedly back toward the vertical, to add softness to the halt. These are soft flexions, and do not involve an excessive bobbing of the head.
5. Sliding stop, if required for your event (reining, western riding, roping)
   a. The hind legs should be grounded parallel to one another as the stop is begun.
   b. The slide and stop should be on the line.
   c. The horse's mouth should remain closed.
   d. The horse's head and neck should be elevated during the slide, but the horse should not be above the bit.
   e. The horse should settle and stand quietly upon halting.

Other Movements

The Rein Back:
1. Straight backing with the correct sequence of legs
2. Willing flexion of the head in backing
3. Speed in backing, if required for your event
4. A square, balanced halt after the rein back, with a willingness to stand quietly, relaxed but alert

Circles:
1. Even speed and movement on the line both constant
2. Small circles at slower speeds with movement on the line
3. Larger circles at faster speeds with movement on the line
4. Accuracy in performing absolutely round circles

Leads:
Early in intermediate schooling, work on very good canter departures with the horse reliably beginning the canter on the inside lead. Departures should be prompt, smooth and precise.

Simple Change of Leads:

1. A simple change can be taught on a figure eight, half circle or serpentine, across the diagonal of the arena and on a straight line.
2. Teach this sequence first: canter to the trot, trot a few steps until the horse is relaxed, then depart on the new lead.
3. Later, teach this sequence: canter to the walk, walk a few strides until the horse is relaxed, then depart on the new lead.

Flying Change of Leads:

1. Teach the flying change when the simple change has been mastered.
2. The horse must change leads both front and behind, producing a united canter on the new lead.
3. There should be no undue resistance during the change.

Turn on the Forehand:
1. Perform this turn from the halt, with the horse's head and neck straight as the hindquarters are moved around the stationary forehand.
2. Hindlegs should cross one in front of the other as the hindquarters are moved around the stationary forehand.
3. The turn should be smooth and unhurried, with the forelegs simply marking time—mostly up and down—as the quarters move around the forehand.
4. There should be no movement forward or backward as the turn is made.
5. Teach quarter turns and half turns. Teach a full turn on the forehand if you are schooling for trail classes.

Turn on the Haunches:
1. When the turn is performed from the halt:
   a. The front legs should cross one in front of the other as the forehand moves around the relatively stationary hindlegs.

    b. The turn should be smooth and unhurried, with the pivotal leg simply marking time, while the opposite hindleg walks in very small circles around the pivotal leg.

    c. There should be no movement forward or backward, nor should the hindquarters move to either side as the turn is performed.

    d. Teach a full turn on the haunches if you wish, but insure that you perfect the quarter and half turns on the haunches.

    e. There should be no undue resistance, particularly of the head and mouth. The horse should stand quiet but alert upon completion of the turn.

2. When the turn is performed from the walk:

    a. Same criteria for quality of movement apply as when performed from the halt, except:

    b. The front legs should maintain the rhythm of the walk as the forehand turns around the stationary hindquarters.

    c. The horse should walk quietly away from the turn upon its completion.

Pivot:

1. The movement is a rapid quarter- or half-turn on the haunches from the halt.

2. The head and neck are permitted to elevate naturally as the pivot is begun, but resistance or bit evasions should not be present.

3. The horse should softly elevate the forehand as the pivot is begun and look in the direction of the turn, but rearing and throwing his mass to the side is not acceptable.

4. The horse should stand quiet but alert after completing the pivot, unless requested to move forward by the rider.

Rollback:

1. Teach this exercise when the turn on the haunches and the pivot have been mastered.

2. The rollback should be practiced from both the walk and canter, but the rollback from the canter is the more important, time-saving maneuver.

3. The rollback should be a rapid, continuous movement without undue resistance on the horse's part.

4. From both the walk and the canter, the horse should check his forward speed, perform a fluid half turn on the haunches (pivot), and move forward again at the same gait.

5. The horse should ground the hindfoot in the direction which the rollback is to be performed, slightly ahead of the other hindfoot.

6. From a canter on the right lead and a rollback to the left, the horse should canter away on the left lead. From a canter on the left lead and a rollback to the right, the horse should canter away on the right lead.

Spin:

1. The spin is taught after the turn on the haunches and the pivot have been mastered. Omit this movement if it is not required for your event, but do perfect the pivot.

2. The spin may be performed from the halt, walk or canter.

3. The spin should be a rapid, fluid full turn on the haunches. More than one full turn (up to three) may be required in some reining patterns.

4. When the spin is performed, the head and neck should be carried naturally. The horse should not be above the bit, behind the bit or show undue resistance from head to tail.

5. The majority of the horse's mass is carried over the hind limbs. The hindlegs should be brought far forward and under the horse in preparation for a spin.

6. With his front legs, the horse should "paddle" smartly around the stationary hindquarters. He should not rear or throw his mass to the side.

Sidepass:

1. At this level, the horse crosses his front legs and back legs, one in front of the other, as he moves to the side.

2. The sidepass is a true lateral movement; the horse should remain straight while moving to the side. He should not step backward or forward.

3. The horse should be capable of sidepassing over an obstacle raised above ground level, or between sets of obstacles raised above ground level.

4. The horse should be capable of sidepassing for reasonably long distances, up to 24 feet, and without sacrificing the quality of his movement to the side.

Exercises To Be Practiced

1. All of those exercises specified within the elementary level of schooling.
2. Accurate circles of all reasonable sizes
3. Two speeds at the walk
4. Three speeds at the trot
5. Two speeds at the canter
6. Galloping—occasionally, or if required for your event
7. Prompt, soft, precise halts
8. Excellent backing with direct flexion of the head and with speed, on occasion
9. Simple change of leads
10. Flying change of leads
11. Turn on the forehand: quarter, half and on occasion, full turns
12. Turn on the haunches: quarter, half, and on occasion, full turns. Performed a step at a time, not as one continuous movement
13. Pivots: quarter and half turns performed from the halt
14. Spins: if required for your event
15. Rollback: rapid half turn on the haunches from the walk and canter
16. Sidepassing with good quality of movement
17. Serpentines at the trot, and at the canter with simple or flying changes of leads
18. Figure eights at the trot, and at the canter with a flying change of leads at the midpoint of the two circles comprising the figure eight
19. Sliding stop, if required for your event
20. Barrel, pole, western riding and reining patterns as a matter of good schooling, even if these are not your events. In this case, practice these patterns at moderate speeds. If desired, substitute the simple change of leads for the flying change of leads. Substitute a prompt square halt for the sliding stop. Substitute a full turn on the haunches, step by step, for the spin.
21. Riding on contact at the walk, ordinary trot and ordinary canter, if you wish to school for the English pleasure classes (hunt seat)
22. Low jumping

Quality of the Horse's Movement

1. Stabilization at three speeds of the trot and two speeds at the canter
2. Movement on the line for circles of any size and during upward and downward transitions, including the halt and the rein back
3. Engagement as a constant feature of all gaits
4. Impulse forward during showing, and whenever requested by the rider during schooling (which should be most of the time)
5. Prompt, soft and precise transitions
6. Softness, precision and good movement on the line for all exercises and ring figures
7. Direct flexions of the head and neck as an aid in softening all movements, especially downward transitions. The mouth should remain closed and the horse should not drop behind the bit. The horse should always accept the bit.
8. Willing flexions of the head and neck to assist the horse in producing the slow forward gaits of the jog and lope, and to improve the quality of movement at these gaits and when backing
9. Longitudinal and lateral agility exhibited by the satisfactory performance of all of the ring exercises and movements of the intermediate level of schooling

Showing (Major Events)

1. Junior or senior western pleasure
2. Junior or senior English pleasure
3. Junior or senior reining
4. Barrel racing, for horses four years or older
5. Pole bending, for horses four years or older
6. Roping, for horses four years or older
7. Junior or senior trail
8. Western riding

9. Stock horse classes
10. Appaloosa rope race, preferably for Appaloosas three years or older
11. Appaloosa steer daubing, preferably for Appaloosas three years or older
12. Cutting, provided you can obtain assistance from an experienced cutting horse trainer

Formal Testing Situations:
1. AHSA Medal Classes
2. Obtaining a Register of Merit (ROM) within any breed association, or an AQHA Champion or its equivalent in any breed association
3. Competing in the ribbons at a national breed show or at an A-rated show of the AHSA or any breed association
4. National Riding Commission rider rating examinations (western section) at the number two and three levels. This is a rider rating, but does require a horse schooled to a middle or high-intermediate level

THE ADVANCED LEVEL

The Purpose of Schooling at the Advanced Level

To obtain the best possible performance from each horse

The Rider's Control Technique

Same as at the intermediate level

Forward Movement

1. Same as at the intermediate level
2. Movement of a high quality always maintained
3. Consistent direct flexions for all downward transitions
4. Semicollected gaits performed occasionally

The Walk:
Same as at the intermediate level

The Trot:
1. Same as at the intermediate level, but with particular emphasis on engagement and forward impulse
2. The semicollected trot
3. More lengthening than quickening of the stride in the extended trot

The Canter:
1. Same as at the intermediate level, but with particular emphasis on engagement and forward impulse
2. The semicollected canter

The Gallop:
Same as at the intermediate level

Transitions

Upward Transitions:
1. Excellent quality of movement maintained from the last stride of the slower gait through the first stride of the new, faster gait

Downward Transitions:
1. A consistent use of direct flexions of the head and neck to soften downward transitions, and to make them smoother and more precise. Horse is not above or behind the bit and remains well balanced over his haunches during transitions.

Halting:
1. Quality of movement maintained until the halt is achieved
2. Halts always square
3. Direct flexion with the mouth closed for all halts and sliding stops

Other Movements

The Rein Back:
1. Same as at the intermediate level
2. Halting from the trot, backing, and resuming the trot without any intermediate strides at the walk
3. Halting from the lope or canter, backing, and resuming the canter without any intermediate strides at the walk or trot
4. Consistent direct flexion of the head and neck when backing; horse never above or behind the bit

Circles:
1. Same as at the intermediate level
2. The volte (pronounced vol-tay)—a circle six meters (about 21 feet) in diameter—at all three gaits

Leads:
1. The horse should take either lead, inside or outside, as requested by the rider.
2. Teach the counter-canter along *gradual* turns or circles

Simple Change of Leads: Same as at the intermediate level
Flying Change of Leads:

1. Same as at the intermediate level, but with great emphasis upon the horse's quality of movement and his lack of resistance
2. For a very good flying change, the same even speed of the canter maintained prior to, and after, the change

Turn on the Forehand:
Same as at the intermediate level

Turn on the Haunches:
1. Same as at the intermediate level
2. When performed from the walk, with particular emphasis upon the lack of resistance and on maintaining the rhythm of the walk with the front legs as the turn is performed

Pivot:
1. Same as at the intermediate level
2. Particular emphasis upon the lack of resistance on the part of the horse

Rollback:
1. Same as at the intermediate level, but with particular emphasis upon the lack of resistance on the part of the horse
2. Cantering away on either lead as requested by the rider

Spin:
Same as at the intermediate level, but with particular emphasis upon the lack of resistance on the part of the horse

Sidepass:
1. Same as at the intermediate level

Exercises to Be Practiced

Add the following to the intermediate-level ring figures and exercises:

1. The counter-canter
2. The volté

Quality of the Horse's Movement

1. Excellent gaits
2. Excellent transitions
3. Excellent ring figures and exercises

Showing

All western classes

Formal Testing Situations:

1. Same as at the intermediate level, and
2. AQHA Superior (event) Horse, or the equivalent in any other breed association
3. Affiliated National Riding Commission rider rating examinations (western section) at the number one level. This is a rider rating, but requires a horse schooled to a high-intermediate or advanced level.

Chapter 6

SCHOOLING AT THE ELEMENTARY LEVEL

This chapter describes the use of elementary control techniques in beginning the schooling of the very green horse correctly. Elementary schooling is directed toward two specific areas.

1. The mental education of the horse includes:
    (a) the correct response to each of the aids employed by the rider (see Table III, Elementary Level of Schooling, The Rider's Control Technique)
    (b) obedience and quick and definite responses to each of the aids
2. The physical education of the horse includes:
    (a) the gaits
    (b) circles and turns
    (c) stabilization—an even speed at each gait on loose reins
    (d) downward transitions: obedient, prompt and on the line for the canter-trot, trot-walk and walk-halt
    (e) upward transitions: obedient, prompt and on the line for the halt-walk, walk-trot, trot-canter and later, the walk-canter
    (f) the rein back: straight backing
    (g) engagement
    (h) forward impulse: at least minimal engagement and alertness during forward movement
    (i) the turn on the forehand (optional)
    (j) the turn on the haunches from the halt
    (k) the sidepass for short distances
    (l) longitudinal and lateral agility

The elementary level of schooling requires that you teach the horse the exercises listed above. Use the techniques of elementary control whenever possible as you teach new lessons to the horse: a leading rein when first teaching the horse to circle or turn, leg aids used in a tapping or kicking manner to help the horse understand what is required of him, a very liberal use of voice commands and the definite vertical use of weight both to assist the horse to regulate his forward speed and to signal each transition clearly in advance.

As schooling at the elementary level continues, you will begin to employ progressively more sophisticated control techniques in practicing and improving the horse's performance for lessons already taught. All of the rein aids will be introduced; leg aids will be used in a more sophisticated squeezing manner, rather than with tapping or kicking. You will be able to use fewer voice commands. You will begin to employ your weight laterally, as well as vertically, in order to achieve a softer and more precise performance.

Elementary schooling is the base from which higher levels of schooling are developed. Like all worthwhile projects you undertake, you must begin somewhere. You must begin by taking a first step, by walking forward toward your goal, and so we begin with the walk.

THE WALK

When mounting the green horse for the first time and teaching the walk, use your aids correctly and in the correct sequence from the beginning: sit, say *Walk* briskly, tap or squeeze with both legs at the cinch. Use your aids in this order: weight, voice, legs.

When first mounted, many green horses are often reluctant even to begin moving forward

142

from the halt. In this case, substitute a kicking leg or legs at the cinch to encourage the horse to move forward. As he begins to walk, insure that your reins are loose enough to permit him freedom of the head and neck. Do not let your reins interfere with the natural balancing gestures of his head and neck as he begins to move forward and accustom himself to your weight for the first time.

Steering and turning are initially accomplished with a leading rein. Move your left hand outward and to the side for a left turn, and your right the opposite way for a right turn. As you employ the leading rein to steer the horse for the first time, do not forget to also use your legs, even just mildly. For a left turn, use a left leading rein and your right leg tapping or squeezing lightly at or just behind the cinch. In other words, begin to educate the horse to the leg as well as the hand for turning.

Since your ultimate aim is to develop a forward-moving walk with engagement and impulse, do not be too hasty in attempting to slow or control the speed of the walk with your hands. Allow the horse to walk forward energetically, with long, low strides, whenever he is so inclined. Slowing the forward speed of the walk in order to halt is accomplished by sitting, using your voice and using two direct reins of opposition.

Two problems are usually encountered when teaching the horse to walk. The first occurs when the horse on his own insists upon halting each time the walk is begun. The second occurs when the horse on his own insists upon breaking to the trot each time the walk is in progress.

If the horse tends to break from the walk to the halt, first check your own position design (Chapter 2). Make sure that your reins are loose and that your leg is quiet except when used purposely to urge the horse forward. Use your voice authoritatively, and employ your urging legs in a tapping or kicking manner to reestablish the walk. Remember, one important aim at this level of schooling is to obtain quick, definite responses to your aids. Smooth responses to your aids will be possible only after obedience has been learned.

If the horse tends to break to the trot, be very definite with your hands. Remember to use your voice in advance of your reins. Sit and check rather hard with two direct reins, but *do not hang* on the horse's mouth. Follow each check with a release in rein tension if there is any inclination whatsoever on the horse's part to obey your

hands. Use your voice in a soft tone to say *Walk* just before each check. Make sure that your upper body has a good design of position and that you are using your weight effectively. Check your lower leg position to be sure that your leg has not drifted rearward on the horse's side. When the walk has been achieved again, say *Good* or give the horse a pat on the neck. When the horse maintains the walk quietly, be sure your reins are loose.

Generally, your legs should remain as passive as possible (though not loose or swinging back and forth), except for an occasional tap or squeeze to promote a steady forward pace. However, a tapping or squeezing leg can be employed behind the cinch to begin to keep the horse's haunches on the line as he walks forward. Use a left tapping or squeezing leg to the rear of the cinch to move the horse's haunches to the right, and vice versa. A leading rein will assist him in keeping the forehand on the line, and this same rein aid will be used in teaching him to turn as he approaches the ends of your ring or arena.

Too often while both schooling and showing, riders tend to treat the walk as a rest period for the horse as well as themselves. It is not, at least for these two activities. Ask your horse to work all of the time while he is being schooled or shown. The walk is one of the three principal gaits of the horse. It represents fully one-third of the horse's repertoire of forward movement, excluding the gallop. Assign definite importance to developing a walk of good quality (Picture 110). Teach an energetic, free, forward-moving walk. It will enhance the horse's suppleness, cooperation and obedience to your aids, and movement off the line will be less frequent.

Understanding the mechanics of the walk is important to any serious rider, amateur or professional. Later, you will not be able to coordinate your aids with the horse's sequence of legs to teach better transitions and higher-level exercises from the walk if you cannot understand and feel what is occurring beneath you. Understanding and actually feeling the sequence of legs at the walk will be keys to lengthening the stride at the walk, producing square halts, teaching a turn on the haunches from the walk and obtaining prompt canter departures on the correct lead from the walk. Teach a forward-moving walk, on the line.

Your basic objectives in mounting the horse for the first time and teaching the walk should be:

Picture 110. The walk. *Demand that the horse remain attentive to your aids when schooling at the walk. Teach an energetic, forward-moving walk with movement on the line.*

1. To introduce the horse to the voice command *Walk* and, depending upon circumstances, to introduce the word *Slow* in conjunction with check-releases of the reins to control excessive forward speed or the inclination to break to the trot.

2. To introduce the horse to the action of urging legs

3. To introduce the horse to the meaning of the leading rein for turning, and later circling

4. To teach the horse the meaning of two direct reins of opposition used in a check-release manner—to slow the horse if he breaks to the trot, or to halt the horse

5. To begin teaching the horse that movement on the line is required—to begin teaching him the meaning of the rider's holding and displacing legs

6. To teach the horse that an even speed on loose reins is required—stabilization at the walk

7. To teach a forward-moving, energetic walk

8. To encourage a natural carriage of the head and neck when walking forward—free use of normal balancing gestures

If you think about these eight points, you will find that you have already taught the horse a good deal by just beginning a simple exercise such as the walk. You will have already introduced him to two, and possibly three, of the standard leg aids which he will rely upon the rest of his riding life. Two of six possible rein aids will have been introduced, along with the aids of voice and weight. Additionally, you will have begun to teach the horse something about desirable qualities in his forward movement; stabilization and movement on the line. He has already begun to learn obedience with quick, definite responses to your aids.

The way you teach even a simple exercise such as the walk has far-reaching consequences for later schooling. What if your initial schooling for the walk has taught the horse *dis*obedience to the aids used, movement *off* the line and *in*stability of forward speed? Keep in mind that the horse has a good memory; he is apt to remember anything you've taught him—good or bad—the next time he is mounted.

Having set the horse in motion at the walk, you can now begin to teach the halt.

THE HALT

This is the horse's first introduction to performing a downward transition. Use your aids correctly and in the following sequence: weight, voice, reins.

When requesting the halt, you should be sitting upright, not leaning forward. Be sure that your lower legs are underneath you and have not drifted forward or back. Say *Whoa* with authority, but do not shout at the horse. Next, check with both reins, and then release as the horse begins to slow his forward speed. Repeat your voice command and the check-release tech-

nique with the reins until the halt is achieved. Do not allow your upper body to lean forward as you apply tension on the reins, or as the horse halts (perhaps a little too quickly). Use your aids in the order just described: weight, voice, reins. See Pictures 111 and 112.

All other downward transitions are accomplished correctly using this same sequence of aids. Later in schooling, the use of your legs to produce square halts will be introduced, but for now weight, voice and reins are enough.

At first, it is only required that the horse learn the aids for the halt and that he respond promptly. A prompt mental response to your aids should be required from the onset of schooling, but it is quite permissible for the horse to take several strides while physically attempting to slow to the halt. Young horses are often quite unbalanced under the new weight of a rider. While they wish to respond promptly to your aids, they may simply be too unbalanced to do so at first. As schooling

Picture 111. Aids for the halt: the check. *The technique of check and release is important in securing all kinds of downward transitions efficiently and unabusively. This picture illustrates the check, and Picture 112 illustrates the subsequent release of rein tension while teaching the horse to halt promptly. The efficient use of the rider's weight should precede the use of the reins.*

Picture 112. Aids for the halt: the release. *A release in rein tension should promptly follow the check (Picture 111). The release is an integral part of the whole process of check and release. It is an important factor in avoiding all types of resistance on the part of the horse— head tossing, going above the bit, opening the mouth and many others. The release shown in this picture followed the check shown in the preceding picture by approximately one and one-half seconds.*

continues, and the horse begins to understand the aids for the halt and has developed some practice at halting, you may become more demanding. Begin to require very prompt and obedient halts with fewer intermediate strides.

When slowing to the halt, keep the horse on the line. Avoid having either the haunches or forehand drift toward the center of the ring, or toward the rail. Use a displacing leg behind the cinch to control the hindquarters; use a leading rein to keep the shoulders, neck and head on the line. Later in schooling, other rein aids will be used to prevent movement off the line by the horse's forehand.

Halting on the line should be taught early in schooling. More evasions and disobediences to the rider's aids are possible when the horse has the advantage by being off the line. A correct halt is an important foundation for later exercises: prompt canter departures from the halt, pivots, spins, rollbacks and sliding stops. Horses that halt off the line cannot be as relaxed as they should be; any horse is more relaxed when he moves forward, backs or halts on the line.

When halting, the green horse will often insist upon continuing to walk forward. Use your voice and a check-release of the reins to prevent this. If he persists, check your position to see that you are not responsible for the horse's inclination to creep forward. Make sure that your upper body is not leaning forward, that your lower leg is not drifting back or wobbling on the horse's side and that you are not inadvertently squeezing the horse forward with your legs.

If obedient halts become a problem, there are three progressively stronger tactics to use. First, use only your weight, voice and reins (check-release) in the normal manner. If the horse ignores

Picture 113. Forcing the halt. *The rider's back is braced; the shoulders are inclined behind the vertical. The arms are stiffened and a definite rearward check of the reins is used, but the rider's hands remain soft and unabusive. Note that in this picture the rider's little finger is giving forward. It is the rider's aggressive use of weight, not an abusive use of reins, which forces the halt.*

this, use both your hands *and arms*, in addition to your other aids, to stop the horse. If this second effort is disobeyed or not understood, use your hands, arms *and shoulders* very strongly. In this case, your shoulders should be inclined slightly behind the vertical, and your back should be braced. You should have the feeling that you are pulling your seat deeper into the saddle (Picture 113). If you use this method to force the horse to pay attention to your hands, be sure that he is bitted in a snaffle, bosal or some type of reasonably mild bit. Do not employ this scheme of aids on regular basis; use it only to correct occasional disobediences to the reins, or to demand the attention of an inattentive horse when requesting the halt. Return to soft aids when your point has been made.

At this level of schooling, always give the horse advanced notice before using your reins. Use your voice and weight; then use the reins in check-release manner, and use them softly, except when the horse is ignoring your hands. Disobedience to your hands should be punished with the reins, but remember to return to soft aids for subsequent requests to halt. The release part of the check-release is the horse's reward for his obedience to the check. When a rider cannot remember that the release is part of the aid, the horse usually begins to open his mouth and toss his head.

At the halt, the horse should be willing to stand still on loose reins. From time to time, insist that the horse stand quietly, without attempting to creep forward for reasonable lengths of time. The horse should stand in a relaxed but alert manner, with his head and neck in a natural position.

At this level of schooling, do not be concerned if the horse does not halt squarely. This can be taught later in the elementary level, or in the intermediate level (square halts are discussed in Chapter 7). To obtain a square halt, except by luck, the rider uses mild urging legs as he asks the horse to halt, and this would be a confusing signal for many green horses: the hands would be saying stop, while the legs would seem to be saying go forward. At this level, you *can*, however expect a horse to stop with front legs parallel to each other. Squaring the forelegs can be accomplished by using your reins just as the horse comes to a full halt. Squaring the hind legs must be accomplished by the rider's legs, not his hands.

THE TROT

For the trot, use the same aids as for the walk: weight, voice, legs. In this case, however, use your voice a little more briskly to say *Trot*. Use your urging legs more actively to increase the horse's forward speed to that of the trot.

You are teaching a green horse to trot for the first time under the new weight of a rider. Your initial goals: a prompt response to your aids in beginning the trot, a reasonably slow, steady forward speed at the trot—stabilization at the trot (Picture 114). Worry about teaching variations of the trot later: there is plenty of time to teach the jog, ordinary trot, fast trot or extended trot. At this point the horse doesn't even know how to neck rein; he has barely come to understand what is required by your leg aids, he only understands two of six possible rein aids, and his only experience in performing upward transitions has been in moving from the halt to the walk.

Begin the trot from a forward-moving walk. Be sure that you are sitting in rhythm with the horse's efforts at the walk, and say *Trot*. Use your urging legs to increase the horse's forward speed until he breaks to the trot. Use them in a tapping or squeezing manner, whichever is required. If the horse remains reluctant to move into the trot, use a louder voice and kicking legs.

If the trot is too fast at first, repeat the command to trot, but this time use your voice softly. Check and release with the reins in rhythm with the trot that exists, or in rhythm with your voice if you must repeat the command to trot several times. Do not lean forward, and be sure that your legs are not irritating the horse by swinging back and forth, wobbling or drifting rearward. Do not hang on the horse's mouth with the reins; release the rein tension whenever he is inclined to obey the reins by slowing down even a little. You can use your reins again if the subsequent speed still remains too fast.

If the horse is reluctant to increase his speed

enough to break to the trot, or if he breaks back to the walk as soon as the trot is established, resort to a kicking leg (still in the normal urging position) to urge him forward. Teach the horse that you require prompt responses to aids. If you frequently encounter disobedience from the horse in moving rapidly from the walk to the trot, or if he ignores the fact that he is to continue trotting until instructed to walk or halt, reinforce your urging legs with a spur, crop or the ends of split reins. If you employ a crop or split reins to reinforce your urging legs, don't hit the horse just anywhere. Use your crop or split reins directly behind either of your urging legs to reinforce their action.

When a reasonable speed of the trot has been achieved, be sure that your reins remain loose. If the forward speed of the trot becomes erratic, you may only need to use your voice either in a sharp tone to speed him up or prevent a break to the walk, or in a soothing tone to slow him down. You may need a slight use of urging legs, or a brief check and release to supplement your use of voice.

Once the trot is in progress and the horse is moving at a fairly steady pace, two options are open to you. You may either post or sit to the trot. If the trot is rough, or a little fast at first, posting may be preferred, both for the comfort of the horse and the comfort of the rider. If you choose to post, remember that the higher you post, the faster the horse will be inclined to move. Posting low, with your crotch close to the saddle, and softly will aid the horse in developing a slow, rhythmic trot. Posting gives you time to teach the horse with your voice and hands to regulate his speed, while not disturbing him by bouncing in the saddle. Posting allows the horse to practice the trot, while allowing the rider to teach the horse a slow even pace so that he or she can begin sitting the trot.

When the horse has learned a slow speed at the trot, begin to sit to the trot. The sitting trot has some distinct advantages, provided that you can sit without bouncing. First, you can use your legs more effectively when sitting. They can be used more efficiently for the purposes of keeping the horse next to the rail, or for urging him forward if he is inclined to break to the walk. When sitting, you can keep your legs extremely quiet and nonirritating; when you post, some squeezing of the horse's sides will be unavoidable each time you rise.

While posting can be conducive to producing a

Picture 114. Sitting as an aid to teaching the trot. *When the horse is first taught to trot, the rider's ability to sit in rhythm with the trot, even with erratic changes in pace or rapid shifts in the horse's balance (as are occurring in this picture), is vital to ultimately developing a slow, steady trot. Sitting well also enables the rider to use his hands and arms smoothly and independently, while coping with fluctuations in the horse's speed and balance at the same time. Here the rider remains sitting well to control the horse's speed, while at the same time using his hands and arms for a completely different task—teaching neck reining.*

rhythmic trot, it also encourages slightly faster forward speeds. Additionally, when you are sitting it is easier to use your weight from side to side to influence the movement on the line.

Teaching the trot from a standing position is usually inadvisable. First, you should be teaching the horse that the use of your weight precedes each upward transition. Second, you should be teaching the horse to maintain a slow forward speed in response to your weight. In the standing position, some forward inclination of the rider's upper body inevitably occurs. This forward inclination, with no weight in the saddle, only teaches the horse to hurry forward. Teaching a slow speed at the trot from a standing position means that you will have to teach regulation of speed only with your hands; you will be schooling the horse to listen only to your hands, rather than to your weight and hands, as you should be doing.

When teaching the trot, encourage movement on the line. Use a holding or displacing leg to prevent the horse, primarily his haunches, from coming off the rail. A leading rein will assist you in controlling the forehand. Later in schooling, after the horse better understands two direct reins used as a check-release and the leading rein, you may use an indirect rein in front of the saddle horn to help keep the horse's forehand on the line, next to the rail.

Remember that your objectives here are to teach a prompt transition from the walk to the trot, a reasonably steady slow forward speed (stabilization) and forward movement on the line. Secondary considerations are teaching a transition from the halt to the trot, with very few steps at the walk in between, and teaching a prompt halt from the trot, again with very few walking steps during the transition. Encourage a natural carriage of the horse's head and neck at all times.

The green horse, under the weight of a rider for

the first few times, generally finds the trot to be the most comfortable gait at which to accustom himself to his new burden (see Chapter 1, Sequence of Legs at the Trot). I have seen many young horses, very nearly unable to walk in a straight line when first mounted, perform reasonably well at the trot. Some of these horses were capable of performing fairly accurate circles from the very onset of schooling at the trot.

When the horse has been schooled to a point where he understands your sequence of aids for an upward transition (halt to the walk, walk to the trot); when he understands the use of legs generally; when he understands the use of reins generally; when he can maintain a stabilized walk and trot, begin to teach the canter.

THE CANTER

Teach the canter initially from the stabilized trot. The sequence of aids in asking for the canter are basically the same as for any other upward transition: weight, voice, legs—with the addition of a slight outside opening rein as you ask for the canter.

In preparation for the canter, use a slight leading rein to turn the horse's head to the outside, toward the rail. Sit and do not lean forward; remember this especially if you were previously posting at the trot or standing in your stirrups for any reason.

To begin the canter, say briskly *Canter* or *Lope*, and ask for the canter by using your outside leg actively behind the cinch. Use your outside leg in a tapping, squeezing or even kicking manner. Although your outside leg actually requests the canter (your right leg for a canter on the left lead, and your left leg for a canter on the right lead), you may at first find it necessary to urge the horse forward also with your *inside* leg squeezing or tapping at the cinch. Depending on the horse's willingness to begin the canter from the trot, the rider's outside leg may be used in either a squeezing manner, a more demanding tapping manner or a severe kicking manner.

You will find that most horses when first attempting the canter, will just sort of run into it. This is fine. Your first priority is to obtain the canter, on any lead, from the trot.

Your second priority is to maintain the canter—to give the horse practice in cantering. Once the horse has caught his balance at the canter, you can begin to worry about other matters: obtaining the correct inside lead, maintaining a reasonably slow, steady forward speed and remaining on the line. Picture 115 shows a young gelding cantering for the first time.

When teaching the canter, be sure your reins are loose. If you have momentarily taken hold of the horse's mouth with the reins because he merely wants to trot faster rather than breaking to the canter, be sure that you release the rein tension as soon as the horse begins to take the first cantering stride. This is important. Too often I see riders using their weight, voice and legs correctly to teach the canter, but just as the horse obeys their request by taking the first cantering stride, these riders inadvertently bump the horse in the mouth with the bit, sometimes quite severely. They do this for one of two reasons. First, their reins may simply be held too short. As the horse extends and lowers his head and neck in preparation for the first full stride at the canter, he contacts the bit. He bumps into it. Second, the rider may attempt correctly to compensate by following the downward balancing gestures of the horse's head and neck with his hands and arms, but his timing is off. The rider is not quick enough to extend his arms forward to follow the horse's head and neck as the canter is begun: the horse gets bumped in the mouth anyway.

The green horse quickly becomes confused whenever the rider instructs him to canter and in the same instant instructs him with his hands to slow down, trot or halt.

There are many variations of the canter: lope, ordinary canter, fast canter, semi-collected canter, countercanter, and so forth. However, at this stage in the horse's schooling you only need to teach one slow, even speed at the canter on loose reins. At the very first, nearly any speed of the canter is acceptable, so long as it is not excessively fast or dangerous. The important thing is that you afford the horse practice in cantering—that you allow him first to catch his balance and then to slow and stabilize his forward speed on loose reins.

Sitting well and in rhythm with the horse's efforts will greatly assist the horse in maintaining an even speed at the canter. Also, if you remember to sit upright as you canter through the corners of the ring, your horse will perform better. His forward pace will be steadier, he will be less inclined to break to the trot and you will be able to use

Picture 115. Young horse cantering for the first time. *This is quite a typical picture of a first canter. Note that the canter departure was not prompt—the horse typically ran into the canter from the trot; this is evidenced by the very wide-spread attitude of the front legs. The length of the stride at the trot had become quite long as the horse approached a speed so fast that only a canter would permit him to move forward at an even faster pace in response to the rider's urging legs. That the horse is quite strung-out behind is evident; this is also quite typical of a horse beginning his first canter. Note the very stiff attitude of the horse's head and neck. With practice, a natural carriage of the head and neck will be regained as the normal balancing gestures of the head and neck are re-established.*

your legs more efficiently to keep his haunches on the line. Picture 116 illustrates some of these points.

The inclination of most horses when first learning to canter is to slow down and break to the trot. This is understandable since most are already unbalanced by the new weight of the rider. Also, remember that the canter is the least stable gait. The problem of beginning the canter and then slowing down, usually breaking to the trot, is compounded whenever the horse must also turn a corner as he canters.

Be patient, but continue to demand the canter for progressively longer distances each schooling session. Continue to demand the canter until the entire circumference of your schooling area can be negotiated without the horses breaking to the trot. Sit, use your voice and use your outside leg actively tapping or squeezing behind the cinch. Also, use your inside leg, actively squeezing at the cinch, if this seems to help.

Most authorities agree that the rider's inside leg, squeezing at the cinch in rhythm with the canter, is responsible for maintaining the canter. I believe

Picture 116. Sitting as an aid to teaching the canter. *This young rider is using her weight effectively by sitting in rhythm with the horse's efforts at the lope. Effective use of the rider's weight—as opposed to use of the reins—is the preferred way to control the forward speed of the horse at the canter. Sitting well at the canter (i.e., not "perching") also permits the most effective use of the rider's leg aids.*

this is true for the schooled horse, but does not necessarily apply to the unschooled horse. At first, you may find your outside leg is more effective in maintaining the canter; this outside asking leg may make more sense to the horse.

Clucking with the voice can be a useful technique along the same lines. Clucking can be useful to help the horse maintain his pace at the canter, and to prevent him from slowing to the trot. However, I would discourage you from continuing this voice aid too long. Discontinue its use as soon as possible and instead use the command *Canter* in conjunction with your legs. After a while, clucking becomes a habit for the rider and an admission of sorts that you cannot really use your legs effectively to maintain the canter or to increase its speed when necessary.

When the horse has caught his balance, and his canter departures from the trot are reasonably prompt and reliable, begin to insist on the correct

lead: the left lead when cantering to the left, and the right lead when cantering to the right.

Obtaining the Correct Lead

Several methods for obtaining a canter departure will be discussed in Chapter 7. At this stage of schooling, concentrate on consistency in the use of your aids, and teach the type of canter departure the most easily understood by the horse—the one most apt to produce the correct inside lead. Use the following sequence of aids to request the canter on the inside lead:

1. As you prepare to canter, use the outside rein to turn the horse's head slightly to the outside, toward the rail or wall.
2. Sit upright. Do not lean forward as you request the canter. If it is necessary for you to stand or lean forward, do this only after the canter has begun.

Picture 117. Beginning the canter from the trot. *A prompt canter departure on the left lead begins with grounding the right hindfoot; this comprises the first beat of the newly-established canter, or lope. Of course, at the trot the right hind leg and left foreleg are simultaneously advanced as a diagonal pair of legs. Thus, the rider's request for a canter departure on the left lead from the trot should be made as this particular diagonal pair of legs is actually advanced—but before either of the feet is subsequently grounded again. The rider in this picture is (correctly) in the process of requesting a canter departure on the left lead at, or even just slightly before, the instant at which this photo was snapped.*

3. Use your voice. Give the verbal command *Canter* or *Lope.*
4. Use an outside leg actively behind the cinch to ask for the canter departure. When first teaching the canter, tap or kick with the outside leg. As the horse learns the routine, as he learns what is required of him, use an outside squeezing leg to request a departure at the canter.

Use the outside rein/outside leg scheme just given in order to obtain the correct lead when beginning the canter. More than most methods, this method is designed to insure the correct lead. Asking for the canter while trotting around a corner will initially provide you with added insurance in obtaining the correct lead.

After you have taught neck reining (discussed

later in this chapter), the equivalent aids for securing a canter on the correct inside lead will be these:

1. An inside bearing rein to turn the horse's head slightly to the outside, toward the rail or wall
2. Weight—sitting in the manner already described
3. Voice
4. An active outside leg used behind the cinch to ask for the canter departure

Whenever a wrong lead is taken, quickly bring the horse back to the trot. Do this softly, because he did obey your request to canter, even if it was on the wrong lead. Get your position organized, and immediately ask for the canter departure on the inside lead again.

As the elementary level of schooling continues, you may want to teach very prompt canter de-

Picture 118. Beginning the canter from the walk. *To obtain a prompt canter departure on the correct lead from the walk, you must understand the sequence of legs at the walk. This horse is correctly beginning the first stride of a left lead canter with the right hindleg. The rider had to recognize that at the walk the right hindleg would be the next to be advanced and grounded as the horse began to bear weight on his left front leg. Thus the rider appropriately timed his request for the canter.*

partures, on the correct lead, from both the trot and the walk.

To obtain a prompt departure from the trot on the left lead, for example, ask with your right leg just as the horse begins to advance his left foreleg (Picture 117). Insist, with your outside leg, that the canter be started with an absolute minimum of trotting steps. If necessary, reinforce your leg with a crop, spur or split reins.

Obtaining a prompt canter departure from the walk is a little more difficult, but this is how it is done. For a departure on the left lead, ask for the canter with your right leg just as the horse is beginning to bear weight on his left front limb. This is the moment that just precedes the advancing and subsequent grounding of the horse's right hindfoot. You will then be in a position to start the left lead canter correctly from the outside right hind limb. A very prompt, smooth and efficient type of canter departure will be the result (Picture 118).

If you are not clear on the position of the

horse's legs underneath you as he walks forward, producing a canter departure on the correct lead from the walk is apt to be a hit-or-miss affair. Either that, or the horse is being terribly kind to you. If you have trouble knowing how the legs are moving, review the previous discussion and also review Chapter 1 on the sequence of legs at the walk. Stand along the rail and observe horses as they walk forward; recall the sequence of legs at the walk and think about the instant at which you would request a canter departure on the appropriate lead.

Aside from teaching prompt canter departures on the correct lead and teaching stabilization at the canter, asking that the horse move on the line is also important. Your inside leg can be used in keeping the whole horse on the rail. You may use your weight to the inside to assist him in turning, or you may find it necessary to use your weight to the outside in order to prevent the horse from cutting corners. Use an outside leading rein to

Picture 119. Turning on the line at the canter. *Here the rider is employing an indirect rein (used in front of the saddle horn) in order to turn the horse's head and neck in the proper direction and to move the horse's shoulders closer to the rail. The rider's indirect rein hand (left hand) is correctly moving back toward his belt buckle; this active hand is correctly placed so that it does not cross the withers to the opposite side of the horse. The rider's non-active hand (right hand) is correctly giving forward as the indirect rein is applied with the left hand. While the correct application of this rein aid enabled the horse to remain on the line as she turned, it would have been preferable to see the rider's hands carried lower and less inclination to lead with his inside shoulder.*

prevent the forehand from drifting off the rail. You may use an inside indirect rein to accomplish the same thing even more effectively (Picture 119).

At the elementary level of schooling, do not worry about developing a lope of high quality. Instead, put your energies into developing a reasonably slow, stabilized canter. Permit a natural carriage of the head and neck and free use of balancing gestures. Work on prompt canter departures and on obtaining the inside lead. Teach movement on the line when the canter begins and while it is in progress. Stay next to the rail, and do

not cut corners as you turn at the end of your schooling area or ring.

DOWNWARD TRANSITIONS

The downward transitions include the canter to the trot, walk or halt; the trot to the walk or halt; and the walk to the halt. Regardless of which of these transitions you wish to perform, the general formula for the use of your aids remains the same. Use your weight first, then your voice and finally your hands, by checking with both reins. For example, if you were cantering while in the standing position and you wanted to walk, you would do the following: sit in the saddle and bring your shoulders back to the vertical, clearly say *Walk*, and check with the reins. Do not hang. Release the tension on the reins as the horse starts to slow down. The sequence of the rider's aids should remain the same for every downward transition.

The use of the rider's weight deserves further discussion. Nearly every horse is capable of perceiving very slight changes in the rider's position and weight distribution. This is true no matter how heavy or how well padded a saddle may be. Whenever the rider ceases to sit in rhythm with the horse's movements or stops giving with any portion of his back, the horse perceives this change; it makes him somewhat uncomfortable. In response to his discomfort (the added pressure on his back), a horse will usually slow down in an effort to move with the motion of the rider.

For a very green horse, the use of the rider's weight will have some effect, but not a dramatic one. The horse must learn the routine of downward transitions, and the use of the rider's other aids (voice and hands) help the horse to better understand weight. For an intermediate-level horse that is tuned to the rider's weight, a slight bracing of the back may be all that is needed to

Picture 120. Softly demanding a prompt transition from a green horse. *This green horse was running away at the trot. The rider has demanded the walk with the intention of resuming a steadier trot. The rider has used his weight (while leaning a bit too far back), has braced his back and has asked the horse with his hands to slow his forward speed. All in all, an unabusive request for a downward transition from the trot to the walk, considering the previous attitude of the horse.*

bring him from a canter to a walk. Other aids may be unnecessary.

When first teaching any horse about downward transitions, give him the benefit of the doubt if he is initially unresponsive. Let him learn the routine: weight, voice, reins. After using your weight to signal a decrease in forward speed, repeat your voice and rein aids as often as necessary, and as softly as circumstances will permit. As you continue to practice downward transitions, increase your demand for fewer and fewer strides before the horse assumes the new slower gait. Begin to demand promptness in these transitions, while keeping them as smooth as possible (Picture 120).

Punish outright disobedience for any particular downward transition with your hands. Be rough if necessary. Ultimately, a refusal to slow promptly to a new gait is a disobedience to your hands: even though you have used your weight and voice correctly. If you find it necessary to administer a

"tonsillectomy" with the bit to achieve obedience to your request, then do so. Then assume that the horse has learned his lesson, and return to soft hands the next time you request the same transition. If he is obedient, tell him so with a word or a pat on the neck.

Insist that the horse remain on the line during downward transitions. Use a tapping or squeezing leg to move the haunches back on the line if these tend to drift to either side as he slows his forward speed to assume the new slower gait or the halt. If the horse is reluctant to move his haunches to the side in response to your active leg, use a crop behind your active displacing leg. Raise a 24-hour welt if necessary.

Use a leading rein to prevent the horse's head and neck from becoming crooked as the downward transition is in progress *if necessary*. Do not hang on the outside rein without reason; do not use the inside rein to prevent something that may not occur.

Picture 121. Conflicting aids for downward transitions. *The rider is asking the horse to increase his forward speed by leaning forward with her upper body, while at the same time asking the horse to slow his forward pace with her hands. The rider is also attempting to slow the forward speed by sitting, but at the same time her lower leg has drifted back, instructing the horse to go faster. If you were this horse, would you speed up or slow down?*

Although not an elementary control technique *per se*, the occasional use of one direct rein to correct a crooked attitude of the head and neck can be very effective. It is more demanding than the leading rein. Also, an indirect rein used in front of the saddle horn is an effective means of moving the horse's shoulders to the side. For example, if you are moving along the rail to the left, and the horse moves his forehand off the rail and to the inside, a left indirect rein will largely correct this situation. Use it with an inside holding leg.

None of the aids given for teaching downward transitions should instruct the horse to go forward (Picture 121). All are intended to slow the forward speed and to produce the desired transition. Later in schooling, you will add mild urging legs to all requests for downward transitions. This urging takes some of the roughness out of these transitions and encourages the horse to remain engaged behind as he assumes the new slower gait. The engagement gives precision to prompt downward transitions.

UPWARD TRANSITIONS

You have already learned how to teach upward transitions: the halt to the walk, walk to the trot and trot to the canter. The transition from the walk to the canter has also been discussed. Remember that the correct sequence of aids for all upward transitions is 1) weight, 2) voice, 3) legs. If you must use your reins to control the horse's forward speed in advance of the transition or to turn the horse's head slightly to the outside for a canter departure, employ your reins immediately after using your weight, but before using your voice and legs.

When first teaching upward transitions, do not demand that the horse immediately canter from the trot. Allow the horse to remain calm and to take several more trotting steps before breaking into the canter. The very green horse may be permitted to take a few quicker steps at the trot, while a more schooled horse should not be permitted to quicken his stride at the trot, and should respond more promptly to the aids for the canter departure.

Remember, the correct use of weight requires that you simply remain upright and sit in rhythm with the horse's efforts in advance of each upward transition. Do not however, brace your back as

you would for a downward transition. Do not hang on the reins or otherwise discourage the horse from assuming the new, faster gait.

Remember your objectives at this level of schooling: quick and definite responses and obedience to your aids.

TURNS AND CIRCLES

Rein Aids

While the leading rein is the primary rein aid in initially executing circles and turns on the very green horse, bear in mind that there are actually four rein aids which may be commonly employed for purposes of turning the horse's head and neck. They are:

1. The leading rein (for early schooling)
2. The neck rein (for later schooling, showing and for actual working situations)
3. One direct rein
4. One indirect rein (used in front of the horn as an aid in displacing the horse's shoulders to the side, but also having the action of turning the horse's head and neck to the side)

Any of these rein aids may be employed to the rider's advantage from time to time in producing circles and turns. The very green horse, not yet accustomed to the neck rein, will necessarily be schooled to these movements using the leading rein at first, but this does not automatically exclude the rider from employing a single direct rein or an indirect rein when needed. Similarly, when the horse has been taught neck reining and responds well to this technique, the rider may still employ a leading rein to teach a new lesson, or any other rein aid if appropriate for a certain situation.

Circle Figures

The full circle is a perfectly *round* figure. It is not oblong, oval, egg-shaped or any other shape which is not round. While this discussion centers on teaching full circles, there are several variations of a full circle which should also be taught to any horse. They are:

1. The full circle (Picture 122)
2. The half circle and reverse (Picture 123)
3. The half circle in reverse (Picture 124)

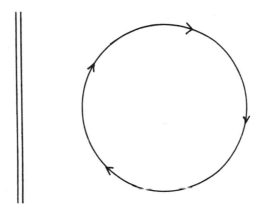

Picture 122.   The full circle. *Circles must be round. The rider's eye control and concentration are vital if the movement is not to be spoiled. Circles provide an unabusive way of controlling forward speed during early schooling. They are essential in stabilizing the horse at all gaits, and tend to improve the quality of movement and carriage of the head and neck.*

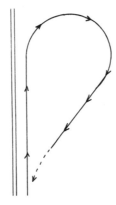

Picture 123.   The half circle and reverse. *The half circle and reverse is the standard way in which to change directions in the show ring. It is performed at the walk and trot on the elementary level.*

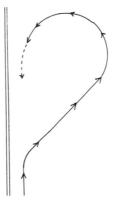

Picture 124.   The half circle in reverse. *The half circle in reverse is another way in which the rider may change directions in the ring while schooling. This ring figure contributes to schooling for lateral flexibility, as well as practicing another variation of the circle itself. Rather good eye control is required on the part of the rider in order to accurately return to the rail.*

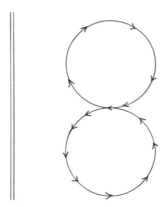

Picture 125. The figure eight. *A figure eight is merely two adjoining circles; it is performed at the walk and trot on the elementary level. At the junction of the two circles, the horse should take several strides on a straight line before moving on the line in the new direction. This figure is at the heart of all reining patterns and is used to teach both simple and flying changes of leads on the intermediate level.*

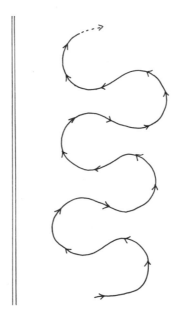

Picture 126. The serpentine. *A serpentine of six loops is shown. This is the maximum number of loops that will comfortably fit in an arena 175 to 200 feet long. This figure is a series of half circles joined together. The horse's body should be straight for several strides when one loop is ended and the next one is about to begin. The serpentine is performed at the walk and the trot on the elementary level. Later, on the intermediate level, serpentines with fewer and larger loops can be performed at the canter with simple or flying changes at the moment when the horse should be straight.*

4. The figure eight (Picture 125)
5. The serpentine (Picture 126)

Your first obligation is to teach full circles. After this technique is perfected, you may want to teach some variations. Practicing variations will help relieve some of the boredom inevitably associated with elementary schooling—for both horse and rider. Also, practicing some of these variations *after teaching the full circle* will be advantageous when you set about to teach neck reining in earnest.

Teaching the Horse to Turn

Early in schooling, each horse must be taught to turn. As you teach any of the gaits, the horse must learn to turn as the ends of the ring or arena are approached. This is a relatively simple process. Your leading rein is used in the direction of the turn to be made; it simply shows the horse where to go, which way to turn. Your inside holding leg helps to prevent the horse from cutting corners as he turns. It assists him in understanding that he should go deep into the corners of the ring as the turn progresses. This same inside leg will assist you in keeping the horse next to the rail and on the line as you approach the first turn at the end of the ring. If you prepare for them, your turns will come out better.

While the leading rein indicates the direction of the turn, and the inside leg prevents the horse from falling in while turning, the rider's outside leg in conjunction with the leading rein tells the horse which direction to turn. Use an active right leg, squeezing softly, to indicate a left turn; use an active left leg, again squeezing softly, to indicate a right turn. Use these leg signals at the cinch, or immediately behind it.

Good turns at slow or moderate speeds require that you sit upright. As you move your inside leading rein hand in the direction of the turn, you may also have to move your outside hand slightly forward in order to prevent the outside rein from tightening as the horse bends his head and neck to the inside. As you use these two hands independently, maintain your position. Do not lean to either side or collapse your upper body forward or back.

Picture 127. Overleaning while circling. *This rider is contributing to the unbalance of a green horse by overleaning in an effort to turn the horse at the canter.*

Teaching the Full Circle

Turning around the corners of a ring is fairly simple; teaching the horse to execute an accurate full circle is a little more difficult.

Most very green horses are unbalanced by the rider's weight at first, and this loss of balance is increased when the horse is asked to circle for the first time. Attempting to perform circles less than 50 feet across contributes to even greater unbalance. Poor control of the rider's upper body may further unbalance the horse (Picture 127).

Your objective at first is to teach a large circle at an even speed. Your further objectives are:

1. To teach the horse to move on the line as he executes the required circle; to have him look in the direction of the turn, and to be sure that his rear feet track in the same arc described by the front feet.
2. To execute accurate circles.

Later in the course of elementary schooling, smaller circles may be taught and performed; your emphasis, however, should still be on producing an even speed on loose reins, movement on the line, and *round* circles.

The aids for teaching circles are no different from those for teaching turns: inside leading rein, inside-holding leg (a supporting leg) and an outside turning leg (at the cinch or even behind it, in a holding position). Again, use your right leg to indicate a left turn, and your left leg to indicate a right turn. Either of the rider's legs may be used by softly squeezing or more actively tapping, as required to produce an accurate circle. If the horse tends to bulge outward on the circle, use your outside leg more actively. If he tends to fall inward, use your inside leg more actively.

Always turn the horse with your legs. Push him as softly as possible away from your outside leg and in the direction of the turn. Use an inside supporting leg to prevent him from falling inward toward the center of the circle.

Circles at the Three Gaits

Teaching circles at the walk is not difficult. The primary problem here is maintaining sufficient forward impulse to permit the horse to execute accurate circles. Green horses that lack energy in their forward movement tend to weave; in particular, the haunches tend to travel from side to

side. With your reins loose, sit in rhythm with the walk. Use urging legs, as well as holding and supporting legs, to improve the accuracy of circles at this gait.

Teaching circles at the trot is probably easier than teaching them at the walk. A great deal of natural stability is provided by this particular gait (Chapter 1). The problem at the trot is to keep the circles accurate and the horse on the line. Steadying the horse's forward speed is a matter of sitting rhythmically with the horse's efforts at the trot and using your reins and legs effectively. Sit up and do not lean to the side. Use your voice to say *Slow*, and use two direct reins if the horse becomes a little too quick. On the other hand, if lack of forward impulse becomes a problem, say *Trot* and use urging legs. Use an outside turning leg and an inside supporting leg to improve accuracy of the circles.

The canter is the most difficult gait for teaching circles. Obtaining an even speed while circling is your first priority. Worry about precise circles and movement on the line later. Most horses, when first being taught to canter along the arc of a circle will exhibit the following fault in the evenness of their pace.

First, they will break to the trot, but as you urge them forward into the canter again, they will only hurry ahead at the trot. Or they will resume the canter, and then spurt ahead.

Remember that the green horse has legitimate balance problems when first learning to canter a circle. It is your responsibility to *assist* him in his efforts. Be determined; use your aids efficiently, but do not be abusive. If the horse breaks from the canter to the trot, use your legs actively to urge him forward; use your outside leg to ask for the canter. Say *Canter*. Use your inside urging leg actively at the cinch. Do not make the mistake of leaning forward. This, only encourages the horse to trot faster.

If the horse picks up the canter again, but spurts forward, sit deeply and in rhythm with the canter. Use your voice to say *Slow*, and your reins to softly check his forward speed. If the horse tends to bulge outward as he speeds up, then use your outside leg very actively in the displacing position to range the hindquarters to the inside, and perhaps use your inside supporting leg less actively.

When the horse has learned to maintain an even pace while circling at the canter, become very particular about obtaining accurate circles and very good movement on the line. Your leg aids should control the movement of the haunches to insure that these remain on the line. Your leading rein indicates the direction of the turn and literally leads the horse's nose along the arc which you wish to describe.

A problem can arise here. With practice at circling, and with a continued use of the leading rein, many horses will begin to fall inward with their forehand: their shoulders, head and neck will begin to drift inward in response to the leading rein. To correct this, use your leading rein less actively; move your inside hand slightly to the inside so that you are using more of a direct rein—a compromise between the leading rein and the direct rein.

In the final analysis, good circles and turns are produced by the rider's legs. The rider may use his weight laterally (Chapter 3) to help the horse perform accurate circles *softly*. Use your weight to the inside if the horse tends to bulge outward on circles; use it to the outside for horses that tend to fall inward as they circle. The lateral use of weight can reduce the active use of both reins and legs.

Eye control is essential to performing accurate turns and circles. You must look ahead, and follow the arc of the circle you wish to describe with your eyes (Picture 128.) If a set of footprints already exists, and these describe an accurate circle that you wish to follow, look ahead and follow these same prints with your eyes. If none exist, then visualize the path you wish to follow, and concentrate on this imaginary circle with your eyes. Look ahead of your horse. If you exercise eye control, every circle or turn you make will

Picture 128. Eye control on circles and turns. *The rider is correctly looking ahead along the arc of a circle, which she wishes to follow.*

come out better. This is just as applicable whether you are teaching a green horse to circle for the first time or riding a finished show ring horse.

NECK REINING

During elementary schooling only three of the six standard rein aids are used consistently: two direct reins, the leading rein and neck reins. At the lowest elementary level, only the two direct reins, used in a check-release manner, and the leading rein are used. The entire course of elementary schooling could actually be accomplished using only these two rein aids, in conjunction with the other three natural aids (voice, weight and legs). Nevertheless, neck reining should be taught at this level of schooling. It is an important means of control for both the working stock horse and the western show horse.

As I pointed out in Chapter 3 teaching the horse to neck rein is not complex or difficult for the average rider. It is simply worked in as schooling progresses. For example, turns and circles are initially taught using only an inside leading rein to literally lead the horse's nose in the direction of the turn. But once the horse has learned to turn responsively to the action of the leading rein, the opposite or outside rein can simultaneously be brought to bear lightly across the neck. This is how you begin to teach the horse to neck rein (Picture 129). You are teaching him to turn away from the bearing rein.

Picture 129. Beginning to teach neck reining. *While this turn is being generated primarily from the rider's left leading rein and his right leg, a right bearing rein is nevertheless being used on the horse's neck. This is the beginning of teaching the horse to move away from the bearing rein—to neck rein.*

Picture 130. Helping the horse to understand neck reining. *The rider here is asking the horse for a left turn. His right bearing rein is asking for a turn to the left (along with his active right leg). He uses a left leading rein to assist the horse in understanding the demand.*

When teaching neck reining, ride with two hands. You may bridge split reins between your hands, ride with both hands on closed reins, or even hold your reins separately. In any case, as you neck rein the horse to the left, for example, move both of your hands simultaneously to the left. In essence, you will be using not only a right bearing rein, but also a left leading rein—a combination of signals easy for the horse to understand (Picture 130). As the horse becomes more accustomed to obeying the action of the bearing rein in the turn, gradually begin to reduce the leading rein effect. No longer move your inside hand so far in the direction of the turn to be performed. Make the horse rely more on the bearing rein for turns and less on the leading rein. As schooling continues, diminish the leading rein effect to the point that the horse begins to rely solely on the bearing rein to perform turns and circles (Picture 131).

From time to time while schooling, ride with the reins held in only one hand to be sure that the horse remains strictly responsive to your bearing reins and has not come to rely excessively on the combined use of leading rein and bearing rein for turns and circles. Punish disobediences and slow responses to the bearing rein quickly and effectively. With a sharp leading rein, jerk the horse's head definitely in the direction of the turn to be made, or use a crop or the ends of split reins smartly on the bearing rein side of the neck to make your point.

As you teach the horse a quick and definite response to the neck rein, do not forget that he must be obedient to your leg as well as your hands. If you are executing a very wide, easy turn to the left, use your bearing rein on the right side of the horse's neck, and use your right leg in a mild squeezing fashion at, or just behind, the cinch. If a sharp turn to the left is required, use your bearing rein on the right side of the neck, but use your right leg in a very definite squeezing manner. Use it in the holding position—push the horse into the turn with your leg. Remember, if you also shift your weight slightly to the left side of the saddle, this will encourage the horse to turn to the left.

Picture 131. Turning with a bearing rein. *After sufficient schooling, this horse willingly turns in response to a bearing rein, no longer relying on a leading rein to assist him in turning. (The rider has exaggerated the use of his rein hand for demonstration purposes.)*

Stand a little harder in your left stirrup, or move your hips to the left slightly.

Neck reins are to be employed as loose reins. It should never be necessary to turn the horse by pulling his head and neck to the side. It should not be necessary to move your rein hand far across the withers in the direction of the turn to be made. Whenever the bearing rein becomes too tight, either your technique is faulty or the horse simply is not schooled well enough to the use of neck reins.

When first teaching neck reining, you will have better success if you employ reins which have some roughness to them: rope reins, braided reins or horsehair reins are all satisfactory. Generally, the relatively unschooled horse will turn away from a rein with a rough texture more quickly than from a smooth one.

Many bits are unsuited to the effective use of a leading rein. Teaching the horse to neck rein, using a leading rein and a bearing rein together, is best accomplished in a snaffle, gag bit, or bosal. If you use a training snaffle with shanks, be sure that these will swivel to the side (Picture 54). Long-

shanked bits are unsuited for continued use with the leading rein: considerable tilting of the bit in the horse's mouth is apt to occur, resulting in fussing and movement off the line with the head.

Even after the horse learns responsive neck reining, always consider a return to the leading rein when teaching a new lesson involving turning of any sort. Use a lead rein or a combination of leading and bearing rein if it will help the horse learn a new lesson or movement (Picture 132).

THE REIN BACK

To back the horse for the first time, sit upright and do not lean forward. Say *Back* and then pull back lightly with two direct reins of opposition. As soon as the horse obeys by beginning to step backward, release the rein tension. Repeat the same action with your reins again, insuring that you release each time a step backward is taken. Ask for only a few steps at first.

It is a common fault of many riders to lean forward as they move their arms and hands rearward

Picture 132. Rein combinations for teaching a new lesson. *In this case, the rider is teaching the horse a turn on the haunches. Even though the horse understands neck reining, this rider is using a right bearing rein and a left leading rein, along with leg and weight aids. The leading rein is helpful to the horse in understanding the new movement; it also helps to keep him looking in the direction of the turn.*

to apply tension on the bit. This is undesirable, as well as confusing for the horse. Not only does the rider lose his position, but the inclination of his upper body to the front tells the horse to go faster *forward*—quite the opposite of what the rider is attempting to accomplish.

Also, while applying rearward tension on the reins to instruct the horse to back, do not simultaneously squeeze with your legs. Again, do not say *Back* with your voice and reins, and *Go forward* with your legs.

Speed in backing is not necessary at this level of schooling, but obedience is. Straight backing should be required from the onset of schooling. Deviations of the horse's haunches to one side or the other are primarily corrected through the time-

ly use of the rider's displacing leg. If the haunches deviate to the right as the horse is backing, use a right displacing leg in a tapping or kicking manner. Later, as the horse acquires more experience in backing, a mild squeezing leg used in the displacing position should be all that is required to keep the horse from deviating his hindquarters to the side. Deviations of the horse's head and neck to the side will also result in crooked backing. Use a leading rein to straighten the attitude of the horse's head and neck whenever this is required. Although not an elementary technique per se, one direct rein of opposition is also an effective means of accomplishing the same thing.

Occasionally, a horse does not respond well to the use of the rider's displacing leg in correcting deviations of the haunches to the side. While he may be quite responsive to the use of a displacing leg while moving forward, for some reason he is resistive while backing. One useful solution for the young horse that has not yet learned neck reining is to employ a strong indirect rein *behind* the saddle horn. If the horse deviates his haunches to the right and will not respond to a right displacing leg, employ a strong right indirect rein behind the horn.

This rein aid is useful in correcting resistance to the rider's use of a displacing leg, but do not rely on it too much. You can use it occasionally if necessary, but obedience to the leg is still the bottom line. The horse is being disobedient to your leg, not your hands. Remember, also, that this rein aid can be extremely abusive to the horse's mouth unless he is bitted in a plain snaffle. If you employ this rein aid, use it correctly. Bring your active rein hand toward your opposite hip; do not cross your hand and wrist to the opposite side of the horse.

The proper execution of the rein back is really a test of the horse's obedience to your aids. From a practical view, roping horses being a notable exception, the rein back actually has very little to do with most types of riding. Backing is chiefly useful in schooling the horse in prompt responses and obedience to the rider's aids. Also, backing is one of the first exercises to be learned in which the horse must carry a good deal of weight on the hindlegs; it is a step toward teaching central balance—a step toward semicollection. Also, if you can begin to teach the horse to willingly flex his head toward the vertical in response to your soft rearward tension on the reins, so much the better. The habit of *willing* flexions of the head and neck, in response to *soft* increases in rein tension, helps to set the stage for higher levels of schooling.

The proper execution of the rein back is a diffi-

Picture 133. Learning to back. *Remain sitting and do not stand in the stirrups, verbalize the command to back, and then employ two direct reins of opposition to initiate a step rearward. As soon as the horse obeys by stepping rearward, then release the rein tension (as this rider has done) before requesting a subsequent step to the rear. The single step rearward, which is shown here, consists of the diagonal pair of legs—right front and left rear—used simultaneously.*

cult, but important, exercise for most riders to teach. The rider's lack of technique often contributes to poor backing, and this lack of technique is the rule, not the exception, at many horse shows. The objectives of a good rein back at the elementary level of schooling are:

1. Obedience to the rider's aid, including voice
2. Straight backing
3. Backing for short distances willingly
4. Backing with the correct sequence of legs—diagonal pairs (described in Chapter 1)
5. A beginning of flexion at the poll in re-

sponse to the rider's soft hands, entailing a release of rein tension each time the horse executes a step to the rear

Pictures 133 and 134 sum up the rider's technique and the horse's quality of movement during the rein back at the elementary level of schooling.

ENGAGEMENT

A very good Appaloosa race horse had been acquired by a friend of mine who was a fine western trainer. This horse had been retired from the race track after a brief but successful racing career. Al-

Picture 134. Better backing at the elementary level. *If you compare this photo with Picture 133, your overall impression will be one of a greater willingness on the part of the horse to cooperate with the rider's aids in executing the rein back. Greater flexion of the head and neck is evident and a greater willingness to employ the hindquarters actively while backing is seen. There is a very definite tendency toward central balance at the moment this picture was taken. When compared with the previous photo, a straighter attitude of the head and neck is quite evident; straighter backing is therefore possible. You will also note some increase in the speed of backing.*

though quite a good speed horse, he had little schooling relating to any events which are normally part of western shows. He was steerable and did not buck often. This was about the extent of his schooling for show ring purposes.

At any rate, and even with this limited schooling, my friend kept insisting that this horse really had something; he was very athletic, and a rider could feel something underneath him quite exceptional for such a green horse.

Well, what this horse had and what my friend could feel as he rode was the quality of engagement in the forward stride. Though green and relatively unschooled by show ring standards, the horse possessed very good engagement of the hind limbs at each gait, due chiefly to his learned ability to advance the hind limbs up under his body as he raced. He was capable of advancing the hind limbs well forward, as well as the front limbs also, and in each case to a greater extent than most show ring horses are called upon to do.

This same horse went on to win or place in many of the western events offered in competition at the national level. And yes, it was necessary to decrease the engagement in this horse's forward stride in order to make him competitive within the western pleasure classes.

Most of us are not often fortunate enough to have the opportunity to start such a horse, one that has already learned a fundamental quality relating to very good movement within the show ring. Many of us start horses from scratch, and if they are to learn what is required of them, and this includes engagement, we must teach them.

To teach engagement, two things are required in advance. First, the horse must be stabilized. Second, the rider must understand exactly what it is that he wishes to teach; he must understand the physical nature and appearance of engagement.

Stabilization is achieved through regular riding, and for the green horse this usually requires schooling at least five times a week. Stabilization is achieved by a rider's maintaining a good working position while schooling. It is a matter of teaching one steady speed at the walk, one at the trot and one at the canter. The horse must be capable of maintaining a steady speed at each gait while being ridden on loose reins.

Although the rider may find it necessary occasionally to use his voice, reins or legs to insure a steady forward speed at any gait, the stabilized horse will maintain a steady forward speed, no slower, no faster, than that which is indicated by the rider. For example, the stabilized horse would maintain a 6 mph trot until asked by the rider to halt, walk or canter; or asked to increase the speed of the trot via the rider's urging legs; or asked to slow the speed of the trot by increased rein tension.

At the elementary level of schooling, the horse is asked to develop an energetic walk, and to remain stabilized at relatively slow speeds of the trot and canter while being ridden on loose reins.

Engagement is really not difficult to understand, and teaching it is only a matter of cooperation between the rider's hands and legs.

At the elementary level, schooling is mostly concentrated on teaching each of the gaits and developing stabilization of speed for each. In the case of the trot and canter, developing rather slow speeds at these gaits is not only desirable from the standpoint of stabilization, but also desirable as you look down the schooling road and think about developing the very slow gaits of the jog and lope.

When stabilization at reasonably slow speeds of the trot and canter has been achieved, then teach engagement. Teach the horse to move forward with engagement first at the trot. Use your legs at the cinch, in a very mild urging fashion, to say to the horse, "Move forward, step up under yourself a little with your hindlegs." Use your hands to say, "Don't speed up as you begin to move forward alertly, and with the quality of engagement to your stride."

When asking for engagement at this level of schooling, you are by no means asking the horse to emulate the forward stride of the English horse or the dressage horse. You are merely asking that the horse not move forward in a strung-out manner (Picture 135). You are asking for a measure of quality to the horse's slow movement at the trot: that the forward swing of the hindlegs (engagement) is at least as great as their backward swing (disengagement).

Your legs should gently ask the horse to be alert and to reach forward a little more with the rear legs, or even to lessen the disengagement portion of the stride (as opposed to actually increasing the forward reach of these limbs).

In either instance, you can produce movement of a better quality—movement that is not lazy, passively resistant and strung out. So long as you can produce movement in which the forward stride is at least as great as the corresponding rearward swing of the hindlegs, you have accomplished your purpose. Whether you do this by in-

Picture 135. Engagement. *This horse is engaged at the trot. The forward swing of the rear legs is greater than their corresponding rearward swing.*

creasing the forward reach of the limbs or by reducing the distance covered by their rearward flight is not too important at the slower speeds of the trot. Your soft hands instruct the horse not to convert this increased engagement into an increase in speed. He remains stabilized.

During elementary schooling concern yourself primarily with teaching engagement at the trot. The reasons for such an emphasis are: First, a brisk walk should have already been developed during very early schooling, so you will not need to be concerned about teaching engagement at the walk. Very likely it is already present. Second, teaching engagement at the slow canter would be desirable, but this is difficult to do when the horse is continually required to maintain a slow pace at this gait. Assessing relative degrees of engagement is a difficult proposition for anyone where slow speeds at the canter are involved. If you concentrate merely on developing engagement at the trot, and insist upon it being maintained during all schooling at this gait, there will be a sufficient carry-over of alertness and probably a minimal sort of engagement at the canter.

It is not necessary that the forward stride of the

rear legs be long in order for engagement to be present. In fact, a slow speed at the trot cannot be preserved with substantial lengthening of the rear legs' forward stride. The rider must not, however, permit the horse to establish the habit of moving forward in a strung-out manner. The forward stride of the hindleg, no matter how short the distance covered, must exceed or at least equal the corresponding distance covered by the rearward flight of this same limb. If you are in doubt about the engagement of the horse you are schooling, have another rider watch as you school the horse at the trot.

The engagement discussed here is satisfactory for the average schooling situation and should be taught at this level. Later in schooling, you will want to teach better engagement for faster speeds of the trot and canter. Engagement at ordinary, medium speeds of the canter will be taught. Also, if your interests include competition in the western pleasure classes, a rather special type of engagement will have to be taught if you are to develop a jog trot of superior quality. This will be discussed in Chapter 7. This special type of engagement is vertical engagement, discussed in Chapter 4.

IMPULSION (IMPULSE)

At the elementary level of schooling, a great deal of emphasis does not have to be placed on impulse. Just be sure the horse remains attentive. Demand that he be alert to each of your aids as he moves forward. Do not permit him to move forward as if his favorite stablemate had just died. Demand that he be attentive as he moves forward, turns, circles, halts and backs.

At the start of each schooling session, gain the horse's attention in an unabusive manner by performing a series of upward and downward transitions. For the average horse, or one that tends to be lazy, perform a series of transitions in quick succession. If the horse is inattentive to your legs, wake him up with a smart use of a crop behind your leg, or with a spur. Do not get yourself into the tiring position of nagging the horse with your legs for an entire hour or more.

For the horse that tends to be a little hot, restrict these transitions to walk-halt, walk-halt, walk-halt. If the horse is inattentive to your hands, settle the issue from the onset; use your weight, voice and reins in a very definite manner. Insist that he listen to your aids.

Remember, impulse forward is mental alertness on the part of the horse. Certainly, it is not unreasonable for you to demand that he remain alert during any schooling session. Impulse forward requires the property of engagement, but the presence of engagement does not have to result in increased speed or gaits which appear hurried. The horse should have the *appearance* of a reserve of energy. He should appear to be capable of lengthening his strides or increasing his speed quickly *if* required by the rider.

As I have said, showing impulse in a still photograph is difficult. The mental state of the horse cannot really be captured photographically. Nevertheless, Picture 136 may help you develop a feeling for satisfactory impulse at this level of schooling.

Picture 136. Impulse forward. *This horse is moving forward at the trot with impulse. He appears alert and keen and maintains good engagement at the trot. There is an appearance of energy about this horse's forward movement, even though the trot is quite slow and steady. The horse is being asked for impulse forward while maintaining a slow, steady trot. He is not being asked for a show ring (pleasure class) frame of movement.*

THE TURN ON THE FOREHAND

The turn on the forehand is always performed from the halt. In order to execute the turn on the forehand, the horse must rotate his hindquarters one step at a time around two relatively fixed forelegs. The forelegs simply mark time, up and down, or in very small steps in place, as the hindlegs walk to the side and describe an arc around the front legs. The usual extent of the movement is the performance of a half turn on the forehand, but quarter turns and full turns may be performed. Picture 137 illustrates the turn on the forehand—a half turn in this case.

The cardinal rules in teaching the turn on the forehand are to insure that the horse's head and neck remain straight as the turn is performed, and that he step neither forward nor backward while turning. The turn should be executed in an unhurried fashion, a step at a time, with the hindlegs. At this level of schooling, the lack of resistance on the part of the horse as the turn is made is an important feature of the movement. A high quality of movement is not emphasized, but if the horse crosses one back leg in front of the other as he sidesteps with the haunches, so much the better.

To teach the turn on the forehand, halt the horse a reasonable distance off the rail. Permit him to relax, and bring him to attention with two mild urging legs. If necessary, use your hands to prevent him from walking forward. If the turn is to be made with the haunches circling toward the right around the stationary forehand, use the following aids.

Use an active left displacing leg, tapping behind the cinch, to displace the haunches to the right. Ask for only a single step to the side, and stop using your displacing leg for an instant. Ask for another step to the side with the haunches, and another, until the desired half turn has been accomplished.

If the horse attempts to step backward as the turn is started or while it is in progress, use your right leg urging at the cinch. If the horse attempts to walk forward, use your hands to check the horse's forward movement with two direct reins of opposition.

In no instance should the rider use his reins to assist the horse in turning. The turn on the haunches is performed only in response to the rider's displacing leg. The rider's hands and op-

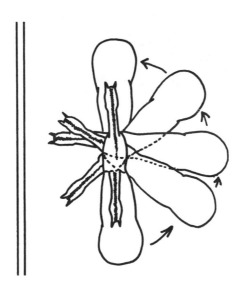

Picture 137. A turn on the forehand performed to the left. *The forehand remains relatively fixed as the haunches describe an even arc around the front legs. The horse should not step forward or backward while the turn is in progress.*

posite urging leg are only used to prevent the horse from moving forward or backward.

Although I generally avoid teaching or practising this exercise regularly at this level of schooling, here are some good reasons *for* teaching it at this point.

1. It is commonly required in most trail classes.

2. A horse capable of performing a nonresistive turn on the forehand will generally move his haunches back toward the rail, in response to the rider's inside displacing leg, whenever movement off the line has occurred. Generally, the horse will yield readily to the rider's leg in maintaining good movement on the line during increases and decreases in speed, as well as when performing all types of transitions.

3. Teaching the turn on the forehand may assist the horse to listen better to your displacing and holding legs, for purposes of more accurate circles and turns (for example, a more obedient response to your outside displacing leg for the horse inclined to drift to the outside with his haunches while circling at the trot or canter).

4. This exercise can help in teaching lower-level riders to coordinate their aids (provided they are careful not to use the reins in an effort to generate the actual turn).

Pictures 138, 139 and 140 sequentially illustrate

Picture 138. Beginning the turn on the forehand. *In this photo, the horse is beginning to execute the turn on the forehand by moving his haunches to the left and around his two "stationary" front legs (the horse should not attempt to step forward, backward or to the side with the front legs). The front legs should only "mark time" as the haunches step to the side, describing an arc around the fixed forehand. The rider is using her right displacing leg to ask the horse to move his haunches to the left. She is also using her weight by pushing her right seatbone toward the left side of the saddle. Her left leg is close to the horse to prevent him from stepping backwards. Her hands are soft, but alert to preventing forward movement. The only flaw in this picture is that the rider has not kept the horse's head and neck straight as the turn is begun.*

a green horse learning to perform the turn on the forehand.

THE TURN ON THE HAUNCHES (FROM THE HALT)

The turn on the haunches is the foundation for three higher level exercises: pivot, spin, rollback. Each of these is merely a variation of the basic turn on the haunches as described here.

To execute the turn on the haunches, the horse must rotate his forehand a step at a time around two relatively fixed hindlegs. The rear legs remain more or less fixed in the sense that the horse is not permitted to step forward, backward or to the side with either of the hind limbs as the turn is in progress.

If the turn is to be made to the left, the left rear leg remains in place as a pivotal leg, while the right rear leg merely walks in very small steps around it. The front limbs continue to step to the side, rotating the entire horse around both of these relatively fixed rear limbs. Picture 141 illustrates the type of movement required in performing a half turn on the haunches from the halt.

The cardinal rules in teaching the turn on the haunches are to be sure that the hindquarters do not step to either side as the turn is performed,

Picture 139. Crossing over during a turn on the forehand. *At the point shown in this photograph, a quarter-turn on the forehand has been executed. However, the rider's intent is to continue the movement until a half-turn has been completed. The horse is correctly crossing over with the hind legs as he rotates his haunches to the left. "Crossing over" with the hind legs is one component in better-quality movement for a turn on the forehand. The rider's aids remain the same as those described in Picture 138—but again, she has not asked the horse to maintain a straight attitude of the head and neck.*

Picture 140. Completing a turn on the forehand. *At this point a half-turn on the forehand has nearly been completed (the horse is not quite parallel to the fence). You can now see the active use of the rider's leg in displacing the horse's haunches to the side and around the stationary forehand. This young rider recognizes that the position of the horse's head and neck is not as correct as it should be.*

and to be sure that the horse does not attempt to walk forward or backward with any leg as the turn is executed. Remember that at this level of schooling a high quality of movement is not necessarily demanded, but the turn should be taught and practiced until the horse can perform this movement without resistance and without moving his haunches to either side or forward or backward.

Again, later success in teaching the pivot, spin and rollback is directly dependent upon successfully teaching the turn on the haunches at this level.

Because you will be establishing contact with your horse's mouth during this lesson, you should use a snaffle bit or some other kind of mild bit. A bosal can also be used for this exercise.

To teach the turn on the haunches to the left, halt the horse in a straight line, parallel to the rail or wall of your schooling area as you are tracking to the left. Allow some room between the rail and the side of the horse, perhaps two or three feet. The rail or wall will be a barrier to prevent the

horse from backing too far as you begin to teach this exercise. Be sure the horse has halted squarely, or even preferably with the pivotal leg (the left rear in this case) slightly ahead of the other (right) rear leg.

Shorten your reins, even to the point of having a light feel of the horse's mouth. Next, allow the horse to relax momentarily. Bring him softly to attention with a mild squeeze from both of your legs, or by vibrating the reins momentarily. If you bring him to attention with your legs, be ready to prevent his walking forward; check lightly with the reins and use your voice if necessary.

For the turn to the left, place your right leg in the displacing leg position, and your left leg in the urging leg position. Your right leg will be used to control the horse's haunches, to prevent them from stepping to the right side as the turn is made. Your left leg will be used to urge the horse forward if he attempts to step back as the turn is begun or while it is in progress.

To initiate the turn, begin to rotate the horse's

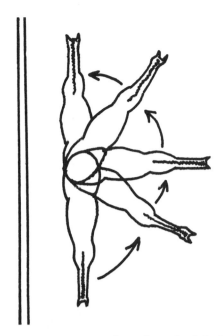

Picture 141. The turn on the haunches performed to the left. *The hindquarters remain relatively fixed as the forehand steps to the side describing an even arc around the hindlegs. The horse does not move forward or backward or attempt to step to either side with the rear legs while the turn is in progress.*

forehand to the left, around the stationary hindquarters, by using both reins. Use both of your hands on the reins, simultaneously moving both hands to the left while applying a slight rearward tension on each rein. Actively squeeze or tap the horse's side with your right displacing leg while at the same time initiating movement of the forehand to the left with the reins.

The simultaneous action of both reins is responsible for generating the turn: a combination of a left leading rein and a right indirect rein used (lightly) in front of the horn. The left leading rein indicates the direction of the turn, and the right indirect rein—almost a bearing rein—assists in displacing the horse's shoulders to the left.

Applying light rearward tension on both reins assists the horse in transferring a good deal of his weight to the hindquarters. Leg pressure from the rider's right displacing leg acts as a sort of wall to prevent the horse from stepping to the right with the hindquarters and merely walking out of the turn. The rider's left leg is used to urge the horse forward in the event that he attempts to back as a resistance to actually performing the turn. The reins, aside from their primary function in generating the turn, can, if necessary, prevent the horse from walking forward.

Pictures 142, 143 and 144 sequentially illustrate a green horse performing a turn on the haunches.

To teach the turn on the haunches to the right, use the opposite rein and leg aids in the manner I have just described. Whether you practice this movement to the left or to the right, it is advisable to teach only a quarter turn on the haunches at first.

When a quarter turn can be performed without resistance and the horse understands that the haunches are not to be moved to the side, begin practicing a half turn on the haunches to the left and to the right. When teaching the half turn on the haunches, you may find that the horse will insist on attempting to step to the side with the rear legs as the second quarter of the half turn is executed. Usually, there is little problem in teaching the quarter turn on the haunches.

Be alert. Use your displacing leg very actively if the horse attempts to move his haunches to the side while turning. Use a crop behind your displacing leg or your spur to prevent this poor movement if the horse ignores the action of your leg. Stepping to the side with the haunches spoils the movement and constitutes no more than a simple turn on the forehand, or a turn on the middle. In this case, the horse will continue to walk to the

Picture 142. Beginning the turn on the haunches. *This horse is just beginning a turn on the haunches to the left, from a halt. Note the rider's simultaneous use of the left leading rein and a right indirect rein in front of the horn. The rider's right leg (not shown) is in a displacing position to prevent the horse from stepping toward the fence with his haunches as the turn is begun. The rider's left leg is "alert" and prepared to urge the horse forward should he try to step backwards as an evasion to performing the movement. The horse is correctly looking in the direction of the turn being initiated.*

side with the forelegs while the haunches step to the side in the opposite direction.

Occasionally, a horse first learning this exercise will become stuck in his tracks as the turn is in progress. He will resist your hands as they move to the side, no matter how forcefully you employ them. If this occurs, simply relax your hands slightly and apply rearward tension to the reins. Complete the turn by again moving both of your hands in the direction of the turn. Continue the turn as the horse shifts additional weight to his hindquarters or as he begins to step backward, but do not actually permit him to step backward.

As the horse begins to understand what is required of him to perform the turn on the haunches, you may begin to employ your reins in a slightly different manner. Instead of moving both hands simultaneously in the direction the forehand is to be rotated, use a combination of a leading rein and bearing rein.

For a turn on the haunches to the left, use a left leading rein and a right bearing rein. Use your bearing rein to indicate the direction of the turn and your leading rein to tease the horse's head in the direction of the turn. As the turn is in progress and the horse obeys your bearing rein, release the tension in the leading rein. Increase the tension in the leading rein again if the horse seems reluctant to continue turning. Use your displacing leg actively by squeezing. As the horse complies by continuing to rotate his forehand about the stationary haunches, again release some of the tension in the leading rein.

Continuous pulling on the leading rein will eventually set up a pattern of resistance on the part of the horse. Sooner, or later, he will become inclined to pull back against a leading rein when tension is continuously maintained throughout the turn. The old saying that it takes two to pull is true.

Picture 143A. Performing the turn on the haunches. *The turn on the haunches to the left is now in progress. The same aids as were described in Picture 142 are still being used. The rider is alert and ready to employ rearward rein tension should the horse attempt to step forward as an evasion of the movement at this point.*

The purpose here is ultimately to generate the entire turn completely off the bearing rein; use the leading rein to assist the horse in understanding this, and then discontinue its use altogether as soon as possible. Return to the leading rein momentarily only if disobedience to the sole use of the bearing rein occurs.

As the horse begins to perform the turn on the haunches reliably, without attempting to walk out of the turn with his hindlegs, you may begin to move your displacing leg slightly forward, closer to the holding leg position. In this position your leg will act not only to assist you in holding the haunches in and preventing the horse from stepping to the side, but it may also be used in a squeezing manner to assist you in indicating the direction of the turn. Varying the pressure of this active leg will also allow you to regulate the speed of the turn, and assist you in generating the turn solely from the use of neck reins.

At this level, keep the turn on the haunches quiet until the horse is well schooled to the movement. Perform each turn slowly, a step at a time. Speed can be added later. When speed is added to the entire movement, you will then refer to this exercise as the *pivot*; and if you begin performing a full turn on the haunches, with speed, you will refer to this as a *spin*.

A rider who has no difficulty in teaching the half turn on the haunches from the halt, in response to the use of a bearing rein and an active holding leg only, may then choose to teach the

Picture 143B. Crossing over during the turn on the haunches. *At this point a quarter-turn on the haunches has been performed. Note that this horse is exhibiting a good quality of movement in that he is "crossing over" with the front legs as he steps to the side. The horse is continuing to correctly look in the direction of the turn being performed.*

turn on the haunches from the walk: walk into the turn, turn and walk away.

To teach this particular movement, use the same aids as for the turn from the halt. In this case, however, you will have to pay considerable attention to the mechanics of the walk since the pivotal leg will have to be grounded or at least advancing forward as the turn is requested.

If the turn is to be made to the left, the horse's left rear leg must be advancing or already grounded ahead of the right rear leg as the turn is begun. You will recall that the left rear leg is advanced immediately after the right front is grounded and begins to travel rearward underneath the horse's right shoulder.

At the walk, the half turn on the haunches is

performed as one continuous movement, with the basic rhythm of the walk preserved as much as possible by the front legs as the turn is executed. If the horse initially overreacts to your use of aids in performing the turn on the haunches from the walk, he will elevate his forehand off the ground as the turn is performed. In this case you have performed a rollback from the walk, a higher-level exercise but not what you intended.

While the rollback is indeed a higher-level exercise than a turn on the haunches from the walk, it should not be practiced at this time. The rollback requires that the horse elevate the forehand in order to turn quickly and begin moving in the opposite direction; it is a time-saving movement, basically. Both the pivot and spin remain to be

Picture 144. Completing the turn on the haunches. *A half-turn on the haunches has nearly been completed (the horse is not quite parallel to the rail again). The rider should not let the horse start moving forward again until he is straight on the rail.*

taught, however, and both of these movements require that the horse maintain at least one front foot on the ground nearly all of the time. The horse needs to remain flat and in control of all four legs in these exercises, so to teach him to elevate his forehand completely off the ground is a mistake at this point. Rearing may be difficult to correct if it becomes a habit at this point.

Not only is the turn on the haunches preparatory for teaching the pivot, spin and later the rollback; it is also a useful exercise for changing directions at the announcer's request in any western pleasure class. To change directions in the arena, a turn on the haunches from the walk, performed smoothly, is apt to make a favorable impression on any judge—more so than a mere half circle.

A final matter involves the position and actions of the pivotal leg. As the horse begins to understand what is required of him, he will begin to set his pivotal leg farther forward and up under his body. In fact, the later exercises of the pivot, spin and rollback cannot be performed smoothly unless the pivotal leg is in fact grounded well forward

of the other hindleg.

Also, the pivotal foot cannot remain in contact with the ground completely throughout the turn, particularly when the speed of the turn is increased. While the pivotal leg must not be allowed to step to the side, forward or backward, it must nevertheless be lifted off the ground briefly at times and returned to the same spot as the turn progresses. Obviously, it must be able to pivot. This periodic elevation and return to the ground by the pivotal leg is a natural part of the turn on the haunches; it is a natural part of the spin and pivot also.

THE SIDEPASS

The sidepass is a true lateral movement. When performing the sidepass, the horse moves only to the side, away from the rider's active leg. There is no movement forward or backward. The movement is illustrated by Picture 145.

To teach the sidepass, halt the horse with his head close to and pointing toward some barrier, such as the arena wall. Allow him to relax, and

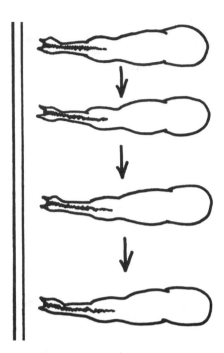

Picture 145. The sidepass. *The sidepass is a true lateral movement. In this diagram the sidepass is being performed to the left, away from the rider's active right leg. When first teaching the sidepass, turn the horse's head slightly in the direction opposite to the actual lateral movement. This puts the horse off balance, encouraging him to reach over with his legs to move in the proper direction.*

bring him to attention with a very mild squeeze with both legs. If the sidepass is to be performed to the left, use a right indirect rein to tilt the horse's head to the right, away from the direction he will actually move. The indirect rein will also serve to displace his forehand in the desired direction. In addition, use a left leading rein, with intermittent tension, to help you coax the horse to the side. Use an active right holding or displacing leg in a tapping or light kicking manner to move the horse to the left. Encourage the horse to step to the left with both the front and back legs. Coax him to the side with an active right leg behind the cinch, with a right indirect rein used in front of the saddle horn.

Do not ask for an extremely prompt response from the horse at first. Encourage him, but be definite and kick with your right leg if this is required to move his haunches to the left. At the same time, coax the forehand to step to the left by using your right indirect rein and left leading rein actively.

At first, the horse will probably move in parts; he will step to the left with the hind limbs, and then he will step to the left with the forelegs, or vice versa. This type of lateral movement is fine until the horse begins to realize what is actually re-

quired of him.

Ask for only a few steps to the side initially. When he performs these, give him a pat on the neck, and say *Good*. Allow the horse to turn to the side and walk along the rail for a moment to relax. Then face the wall again, and practice the sidepass once more.

If you have taught the sidepass first to the left, give equal time to teaching the sidepass to the right. Often, if you teach the sidepass to left first, teaching the sidepass to the right will be a little more difficult, and vice versa.

When teaching the sidepass in either direction, be rough and aggressive with your active leg and also with the reins (if required to accomplish the movement). Frequently, it requires perseverence on the rider's part to get the horse to move even reluctantly to the side. Exercise authority over the horse; gentle means are preferable, but get the job done. Pictures 146 and 147 illustrate teaching a green horse to sidepass to the right and to the left.

When he first learns the sidepass facing a barrier, practically the only evasion open to the horse is to back. When this occurs, use active urging legs at the cinch to move the horse forward again. Re-

Picture 146. Teaching the sidepass to the right. *The rider is using a very active left holding leg to cause the horse to step to the right with both the front and rear limbs. A right leading rein used in conjunction with a left indirect rein, and the rider's active left leg, assist the horse in understanding both the direction and nature of the movement being taught. The horse is looking to the left as he sidepasses to the right. This is typical of green horses first learning this particular movement, because the rider has used the indirect rein. The fence in the background is being used to prevent one of the resistances commonly seen in horses learning the sidepass—walking forward.*

inforce your displeasure with backing by using a crop behind either of your urging legs. The crop should be carried in your left hand when teaching the sidepass to the right, and vice versa.

Rearing is another possible evasion to your aids. Should this occur, use urging legs at the cinch, and say *No* loudly. Keep the head and neck reasonably straight and be sure that your reins are not tight (Picture 148).

Wheeling around away from the wall or barrier is also a possible evasion. This represents an outright disobedience to your hands. Punish it *severely* with your hands. Immediately turn the horse so that he again faces the wall.

If the horse neck reins well at the time the sidepass is first taught, by all means use neck reins to encourage movement to the side: a right bearing rein and right holding or displacing leg tapping or kicking behind the cinch. Later in schooling, it will be expected that the horse perform the sidepass in response to a slight use of the bearing rein and the squeezing action of the rider's active leg. Even later in schooling, a greater quality of movement will be expected. The head and neck should remain straight while the legs, front and rear, are crossed smartly, one in front of the other, as the

Picture 147. Teaching the sidepass to the left. *The rider's aids are an active right holding leg and a left leading rein (not visible) used in conjunction with a right bearing rein.*

horse steps to the side. At some point in schooling you should discontinue the use of a barrier as a means of preventing the horse from walking forward as the sidepass is practiced.

LONGITUDINAL AND LATERAL AGILITY

There is nothing demanding or mysterious here. You have already been teaching both of these qualities as you have taught the horse the elementary level of schooling.

At this level longitudinal agility has already been taught by teaching:

1. Obedience to the rider's urging legs, both for the purposes of increasing the horse's forward speed at any gait, and in response to the rider's request for all upward transitions

2. Obedience to the rider's hands, both for purposes of decreasing the horse's forward speed, and in response to the rider's request for downward transitions

3. Engagement

4. The turn on the haunches from the halt, and from the walk (although this exercise primarily develops lateral agility)

5. The rein back

Lateral agility has already been taught by teaching:

1. Circles and turns in response to the rider's holding and displacing legs and the leading rein

2. Turns in response to the neck rein

3. The turn on the haunches

Picture 148. Resistance to performing the sidepass. *This young filly was being asked to perform a few steps of the sidepass for the first time. She refused the rider's correct use of aids in attempting the movement and only wished to evade the entire matter. However, the fence would not permit her to walk forward, the rider's use of urging legs prevented her from stepping back as an evasion, and his hands would not permit her to turn to either side and walk away along the fence. All in all, he insisted that she perform at least a step or two laterally in obedience to his aids. She refused, and her only way out was up. This is a typical resistance to sidepassing seen in many young horses when placed between the legs and hands of a rider who can efficiently coordinate his aids in preventing all types of evasions.*

4. Movement on the line
5. The sidepass (the ultimate form of lateral agility)
6. The turn on the forehand, if you have chosen to teach this exercise at the elementary level

Some Comments About Head Setting

Head setting is a means of setting or forcing the horse's head into an attitude of direct flexion (Picture 149) or lateral flexion (Picture 150).

While I sympathize with many western trainers who are given unschooled horses and are expected to be out winning very quickly in the pleasure classes with direct flexion of the horse's head and neck, I cannot agree in principle to head setting. The entire purpose of flexions of the horse's head and neck is to improve the horse's performance— to have these flexions useful in improving downward transitions, better movement on the line when circling and so forth. Flexions, to be useful, must be obtained by the rider's aids, primarily his hands. Tying a horse's head back to the saddle

Picture 149. Head setting for direct flexion.

cannot teach him cooperation with increases and decreases in rein tension.

Would I ever set a head? Yes, infrequently, to encourage a horse to give to my hands when everything else has failed and when his schooling is at a point where only better flexions will enhance his overall performance. Performance is the key; I would not set a head merely to obtain an artificial fixed and stiff carriage of the head for a pleasure class.

I would set the horse's head as shown in Picture 149 or 150, depending upon whether the problem was a lack of willing direct flexion or one of insufficient lateral flexion. And I would not set the horse's head and leave him standing in a stall. Since flexions are meant to improve the horse's overall movement, I would turn him into an area where he could move about.

Picture 150. Head setting for lateral flexion.

Chapter 7

SCHOOLING AT THE INTERMEDIATE LEVEL

This chapter describes the use of intermediate control techniques to continue the schooling of the horse beyond the elementary level. You should complete the elementary level in its entirety before beginning to school at the intermediate level. The horse should be capable of performing the three standard gaits: walk, trot, canter. He should be stabilized at the one steady speed you have chosen for each gait. The walk should be forward moving and have some appearance of energy. The trot and canter should be slow, consistent and relaxed.

Halts should be prompt, and the horse should be able to remain on the line as he halts. Backing should be prompt, straight and on the line for short distances. Upward and downward transitions should be prompt and obedient, with the horse remaining reasonably on the line.

The horse's trot should not be strung out. A minimal horizontal engagement should be present. If you have also obtained some of the vertical engagement associated with the increased rhythm and cadence necessary for the jog trot, so much the better.

The horse should be capable of executing a reasonably good half turn on the haunches from the halt. Sidepassing in either direction should be prompt and obedient, and without a great deal of resistance to the rider's leg.

The horse should understand and promptly obey two direct reins of opposition for slowing his forward speed, halting or backing; a leading rein; and neck reins for turning and circling.

The horse should understand and promptly obey the rider's urging, holding and displacing leg aids. The rider should be capable of accurately regulating the horse's haunches with his holding or displacing leg to cause them to remain on the line when moving along the rail, turning, circling or backing. Circles and turns should be accurate, with the horse maintaining a steady forward speed on the line. He should not cut corners when turning.

The horse should understand the use of the rider's weight as a clear signal in advance of any transition, up or down. The horse should understand voice commands including *Walk, Trot, Canter, Whoa, Slow, Back* and some type of verbal reward—the word *Good*, for instance.

If all of these basic requirements have been met, the horse is ready to begin schooling at the intermediate level. If you cheat, take short cuts or leave gaps in the horse's elementary schooling, you may get along rather well for a time, but your lack of preparation will catch up with you someplace in the intermediate level. You will have to drop back, and the time spent in reschooling at the elementary level generally will be much greater than if you had completed the elementary level in the first place.

Schooling a horse at the intermediate level not only requires adequate preparation of the horse, it also requires even greater attention to your own riding. You will have to concentrate harder and constantly strive to improve your position: a steadier lower leg, better use of your weight laterally, sitting in rhythm with the horse's efforts at each gait and so on. You will have to strive to improve or at least maintain greater control and precision in the use of your hands, legs, weight and eyes.

Intermediate-level schooling prepares the horse for successful showing, although lots of high elementary-level horses have been successfully shown by *very* good professionals. Schooling at the intermediate level, if you choose to complete it, teaches the horse everything required for virtually any western event. Of course you will have to practice the specifics of each of these events: barrel and pole patterns, work on live cattle, roping, reining and western riding patterns, and so forth.

Intermediate schooling, like schooling at the elementary level, has two specific goals:

1. The Further Mental Education of the Horse
   (a) Correct responses to each of the aids employed by the rider (see Table III, The Intermediate Level of Schooling, The Rider's Control Technique)
   (b) *Cooperation* with the rider's aids. At the intermediate level of schooling, co-operation on the part of the horse is far different from the mere obedience and quick and definite responses required at the elementary level.

2. The Further Physical Education of the Horse
   In essence, all the things specified for the elementary level of schooling are improved, demanding greater cooperation with the rider's aids—greater softness and precision. The higher-level exercises specified by Table III must also be learned. Some of the main features of the horse's further physical education at the intermediate level are:

   (a) Maintaining engagement and impulse in addition to relaxation and consistency in speed for each of the forward gaits
   (b) Stabilization of two or more speeds at each gait in order to promote greater longitudinal agility
   (c) Maintaining willing, soft flexions of the head and neck in cooperation with the rider's aids
   (d) *Soft* and *precise* transitions, rather than merely prompt and obedient
   (e) Higher-level exercises and movements such as flying changes of leads, pivots, rollbacks, spins and sliding stops
   (f) Improved longitudinal and lateral agility, and an ability of the horse to carry his weight more to the rear—to work off the hindquarters for many high-level exercises

DIFFERENT SPEEDS AT THE WALK

The purpose of teaching more than one speed at the walk is to increase the longitudinal agility of the horse—to teach him to lengthen and shorten his frame head to tail. Teaching increased longitudinal agility enhances his cooperation with your aids, assists him in learning to flex the head softly and cooperatively rearward, and encourages him to learn to shift his weight forward or backward in conjunction with the use of your hands and legs.

Increasing longitudinal agility is one way in which the rider paves the way for teaching useful flexions of the head back toward the vertical as well as preparing for the increased central balance necessary for higher-level exercises such as the pivot, rollback, spin, sliding stop and flying change of leads.

There are three speeds at the walk:

1. Slow walk (of little consequence)
2. Ordinary walk (the desired show ring pace)
3. Fast walk (only a schooling exercise, but a useful one)

The Slow Walk

At the slow walk, the horse merely ambles forward in a lazy and inattentive manner, or he moves forward slowly (but with substantial impulse) because he is frightened or unsure about his surroundings. In either case, there is really nothing here to teach. You only need to let the horse know that at times the slow walk will be tolerated: while taking a break in schooling, along unfamiliar surroundings or trails out of doors and when cooling down after a rigorous schooling session. You want to find a way to tell the horse, "Yes, it's fine to amble forward in an inattentive way. We're taking a break," or "We're through schooling today." Use looser reins, a change in your position, or any other means to convey this message to the horse. However, also remember that if you are schooling inside an arena, the horse should remain along the rail. He should not wander about the entire area.

The Ordinary Walk

At the ordinary walk, the horse engages his rear limbs well up under his body in response to the rider's urging legs at the cinch. He simply shows good horizontal engagement of the hind legs. The ordinary walk is one with a sense of energy about it—a sense of forward impulse. It is a walk that will take you from one place to another before you grow old and grey; however, it is not so vigorous or fast moving that the horse could not sustain it over a reasonably long distance without suffering exhaustion.

The ordinary walk is one that shows some interest on the part of the horse, and shows his attentiveness to the rider and his aids. Good horizontal engagement, reasonable forward impulse and moderate, purposeful speed should be *consistent* features of the ordinary walk. Picture 151 shows a lazy, slow walk unacceptable for schooling or showing. Picture 152 shows an ordinary walk desirable for both of these situations.

Unless you pay attention and demand a reasonable quality to the horse's walk, he will probably be quite happy to continue walking forward in a slow, lazy manner. If, on the other hand, you consistently demand a walk of better quality—an ordinary walk—during schooling, he will quickly

glean that this is the normal routine.

The ordinary walk is performed on loose reins with the rider sitting upright and moving his hips back and forth in rhythm with the horse's efforts. This movement of the rider's hips in the saddle is very much like sitting on the edge of a chair and walking it across a smooth floor with repeated movements of your hips and pelvis. Above all, however, it is the rider's legs which produce an alert, forward-moving walk with an energetic appearance. The extent to which you actually use your legs to produce and maintain a consistent ordinary walk depends largely on the horse you ride and his natural willingness to move forward.

Two points: first, do not wear yourself out by continually squeezing the horse's sides with your upper calves in order to produce a consistent, acceptable walk. Wake him up with a crop just behind either of your urging legs or with a spur. Remind him to obey your urging legs; remind him of what he should have understood in the elementary

Picture 151. Poor quality of movement at the walk. *A lazy, inattentive walk is shown here. The horse has a very short stride behind and a long, trailing, lazy stride in front. The horse's forward movement is completely lacking in impulse. As you study this picture and the following two illustrations (Pictures 152 and 153, also dealing with the walk), compare the attitudes of the horse's head and neck, the position of the rider's upper body and the quality of impulse about the horse's forward movement.*

level of schooling.

Second, using your hips back and forth in rhythm with the horse's own efforts at the walk will help to maintain a consistent pace, and may encourage him to walk forward freely. As schooling continues and the horse understands that the ordinary walk is the normal order of the day, less movement of your hips will be required, and a lighter touch of your leg will be possible.

The Fast Walk

At the fast walk, the horse has to lengthen his stride for a maximum forward stride. The fast walk is primarily a schooling exercise intended to teach longitudinal agility and cooperation with the rider's aids. Producing this type of walk is also a test of the horse's obedience to your aids—primarily your legs.

To lengthen the stride at the walk, use alternating legs in the following way: as the horse begins to move his left front leg rearward, squeeze with

your right leg at the cinch. This encourages the horse to step well forward with the next leg in the sequence of the walk, the right rear leg. As the horse begins to move his right front leg rearward, squeeze with your left leg at the cinch. This encourages the horse to step forward with the next leg in the sequence at the walk, the left rear leg. A mild use of alternating urging legs may be sufficient to lengthen and increase the speed of the walk.

Use your hands and weight to discourage the horse from breaking to the trot. *Hopping* is a form of resistance many horses exhibit when first being asked for the strong, fast walk; in this case, they try to increase their forward speed by trotting rather than by expending the energy to increase the length of stride at the walk. Sit deeply and in rhythm with the forward stride as you did when teaching the ordinary walk. It is easier to coordinate your alternating legs from a good base of support in the saddle, and it is also easier to be more effective with each leg when sitting firmly.

Picture 152. The ordinary walk. *If you contrast this photo with Picture 151, you will note that greater engagement is present in the hind legs; the horse is attentive and willing to work more from the hindquarters. The impression of impulse forward is now present in the nature of the horse's forward movement. Note the horse's head and neck have been elevated somewhat and that the rider has assumed a more forward position with his upper body.*

The purpose of teaching the fast walk, again is to improve the horse's longitudinal agility, to obtain greater cooperation with your aids and to test the horse's obedience to your legs. It is not necessary to develop the fast walk so that it may be performed over long distances. Demanding five or six strides now and then is sufficient for schooling purposes. The response, not the continued practice over long distances, is the object of teaching the fast walk.

Picture 153 shows the horse at the fast, strong or extended walk. You can compare the stride at the fast walk with that of the ordinary walk by comparing Pictures 153 and 152.

DIFFERENT SPEEDS AT THE TROT

Like teaching different speeds at the walk, teaching three speeds at the trot is an exercise in increasing the horse's longitudinal agility—his softness, suppleness and cooperation with the rider's aids. At the intermediate level of schooling there are three distinct speeds at the trot:

1. Jog trot
2. Ordinary trot
3. Fast trot

The jog trot, or simply the jog, is the slowest. There is a definite rhythm or cadence which makes the jog the typical western trot. When this gait is perfected, its forward speed is about five miles per hour. The jog is characterized by a shortened forward stride of both the front and rear limbs. The front limbs are reasonably animated in the knees compared to the faster speeds of the trot; the faster speeds are characterized by longer, lower strides with less knee action. Part of the rhythm of

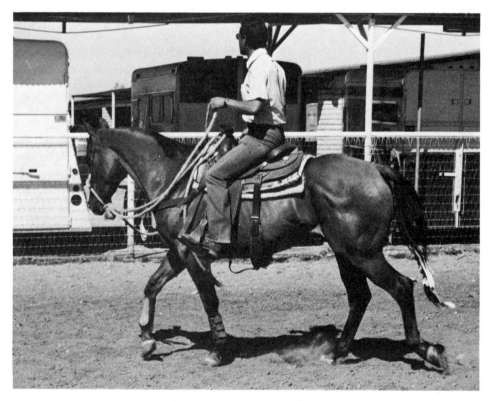

Picture 153. The fast (extended) walk. *Here the rider is asking for a few strides of the fast walk as a schooling exercise. If you contrast this photo with Picture 152, you will note an obvious increase in the horse's impulse forward as well as an increase in his forward speed. Note that the horse's head and neck have been extended beyond that seen in the previous photo and that the rider himself has assumed even a more forward position of his upper body. Obviously the horse is willing to increase his forward speed at the walk in obedience to the rider's increased use of urging legs. (This is an excellent illustration of the lateral nature of the gait which we call the walk.)*

the jog is due to the shortness of the stride, which simply gives the rider more time to feel the rhythm of this gait. This feeling of rhythm is due as well to the good vertical engagement of the hindlegs shown by many of the better horses. As long as the jog's speed remains consistent, the shortness of stride makes it comfortable to sit, even for beginning riders.

Not every horse is capable of developing a jog trot. For a few horses, you will have to look for events other than western pleasure classes. In addition, regardless of whether the horse is capable of developing a pleasant jog trot, you may simply choose to not school for this type of trot. If you have no interest in schooling or showing pleasure horses, there is no reason to teach the jog.

But you will still need to teach at least a reasonably slow trot. If you omit teaching a slow trot, you will only have two speeds of the trot remaining: the ordinary and the fast. Realistically, you will do little schooling at the fast trot. Teaching three speeds at the trot is a natural and logical way to teach the horse longitudinal agility. And teaching three different speeds at the trot does not require a great deal of time or technique.

With increased longitudinal agility, teaching exercises which require the horse to work off his hindquarters becomes easier. Schooling the horse willingly to shift his weight rearward for rapid halts, pivots, rollbacks and similar movements becomes easier as well. With increased longitudinal agility, flexions of the head—useful in assisting the horse to shift his weight rearward—are learned more quickly.

Some riders feel that teaching a horse the ordinary and fast speeds of the trot impairs his ability to learn the jog trot, or even just a slow trot. I could not disagree more. First of all it is your option to teach only a slow, stabilized trot, *before* teaching faster speeds at the trot. However, schooling for three speeds of the trot (longer and shorter strides at the various speeds), will increase the horse's longitudinal flexibility. Learning increased flexibility permits the horse to shorten his stride comfortably to produce a good quality jog—to be flexible enough to execute the slow, precise movements of the jog trot.

Teaching the horse different speeds at the trot also tunes him to your use of urging legs. The horse taught to move forward from the rider's leg is less inclined to drop behind the bit when asked to flex his head back and toward the vertical.

Teaching the Jog Trot

To teach the jog trot is not really difficult, if you do not demand immediate perfection. Generally, teach first the slow forward speed required in any pleasure class. Let your horse relax—don't fuss with your reins, legs or weight. Show ring speed is approximately five or six miles per hour.

Next concentrate on adding quality of movement to the jog. Insist with your legs, on mild horizontal engagement, and use your weight and reins to prevent increased speed. Allow the horse at first to maintain a normal carriage of the head and neck. Later, as you routinely school for three speeds at the trot and each of these becomes stabilized, ask the horse for soft flexion of his head rearward while jogging; always be sure that he remains ahead and not behind the vertical with his head.

Employ large numbers of circles as you school for the jog and as you teach soft flexion of the head rearward. These circles may range from 30 to 50 feet in diameter. Place the horse on increasingly smaller circles as he becomes more proficient at maintaining a consistent jog trot. The horse will shorten his frame even more, become steadier and exhibit an even better quality of movement.

Before you begin to teach the jog to any horse, it is probably wise first to mentally review his previous schooling. At this point the horse should be capable of maintaining one relaxed steady speed at the trot; he should be stabilized on loose reins. In addition, the horse should be capable of increasing or decreasing his forward speed in response to the rider's aids. These increases and decreases of speed need not remain especially steady, as long as the horse is initially obedient to your aids, and as long as the initial stabilized trot (which you taught during elementary schooling) *can be reestablished* without a great deal of difficulty. A few horses may have already learned a reasonably good jog trot during schooling for one steady speed of the trot at the elementary level.

To begin teaching the jog, establish the same steady speed at the trot which the horse has already learned. Begin to lightly take hold of the horse's mouth by mildly increasing the tension on the reins. Say *Slow*, and as the horse slows his forward speed and seems willing to maintain it, gradually go to looser reins—particularly if this assists the horse in relaxing at the slower speed. Use the technique of check and release to encourage the horse to maintain the slow forward speed.

Producing a slow jog is primarily a matter of the horse's obedience to your mild use of hands. Additionally, a quiet lower leg, an upright position, rhythm with the horse's movements and a supple lower back greatly help the rider in regulating the speed and consistency of the horse's pace.

Repeatedly performing the jog along a moderate-sized circle generally assists the horse in stabilizing his forward speed. Pick a diameter small enough to assist the horse in pulling himself together at the jog. Insist that he remain on the line. Do not lose sight of your initial objective: to produce a slow, relaxed trot.

Don't attempt perfection at the jog in a single schooling session; if the horse begins to become upset, stiff or resistive, do something else. Canter easily for a while, practice backing or do a few relaxed turns on the haunches before asking him to trot again.

In addition to the technique of check and release and sitting well, the rider may encourage the slow speed of the jog by slightly reducing his leg pressure, *if* necessary. The rider may rotate his toes slightly inward, removing a *portion* of the inner calf from the horse's sides. Some frictional grip should be maintained. If, and when, the horse tries to break to the walk, use that portion of your calf still on his sides to urge him forward slightly.

One could argue that teaching the jog is really a matter of *softly* pulling and pushing: pulling with the reins to slow the forward speed, and pushing with the legs to prevent too much slowing. With patience, softness and an eye toward maintaining a relaxed horse, the rider may convince the horse that life is more comfortable at a slow jog. In short, the horse comes to cooperate with, and not just to obey, the rider's aids.

Once the necessary slow speed has been learned, the rider can begin to concentrate on other matters relating to the jog, such as securing a good transition from the walk to the jog trot. Use mild urging legs at the walk, gradually increasing their pressure until the horse quietly breaks into the jog. A slight check with the reins just as the trot is begun is often helpful in obtaining the steady jog from the very onset.

Be light with your hands. The horse should regard this initial check as a signal. Otherwise, a pattern of anticipation and head bobbing may be established each time the horse is requested to jog. As he begins to understand that he is merely to ease into the jog, raising your rein hand slightly can serve to remind him that he is not to spurt forward initially before establishing the necessary slow forward speed of the jog.

For downward transitions from the jog to the walk, sit and close your legs slightly before checking with the reins to prevent the horse from collapsing on his forehand. These same actions should precede a transition from the jog to the halt. Downward transitions made in this manner help the horse remain engaged with the rear limbs as he assumes a slower speed or halts. These same actions on the part of the rider are essential to square halts as well as being preparatory for higher-level exercises such as the sliding stop.

Some horses will possess engagement and impulse from the onset of learning the jog trot. These horses will continue to travel forward alertly and with engagement as you insist upon *very* slow forward speeds of the jog. These are the good movers, the horses often referred to as *athletic*. Of course, others will tend to become only lazy and strung out as they are schooled for the jog.

If your horse does not readily maintain engagement in a more or less natural way and if you have only taught the speed and not the quality of movement required for a winning trip around the show ring, you should begin to concentrate on engagement.

To teach engagement, use your legs to squeeze *mildly* at the cinch and apply these squeezes in rhythm with the jog. Ask the horse to remain alert. Ask him to engage his hind limbs, but do not allow him to increase his forward speed. Use your hands and weight to prevent the horse from hurrying ahead. As the horse comes to understand that you are demanding an engaged quality of movement, even at the slow speed of the jog, he will begin to move with greater cadence or rhythm, and become less strung out. Certainly, you do not have to squeeze continually, even with very mild legs, as the horse travels forward—only enough to wake the horse up.

Engagement in forward movement comes from the rider's leg; control of forward speed from the rider's hands and weight. As you teach engagement at the jog, you will find that impulse forward seems to follow naturally.

As the horse becomes better schooled, not only at the jog but at everything he is asked to do, he will become more flexible from head to tail. As he begins to soften in this way, begin to ask for soft flexions of the head rearward to assist the horse in shifting more of his weight to his hindlegs. These mild flexions will increase the quality of the jog (or any slow gait for that matter), and they will be useful for other exercises and movements as well. A horse that willingly comes back to your hands without falling behind the bit or opening his mouth is one that demonstrates cooperation beyond the elementary level.

A jog trot suitable for the intermediate level of schooling is shown by Picture 154. Note the rider's position and the horse's overall quality of movement.

Teaching the Ordinary Trot

The ordinary trot is not difficult to teach. It is probably a bit faster than the stabilized trot which you first established at the beginning of elementary schooling, and certainly it is much faster than the jog which you taught later. Seven to eight miles per hour is the normal speed of an ordinary trot.

In contrast with the jog trot, the ordinary trot should demonstrate a longer stride and greater horizontal engagement. The horse should reach forward with his legs and cover ground in a more efficient way—with longer and lower strides, less knee and hock action. In the show ring, the ordinary trot is used in the English pleasure class.

The rider may either sit, post or stand at the ordinary trot. If you are in an English pleasure class in the show ring, of course you would post to the trot. If you are merely trotting into the arena for a pole, barrel or roping class, you will prefer to stand. If you trot pole and barrel patterns as part of your schooling, you will probably prefer to stand as well, though your weight and legs are most effective at the sitting position.

To produce an ordinary trot, use your urging legs to push the horse forward. If he is reluctant to go forward, supplement your leg with a spur or

Picture 154. The jog-trot. *Slow forward speed, good vertical engagement of the legs, the maintenance of impulse and soft rearward flexion of the head sum up the jog at the intermediate level of schooling. That the horse is willingly flexing the head rearward is evidenced by the softness shown in the rider's fingers. Note that the rider's lower leg is on (not off) the horse's side.*

crop, and perhaps post or stand. When first performing the ordinary trot, most horses will raise the head and neck in response to the increased use of leg aids. As they begin to relax at the new speed, the head and neck will return to a normal position. If you ride on contact at the ordinary trot, as in an English pleasure class, the horse will normally raise his head and neck slightly in response to both your increased rein tension and the greater use of your urging legs.

Performing downward transitions from the ordinary trot to the walk or halt, is one way of encouraging the horse to willingly flex at the poll. He should bring his head softly back toward the vertical as he slows his forward speed, provided you demand smooth rather than quick or abrupt downward transitions.

After you have schooled for the jog and the ordinary trot, occasionally perform transitions from one speed to the other. This exercise will increase the horse's responsiveness to your aids, promote flexions of the head during downward transitions, teach greater longitudinal agility in general and tend to keep him listening to you throughout the entire schooling session.

If you move from the jog to the ordinary trot, or vice versa, be sure that each speed of the trot is well stabilized before asking for the next. Eventually, as the horse reaches a higher intermediate level, transitions from one type of trot to another may be spaced at very short intervals.

The ordinary trot is shown in Picture 155.

Teaching the Fast Trot

The fast trot is produced by urging the horse forward with both legs until he has exceeded the speed of the ordinary trot. The stride of the horse is quickened; hence, the speed of the trot is greater—about nine or ten miles per hour. The schooled horse will lower and lengthen his head and neck slightly as the fast trot is performed.

The rider should either post or stand for the fast trot. In Chapter 3, I discussed the use of vertical weight while posting to regulate forward pace at the trot. Roughly speaking, you post higher to go faster.

Picture 155. The ordinary trot. *At the ordinary trot the horse's stride is lengthened. The emphasis is upon greater horizontal engagement. If the horse is ridden on loose reins, then some extension of the head and neck should occur beyond that seen for the jog.*

The Fast Trot Versus the Extended Trot

The extended trot, which I have actually designated as an advanced exercise, is not so much a quickening of the pace beyond that for the ordinary trot as it is a lengthening of the stride; while the stride is lengthened, the rhythm of the extended trot remains more or less as it was at the ordinary trot. There will, however, always be some increase in overall speed as the stride at the extended trot becomes longer.

It is difficult, from a conformation standpoint, for many cold-blooded horses to increase their length of stride beyond that for the ordinary trot. Pushing them beyond the ordinary trot only produces a quicker trot—the fast trot—rather than an increased length of stride without a substantial increase in the horse's overall forward speed.

However, with the continued infusion of thoroughbred breeding into many of the western breeds, you will see more truly extended trots, rather than trots which are merely faster. In the show ring, whenever an extended trot is called for, you still see quite a mixed bag: trots lengthened without much increase in forward speed (correct), trots that only become faster (incorrect), and even trots that show a lengthening of the stride (proper) but with a great increase in speed also (improper).

One of the advantages of a true extended trot is that the horse is less likely to break to the canter. In fact, trotting faster and faster is the way most green horses learn to canter for the first time.

To produce an extended trot, ask with your legs and weight that the horse lengthen his stride at the ordinary trot. At the same time, ask with your hands and weight that he maintain the basic rhythm and speed of the ordinary trot. One way to do this is by using your legs actively to ask for a lengthening of the stride, while using your weight to request that he not speed up; post lower as you use your legs, or, even better, sit. Supply the horse with a little more rein at first so that he can comfortably extend the head and neck slightly. Subsequently increase the rein tension a little to say "no faster."

If your horse is not capable of lengthening his stride beyond that for the ordinary trot, you will have to settle for trotting faster whenever an extended trot is called for. If he is capable of good lengthening beyond the ordinary trot, don't try to conquer the world in a day. Settle for a *little* lengthening without a measurable increase in speed at first. Improve on the extended trot slowly and quietly as you continue intermediate schooling.

A horse performing at the extended trot is shown by Picture 156.

DIFFERENT SPEEDS AT THE CANTER

Teaching different stabilized speeds at the canter increases the horse's longitudinal agility. He will be more capable of increasing or decreasing his forward pace promptly and smoothly. He will be better able to lengthen or shorten his entire frame.

Practicing different stabilized speeds at the canter will assist the horse in learning to shift his weight forward and backward, depending upon whether fast or slow forward speeds are required. This same practice will help him learn to flex his head softly rearward for prompt and smooth downward transitions, and when slow forward speeds at the canter are necessary. He will also learn to willingly extend his head and neck whenever faster forward speeds might be required. All of these actions enhance the horse's longitudinal agility.

Schooling aside for the moment, very nearly every western performance horse will be required to learn and use at least two different stabilized speeds at the canter:

1. Lope
2. Ordinary canter

The Lope

The lope is in general the slowest forward speed of the canter you can teach without having the horse in danger of constantly breaking to the trot.

The lope is a slow, rhythmic gait generally quite comfortable to sit. The stride at the lope is shorter than that for faster speeds of the canter, and good vertical engagement should be present in the hindlegs of schooled horses. At the lope, greater knee action will be seen than at the faster speeds of the canter because of the shorter strides.

A lope taught with the rider's four natural aids, not gadgets, and with a good design of position is a free-moving gait with natural balancing gestures of the head and neck, the qualities of slow forward speed, very good stabilization and a purposely shortened gait. A perfectly acceptable lope can be produced with the horse maintaining a

Picture 156. The extended trot. *The extended trot requires that the horse lengthen the stride beyond that seen for the ordinary trot, but without (and this is the catch) increasing his overall forward speed. The horse in this picture is initially being asked for a few strides at the extended trot as a schooling exercise. By comparing this with Picture 155, you will see that he has correctly lengthened the stride in response to the rider's urging legs and that he is correctly attempting to control his forward speed in response to the rider's use of reins as the stride lengthens. Though the horse is beginning to fall behind the bit as he attempts this exercise, with practice he will be able to execute several strides at the extended trot while accepting the bit and softly extending the head.*

natural carriage of the head and neck; flexion of the head is not necessary to produce a lope of good quality (Picture 116).

On older and more schooled horses, flexions of the head are appropriate when loping in the show ring. Soft flexion of the head will produce gaits a little more vertically engaged. Greater impulse will be seen, but without the necessity of increasing the horse's forward speed. Slow forward speeds with excellent quality of movement can be more easily produced (Picture 157). Also, a horse schooled to willing flexions of head is more inclined to use repeated flexions to enable him to drop from the lope to a slower gait or the halt, promptly and *smoothly,* with his rear legs up under him while maintaining good engagement (see Picture 158). With poor engagement, the horse collapses forward on the forehand as the downward transition is made.

Older, more schooled horses have had the time to learn great longitudinal agility, and to learn those exercises which help the horse shorten his frame and shift his weight rearward (Picture 159). They have come to understand the benefits of co-operating willingly with the rider's hands in shifting their weight, and the benefits of flexion help them achieve this.

But to demand that the horse learn the lope and also place his face on, or near, the vertical from the onset is entirely unreasonable. A natural carriage of the head and neck, with only a hint of flexion, will usually win over a horse that carries his head stiffly flexed at the poll, drops behind the bit whenever the rider uses his hands, moves forward in a strung-out manner because flexion has been demanded too soon and collapses forward on each downward transition from the lope because he maintains stiff flexion and strung-out move-

Picture 157. The lope performed with soft direct flexion of the head and neck. *The overall quality of movement at the lope is improved whenever soft rearward flexion of the horse's head is added to the other good qualities of forward movement: engagement, impulse, movement on the line and longitudinal agility. Flexion of the head rearward without maintaining these other good qualities of forward movement is not very useful.*

ment as he decreases speed.

To teach the lope is a little harder than teaching the jog trot, simply because the horse's forward movement is a little faster, and there is less time for you to respond softly with your aids or adjust your position. Of course, the lope is also a less stable gait than the trot from the standpoint of mechanics in motion (Chapter 1).

When beginning to teach the lope, you must understand three things:

1. Your schooling at the elementary level must be complete, especially for prompt and obedient responses to your aids for upward transitions and a stabilized canter at any reasonable forward speed.
2. The jog, or slow trot, must be stabilized.
3. When first requesting a canter departure from the jog or walk (if your horse is already particularly obedient to the aids for this transition), be sure that an *immediate* transition to the canter is obtained in order

that the pace of the lope can be (roughly) established *from the onset.*

A canter of any type may be produced by simply increasing the speed of the trot until the canter is obtained. In other words, if your horse does not promptly respond to your aids for a canter departure, an initial trot of eight miles per hour is likely to end in a canter begun at ten or twelve miles per hour. A jog at six miles per hour will probably result in a canter that begins at eight or nine miles per hour—a better situation for producing the lope.

But let's assume that you did your homework at the elementary level of schooling and successfully taught prompt, obedient responses to your aids. You can establish a stabilized jog, and request a canter departure in the normal manner.

If your horse responds promptly to aids for a canter from the jog the approximate speed of the lope will be established from the onset. It will only

Picture 158. Direct flexion used for better downward transitions from the lope. *Willing flexions of the horse's head enable him to perform downward transitions from the lope smoothly and promptly. When halting from the lope as in this picture, these same rearward flexions assist the horse in halting quickly, with his rear legs up underneath him, and without collapsing on the forehand. Provided that he does not drop behind the bit, better longitudinal agility and cooperation with the rider's aids is demonstrated by the horse employing direct flexions during downward transitions from the lope.*

remain for you to control the speed of the lope. The promptness of the canter departure is critical since the horse that attempts to run into the lope from a fast trot has already established a speed for cantering far in excess of the lope. You may establish the lope from the walk also, but this is a little more difficult at first unless your horse can respond to your aids promptly enough so that several hurried intermediate strides at the trot do not occur. Later, for show ring purposes, you will have to school for the transition from the walk to the lope.

At this level, a prompt departure on a stabilized horse from either the walk or jog will produce a lope—at least initially. It only remains for you to control the forward speed so that it does not quicken and to work at stabilizing the speed. Stabilization at the lope is first accomplished by loping many small or medium circles. Later, stabilize the horse along straight lines.

At first it may be necessary to retard the horse's forward speed with your weight, voice and reins (check-release). As stabilization at the lope improves, it becomes more a matter of *not* using aids which say go faster, rather than of using aids to retard the horse's forward speed. As stabilization at the lope become very reliable, better vertical engagement can be added by sitting in rhythm with the lope and using your legs mildly at the cinch. By mildly bracing your back and occasionally increasing your rein tension slightly, the horse is reminded of the slow forward speed that is required.

Mild flexion of the head will begin to occur naturally in response to all of your continued schooling at the intermediate level, and in response to a change to a curb bit when the horse is ready. The horse is ready when he no longer requires your hands to maintain a steady, forward speed at the lope.

Picture 159. The lope performed with very good direct flexion of the head and neck. *Very good direct flexion of the head rearward, with the face literally carried on the vertical, is entirely appropriate for older schooled horses who have had the time to learn great longitudinal agility through schooling for a variety of exercises. The horse shown in this photograph is one of these horses. Here he maintains excellent direct flexion while performing a flying change of leads at the lope.*

The Ordinary Canter

The ordinary canter is a forward-moving gait of ten to twelve miles per hour. This is the canter used in English pleasure classes, though many judges prefer one a bit slower. The stride at the ordinary canter is necessarily longer (less knee and hock action) than at the lope.

Teaching the ordinary canter is only a matter of using your urging legs more actively to increase the length of the stride from the lope. The ordinary canter may be performed on loose reins or on contact; sitting, rather than standing, provides a better quality of movement for show ring purposes. (See Chapter 3, Sitting the Canter.) You must sit and not bounce; sit deepest as the diagonal pair of legs is being advanced. Keeping your lower leg steady at the ordinary canter may be a little more difficult than at the lope. Nevertheless, a steady lower leg will assist you in stabilizing the

horse with the least effort on your part.

Substantial balancing gestures are present at the ordinary canter. If you ride on loose reins, you will not have to worry about potential abuse of the horse's mouth. If you ride with shorter reins or on contact, you will have to follow the balancing gestures of the horse's head by moving your hands and arms softly forward once each stride. If you ride with short reins, it is imperative that you remember to follow forward with your arms as the horse takes the first cantering stride from either the walk or trot.

Some horses tend to become heavy on the forehand at this speed of the canter. Maintaining a steady speed while riding on a moderate circle will help to correct this problem. Similarly, performing a series of transitions from the ordinary canter to slower gaits or the halt, and then back again to the canter, will also tend to lighten the horse's forehand. These same transitions have the added

Picture 160. The ordinary canter. *At the ordinary canter the horse must exhibit a faster forward speed than that characterizing the lope. Also, at the ordinary canter a longer, lower "daisy-cutting" stride is preferred; at the lope, considerably more animation (with more knee-and-hock action) characterizes the horse's forward stride.*

benefit of encouraging willing flexions of the head in response to the rider's hands.

The ordinary canter is illustrated in Picture 160.

THE GALLOP

The gallop is a distinctly four-beat gait. It is produced by urging the horse forward with your squeezing legs beyond the speed of the ordinary canter. The gallop is always performed with the rider in the standing position. It is a controlled gait: the horse should remain ready to respond quickly to the rider's aids.

The gallop is required as part of the following events: barrel racing, pole bending, reining horse classes, working stock horse classes, cutting (occasionally), roping and other diverse classes such as the Appaloosa rope race. The gallop, in this case called the hand gallop, can be required as a part of English pleasure classes.

UPWARD TRANSITIONS

Teaching good upward transitions at the intermediate level of schooling is really just a matter of demanding the following qualities of movement for each transition:

1. promptness
2. smoothness
3. lightness
4. movement on the line
5. precision

Use of aids is really no different than at the ele-

Picture 161. A canter departure from the walk. *Regardless of whether you wish to establish a lope, as in this photograph, or an ordinary canter, your departure will be prompter, smoother and more precise if you begin the first stride of the canter on the horse's outside hindleg.*

mentary level of schooling, except that you employ neck reins when upward transitions are made along the arc of a turn or circle, and you use your voice very little. The sequence of aids is identical to that for performing upward transitions at the elementary level except that the use of voice is held to a minimum or absent entirely.

Promptness is obtained by frequent schooling. It requires that engagement and impulse be maintained at each gait. In addition, the horse's legs must be squarely underneath him at the halt in preparation for moving forward at any gait.

Smoothness and promptness may at first seem to be somewhat antagonistic ideas. By smoothness I mean that the horse does not lurch into a new faster gait without the rider's having control of forward speed. Hopping at the trot or canter is another major fault that detracts from the smoothness of upward transitions. Hopping at the trot interferes with the rhythm of the trot; it shows that the horse desires to break to the canter rather than maintain a steady forward trot. Hopping at the canter occurs just as a canter departure is made. In this case, the horse substantially elevates his forehand just as the canter is begun.

Lightness requires that the horse be in a position to move forward readily at any gait. It requires longitudinal agility on the part of the horse; certainly your schooling so far will have made practically any horse light in your hands. Lightness requires consistent prompt responses to your aids. The horse must maintain engagement and impulse at the slower gait preceding the upward transition you request. Lightness of a canter departure from the walk requires that the horse not only respond promptly and smoothly to your aids; it also requires that you begin the canter from the most favorable position of the horse's legs. Begin the canter from the outside hindleg (Picture 161). For lightness, a horse must work efficiently from his rear limbs; he must begin to work more from the haunches than from the forehand. Lightness requires a tendency toward central balance.

Movement on the line is an important quality of any upward transition. Movement on the line for all of the western classes requires that the horse be responsive to neck reins (to control the horse's head, neck and shoulders) to the rider's holding or displacing leg aids (to control the haunches) and to the rider's lateral use of weight (to move the entire horse subtly to one side or the other). Movement on the line for English pleasure horses requires the same responsiveness, but in this case the forehand is controlled with one direct rein of opposition or one indirect rein of opposition rather than with neck reins.

Precision simply means that you can ride forward, select some spot ahead of you with your eyes and perform an upward transition beginning at exactly that spot. The transition at exactly the point you have chosen should be made promptly, smoothly and with movement on the line. Obtaining precision for each of your upward transitions can be helped by posting markers (dressage letters)

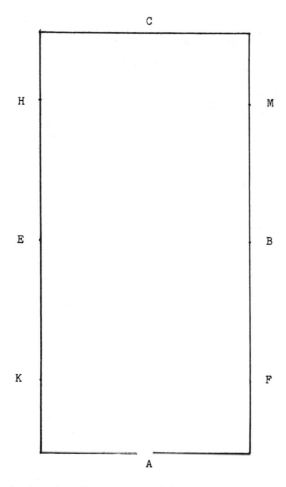

Picture 162. Standard markers (dressage letters) for an arena or schooling area.

along the wall of your schooling area. Standard markings are shown in Picture 162. These letters can simply be painted in black on white, one-foot plywood squares. Using these letters posted around your arena as shown, require that the horse begin the trot at E, or begin the canter at H, and so forth. These letters put the burden of performing any upward transition at an exact spot upon you. This exercise will also tell you how promptly your horse responds to your aids. One hint: as you track forward from M to B, for example, start getting organized, preparing at M for an upward transition that you intend to perform at B.

LEADS

The topic here is how to teach the correct lead at the lope and canter for normal riding situations. In this case the correct lead is the inside lead: the left lead as you track to the left along the rail, or as you circle to the left; and the right hand lead as you track to the right, or as you circle to the right.

At the intermediate level of schooling, there are three ways to teach the correct inside lead at the canter:

WESTERN PERFORMANCE HORSE (USING NECK REINS)

1. inside bearing rein
   vertical weight
   outside displacing leg, squeezing
2. inside bearing rein
   vertical weight
   outside displacing leg, squeezing (active outside leg immediately followed by a slight outside bearing rein)
3. head and neck straight
   vertical weight
   outside displacing leg, squeezing; inside supporting leg

ENGLISH PLEASURE HORSE (USING DIRECT REINS)

1. outside direct rein
   vertical weight
   outside displacing leg, squeezing
2. inside indirect rein and outside supporting rein
   vertical weight
   outside displacing leg, squeezing
3. head and neck straight, two supporting direct reins
   vertical weight

outside displacing leg, squeezing, inside supporting leg

At the elementary level of schooling, before teaching neck reining, you taught the horse to canter on the correct inside lead by using method 1, English Pleasure Horse. After teaching neck reining, you used method 1, Western Performance Horse.

The three methods for obtaining the correct lead at the canter departure are listed in order of their increasing sophistication; method 1 is the least sophisticated, and method 3 the most. The different methods are appropriate for different situations.

In beginning the canter we always look for correct lead, promptness of departure, movement straight or on the line and smoothness and lightness of departure. All of the methods listed are designed to produce both the correct lead and a prompt departure. The major differences among the three methods is the straightness of the departure itself.

The first method reliably produces a canter on the correct lead, since the horse is forced to maintain a leading leg even before the rider requests the canter with his own outside leg. The slight inside bearing rein turns the horse's head to the outside and insists that the correct inside lead be taken as the canter begins. The problem with this method is that good movement on the line is not always achieved, because the head and neck are carried to the outside while the haunches are carried inward.

The second method produces slightly better movement on the line, since an outside bearing rein is used to straighten the head and neck as the rider's outside leg requests the canter. The benefit of a reliable inside lead is also obtained by the initial use of an outside bearing rein followed by the request to canter.

The third method insures the utmost straightness of the horse as he begins to canter. In this respect, this is the most sophisticated method of obtaining a canter departure. The emphasis on a straight head and neck and the additional use of the rider's inside leg to maintain the haunches in a straight attitude allows the canter to begin with the horse very much on the line.

Use the method that best suits your needs. The first method is generally superior for teaching green horses to begin the canter on the correct lead. If you teach, your less experienced riders will also find it the easiest and most reliable way to obtain a canter on the correct lead.

If your riding goals demand increasingly better movement on the line in beginning the canter, you will prefer either the second or third method of performing a canter departure.

DOWNWARD TRANSITIONS

The use of aids in producing good downward transitions at the intermediate level is not very different from the use at the elementary level. The sequence of your aids remains the same—with one important exception. Use your weight first (as always), then your reins (as always), but simultaneously use your legs to insure that the horse remains well engaged as he slows his forward speed to achieve the new slower gait. Close your legs on the horse's sides just as you use your weight and reins to ask for a slower gait or a prompt, square halt.

At this level, the horse has become more flexible, more educated and better schooled to all of your aids. Obtaining truly good downward transitions is mostly a matter of recognizing the qualities of movement required and insisting that the horse display them. The qualities of movement which constitute a good downward transition are:

1. Maintained engagement
2. Smoothness
3. Promptness
4. Maintained movement on the line
5. Precision

Insist upon each of these points every time a downward transition is performed. Use your aids effectively and in the proper sequence.

Use your weight first. Sit up and brace your back. Depending upon whether you want a very smooth downward transition with the horse taking several steps at the old gait before breaking to the slower gait, or whether your demands are for a very prompt downward transition, you will brace your back less or more severely. In either case, ceasing to give with your back is the first signal to the horse that a downward transition may be required.

Follow your use of weight with your use of reins: check and release. As soon as your hands have slowed the speed, both your legs and hands must act to insure that the proper speed, engagement and rhythm are present as the new, slower gait is begun. Of course, this requires good coordination of aids as well as a knowledge of the individual horse's quirks.

Maintaining engagement as downward transitions are performed is mostly a matter of using your legs. However, closing your legs on the horse's sides should not take precedence over the use of your weight and rein aids. Your legs should only supplement these aids to prevent the horse from simply dying on the forehand as the transition is performed, or to prevent him from propping on the forehand rather than bringing his rear legs forward underneath him.

Smoothness is a relative matter. Sometimes you will require only a slow transition to a new gait, and at other times you will require a very rapid downward transition, but one made without the horse bouncing or propping on the forehand. The effective use of your weight in coordination with the use of your legs and hands is the best way to achieve smoothness in either case. A series of balancing flexions will permit even smoother downward transitions to be performed. These flexions will normally develop with continued schooling, in conjunction with your soft use of reins to slow or halt the horse.

Promptness in all aspects of riding should have been taught in the elementary level of schooling. At the intermediate level promptness is still a requirement, but a good quality of movement is also demanded; promptness should be coupled with the maintenance of engagement, smoothness, movement on the line and precision for each downward transition.

Should your horse try to move off the line, then maintaining movement on the line for downward transitions is accomplished in exactly the same manner described for upward transitions: bearing reins, displacing leg and the lateral use of your weight, if necessary.

Precision for downward transitions can be enhanced by using the same standard dressage letters described in the previous section on upward transitions. The key is to plan ahead. Get organized, think about the correct use of aids and execute a particular downward transition with the first stride at the new slower gait occurring just as you reach the letter selected.

HALTS

Stopping the horse is no more than a special case of downward transition. The rider's use of aids remains the same, but good halts are difficult to achieve for the same reasons that smooth transitions and decreases in pace are difficult. They demand excellent coordination of the rider's aids. The basic requirements for good halts are:

1. Promptness
2. Smoothness
3. Precision in stopping exactly at some predetermined point, and halting squarely at this point
4. Engagement maintained as the horse's forward pace decreases and he begins to halt; the horse's appearance of being gathered and alert to a subsequent command; the appearance of being ready to go forward or back at an instant's notice once the halt has been achieved
5. Standing still at the halt
6. Standing squarely at the halt in nearly every instance; or standing with the front legs parallel to one another, but with one back leg slightly ahead of the other in the special case of pivots and spins

This list is really no more than a rehashing of the criteria established in the section on downward transitions.

Square halts are not accomplished with the rider's use of reins alone, except by luck. While the front legs may indeed be regulated with the reins and the rider's eyes (by glancing down), hands alone will seldom succeed in aligning the rear limbs squarely at the halt. Use your legs as you halt to bring those of the horse squarely underneath him. You will have to use your legs—one more strongly than the other at times—to bring a particular back leg squarely in line with the opposite hind leg.

BACKING

During schooling at the intermediate level, the rein back, or simply backing, should be accomplished in the following manner:

1. Back straight for any short distance, keeping the horse alert and using the forward sequence of legs at the trot in reverse.
2. Control the number of steps taken.
3. Back without resistance or evasions.
4. Back with the same good qualities of movement you would demand if you were establishing the walk after halting—alertness, smoothness, promptness and good engagement (actually, good disengagement in this case).
5. The horse should use direct flexions in softening the movement while backing, and at the same time bring the croup slightly underneath (a form of semicollection at the rein back). The rider should softly encourage one direct flexion for each diagonal pair of legs to be moved: one diagonal pair making one rearward step.

Just prior to backing, it is often helpful to close your legs slightly on the horse's sides to ask for his attention. By doing this you are in essence saying, "Be prepared to respond to my aids—whether for backing, a turn on the forehand, a turn on the haunches, a departure at the canter from the halt or whatever I might ask."

Backing is accomplished primarily with the reins and rider's weight. You will want to open your shoulders, look ahead and sit firmly before using your hands to ask the horse to back. Check and release to initiate backing for the desired number of steps. Check to move a diagonal pair of legs rearward, but release as the horse complies by beginning to take a step backward. Repeat this process for each step.

Evasions of the haunches to the side are common occurrences. Correct these with your displacing leg. Use the reins if the forehand begins to drift sideways.

If the horse has previously learned good longitudinal agility through performing different speeds at the three gaits, he will understand something of direct flexions of the head. Direct flexions are useful in producing clean, straight backing.

As a rule, never back and just stand there. Walk forward almost immediately after completing the rein back to your satisfaction. If you must repeat the rein back immediately for schooling purposes, walk forward a step or two before halting the horse in preparation for repeating this movement. Don't initiate further backing from your original position at the halt after the first rein back has been completed.

While schooling for good backing, be careful not to immediately school the horse for certain other exercises. For example, schooling for the turn on the forehand requires that you apply slight rearward rein tension to prevent the horse from walking forward during the turn. This same rearward rein tension, used too soon after a vigorous lesson in backing, will indeed prevent the horse from walking ahead during the turn on the forehand. The result may well be a horse that obligingly steps back—an evasion of the technique. Keep this sort of thing in mind as you move from schooling for the rein back to schooling for other exercises.

Never incline your upper body forward while schooling for the rein back. If you do, the horse will either answer with resistance to your hands, because your weight aids say go forward, or you will not be able to control effectively the horse's movement on the line as he backs. More than likely, you will encounter both resistance to backing and crooked backing.

CIRCLES AND TURNS

Use your eyes to follow whatever circular path you wish the horse to describe. Use your bearing reins to regulate the forehand of the horse, making the head, neck and shoulders follow the circular path.

As a general rule, both legs should be used, even only slightly, to keep the horse on the line when turning in any direction. If your inside leg is used to prevent the horse from falling inward on a circle or turn, your outside leg should also be used slightly to prevent the haunches from skidding outward and to indicate the direction of the turn.

Use your weight laterally to assist the horse to remain on the line. The lateral use of weight will never have quite the effect that your legs or reins will, but it can be of definite assistance in promoting better movement on the line. The use of weight to the side provides fine regulation in moving the horse slightly in one direction or the other.

SIMPLE CHANGE OF LEADS

A simple change of leads is performed by breaking from the canter to the walk or trot, taking a few strides at this new gait and resuming the canter on the opposite lead. As you will see, these simple changes of leads are performed in conjunction with certain ring figures so that the horse will be on the correct inside lead once the canter has been resumed.

Teaching the simple change of leads is generally intended as preparation for schooling for the more complex exercise called the flying change of leads. The flying change is made at the canter without first breaking to a slower gait. No matter how athletic the horse or how capable the rider, the horse can benefit from at least an introduction to the simple change of leads prior to undertaking the flying change of leads. By learning the simple change of leads, the horse will acquire a greater measure of longitudinal agility, and he will have a better understanding of what is required as you begin to teach the more demanding flying lead changes later.

If you are a junior rider, you will find that the simple change of leads performed along a straight line or at the center of a figure eight may be asked as a special test in stock seat equitation classes. If you teach riding, instructing your students in the simple change of leads will add to their riding competence.

A simple change of leads may be taught by performing it:

1. At the center of a figure eight.
2. While riding a serpentine.
3. Toward the end of a half circle.
4. Across the diagonal of an arena.
5. While riding in a straight line but away from the arena wall or rail—as you ride down the center of the arena, for example.

Pictures 163 through 167 show the appropriate way to perform the simple change of leads in the five instances just listed. Instructions on when and how to perform the simple change of leads for each particular ring figure are given in the captions. Before you begin to teach the simple change of leads, however, let me give you some general instructions about this exercise.

1. Begin by securing the correct inside lead at the canter for the direction in which you are traveling.
2. Use your aids as you normally would to secure a downward transition from the canter to the walk or trot.
3. Be sure the horse is straight, head to tail, as he takes a few strides at the new, slower

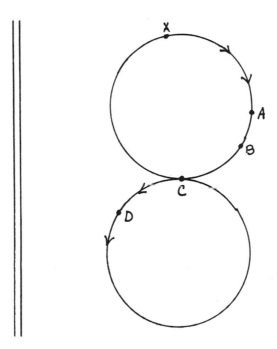

Picture 163. Simple change of leads, on a figure eight. *First, depart on a right lead canter at X. At A, begin preparing for a downward transition to the trot or walk. At B, perform the transition to the trot or walk. Begin preparing for a canter departure as you trot or walk toward C. At C, insure that the horse is straight from head to tail, then depart on a left lead canter. Canter toward D on the new left lead.*

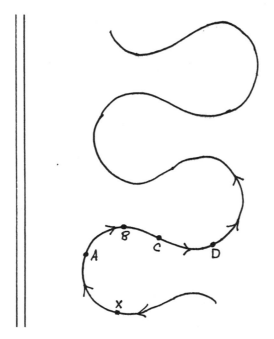

Picture 164. Simple change of leads, along a serpentine. *First, depart on a right lead canter at X. At A, begin preparing for a downward transition to the trot or walk. At B, perform the transition to the trot or walk. Begin preparing for a canter departure as you trot or walk toward C. At C, insure that the horse is straight from head to tail, then depart on a left lead canter. Canter toward D on the new left lead.*

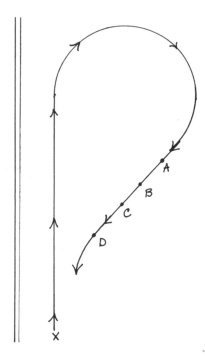

Picture 165. Simple change of leads, along a half circle. *First, depart on a right lead canter at X. At A, begin preparing for a downward transition to the trot or walk. At B, perform the transition to the trot or walk. Begin preparing for a canter departure as you trot or walk toward C. At C, insure that the horse is straight from head to tail, then depart on a left lead canter. Canter toward D on the new left lead. At D, prepare to return to the rail.*

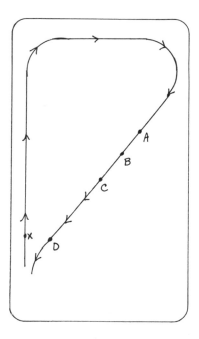

Picture 166. Simple change of leads, across the diagonal. *First, depart on the right lead canter at X. At A, begin preparing for a downward transition to the trot or walk. At B, perform the transition to the trot or walk. Begin preparing for a canter departure as you trot or walk toward C. At C, insure that the horse is straight from head to tail, then depart on a left lead canter. Canter toward D on the new left lead.*

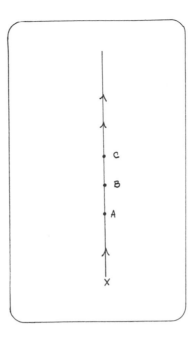

Picture 167. Simple change of leads, along a straightaway. *At X begin the canter on any lead. At A, begin preparing for a downward transition to the trot or walk. At B, perform the transition to the trot or walk. Begin preparing for a canter departure as you trot or walk toward C. At C, insure that the horse is straight from head to tail, then depart on the lead opposite to the one you began at X.*

gait. Each of the five figures illustrated has a straight part, a short distance in which the horse travels in a straight line.

4. Finally, if the horse remains straight, ask for the upward transition to the canter in the usual manner, but on the opposite lead.

The entire sequence for a simple change of leads from the left lead to the right hand lead becomes: canter to the left on the left lead, break to the walk or trot, take a few strides at this new gait, be sure that the horse is straight from head to tail at the slower gait, then ask for a canter departure on the right-hand lead. Do not permit the horse to begin actually turning to the right until the canter on the new lead has been established.

For schooling purposes, performing a simple change through the trot is perfectly all right. If you compete as a junior rider in AHSA stock seat equitation classes, a change through the walk is far better than through the trot, providing your transitions are smooth.

To perform a simple change of leads by allowing the horse to begin turning in the direction of the new lead before it has actually been established is a serious error. Remember, the simple change prepares the horse for learning the more difficult flying change of leads. The flying change of leads absolutely requires that the horse remain straight, head to tail, as the flying change is made midstride in the canter.

As you survey the five illustrations showing the types of figures used to teach the simple change of leads, let me give you a piece of advice. Plan ahead! Some of these figures have very short portions in which the horse may be able to move in a straight line. Plan your downward transition to the walk or trot so that the horse will be straight at this time and that he will remain straight until the new lead is requested.

FLYING CHANGE OF LEADS

The flying change of leads is performed with no interruption of the canter. The horse must continue cantering while the change to the opposite lead is made. The horse must obey your aids in taking the new lead. You must ask for the new lead at *precisely* the correct time. If you do not, the horse will be physically unable to comply with your request.

A flying change of leads is not a difficult exercise for the horse to learn. It only requires a good foundation in schooling to this point, and especially an ability to maintain an even pace at the canter, to be reliable at taking the correct lead in normal ring exercises and to be able to execute a simple change of leads reliably. If he can do all of this, his level of schooling should be sufficient to begin learning how to perform the flying change. Problems in producing a flying change of leads generally do not come from the horse himself, but rather from the rider's timing of the aids.

To teach the flying change of leads, use any of the five ring figures previously given for teaching the simple change of leads. The flying change will be performed along the short straight portions of these figures just as the simple change was, but this time you will not be breaking to a slower gait. Performing flying changes along a straight line, where no change in direction is performed after the lead change has been executed, is the most difficult of the five ring figures shown. Save this one for last; consider it an advanced exercise.

The most critical element in a flying change of leads is timing. *Ask for the flying change of leads just in advance of the period of suspension at the canter.*

This period of suspension at the canter occurs just as the leading leg leaves the ground after passing backward under the horse's shoulder. This is the only possible moment when the horse is physically capable of performing the flying change of leads.

Picture 168 illustrates the period of suspension at the canter for a horse on the left lead: a flying change to the right-hand lead would only be possible at this exact moment. If the rider in this picture had wished a flying change to the right lead, she

Picture 168. The period of suspension at the canter. *All four of the horse's feet are off the ground. This is the only instant at which a horse can accurately perform the flying change of leads, and the rider must request the change just in advance of this particular instant in the stride.*

would have asked for the change with her inside leg (the left, in this case) just prior to the instant shown. She would have asked for the change after the leading leg had been grounded, but before it had traveled rearward far enough to begin leaving the ground again.

The exact moment to ask for the change of leads will vary *slightly* from horse to horse, but your cue to change leads will have to be given after the leading leg strikes the ground, but before it subsequently leaves the ground again. The horse must be able to take advantage of your cue as the period of suspension at the canter occurs.

In other words, the rider must request the new lead as the horse is balanced only on the old leading leg (Picture 169).

Requesting a change to a new lead is simple. Ask for a flying change of leads in exactly the same manner as you ask for any normal canter departure on a particular lead from the walk or trot. Use your weight, legs and reins as always. Your timing in providing these aids becomes critical; you must use them just prior to the period of suspension at the canter.

As you employ your aids to ask for the new lead, you must be certain the horse is straight from head to tail. Do *not* begin turning the horse in the direction of the new lead before the actual lead change has occurred. If you watch reining horses change leads at the canter across the center of a figure eight, sometimes it appears that the rider begins turning the horse at the same time as he requests the flying change. Not so. Admittedly, at the center of a figure eight there simply is not a lot of time in which to make the lead change, but the change is in fact made before beginning to turn the

Picture 169. Asking for the flying change of leads at the correct moment. *This horse is cantering on the right-hand lead. If a flying change of leads to the left were required, then the rider would necessarily have to ask for the flying change at least by the moment shown in this photo—when the left fore, right hind and left hind feet are off the ground. In the next instant, this horse will have passed his body mass over the right front leg and the period of suspension will have begun. It is only during the period of suspension that a horse can physically perform a flying change of leads (and change to a united canter on the new lead).*

horse along the second portion of the figure.

It is best to begin teaching the flying change of leads from slower speeds of the canter. A very pulled-together lope, with good impulse and with the horse's head and neck slightly raised, is for most horses the best frame from which to learn this movement. Physically, a shortened frame will assist the horse in performing the exercise. A horse that carries his head and neck in a very low position and is strung out at the canter is in no position to perform a flying change at any speed. The promptness and correctness of your aids may be of no avail in securing the required change.

Later in schooling, as you teach the flying change of leads for increasingly faster speeds of the canter, you will probably be asking for the change from the standing position. In this case, you will not choose to sit prior to using your leg to request a new lead (and this will be a slight departure from the usual method of sitting in rhythm with the horse's efforts in advance of requesting a lead when making a routine canter departure).

When in the standing position, use your leg in the usual manner for the new lead, but also use your weight by dropping more weight into your inside stirrup: your right stirrup for a change to the right-hand lead, your left stirrup for a change to the left lead. This is a subtle use of weight, not at all a matter of leaning to the side or throwing your weight in the direction of the desired lead. Simply stand a little harder in your inside stirrup as you ask for the new lead with your outside leg. Be careful not to weight this inside stirrup heavily before you begin to request the change with your opposite leg. If the horse begins to turn in response to your use of weight before the lead change is begun, you are apt to have a poor flying change or none at all. The horse simply must be straight as the lead change is actually made.

Problems frequently encountered in performing a correct flying change of leads are:

1. The horse does not change leads at all.
   Generally: The horse was not straight, or. . . .
   The rider began turning the horse in advance of the change, or. . . .
   The rider did not aid the horse for a new lead in advance of the period of suspension at the canter, or. . . .
   The rider did not use his outside leg correct-

ly to indicate a new lead, or. . . .
The horse was too strung out, too heavy on the forehand to perform the change rapidly enough in response to the rider's correct use of aids, or. . . .
The horse's schooling is inadequate to permit him to perform this exercise at this time; lack of longitudinal agility, lack of promptness and obedience to the rider's aids, or a lack of adequate preparation in schooling by first performing the simple change of leads reliably.

2. The horse changes leads in front, but does not change in back; this is called cross-cantering, or a disunited canter. In this case, you will see, or feel, the new leading leg come forward as the rear leg on the *same* side begins traveling *rearward*—the horse fails in establishing a new diagonal pair of legs for the canter on the new lead.
   Generally: The rider's timing in supplying his aids is a "little off," but. . . .
   Cross-cantering may also result from any of those things previously listed under 1.

3. The horse speeds up after making the correct change of leads both in front and behind (a united canter) but he "hurries" forward. This is a flaw in the quality of the horse's movement even though a correct change has been made reliably.
   Generally: Quiet schooling and more practice at performing these lead changes is needed; however. . . .
   Too much practice, demanding too many lead changes in a short time may be at fault; also. . . .
   The rider may have previously punished the horse severely or often because no lead change was made, or a disunited canter on the correct front lead was produced, through no fault of the horse. It was the rider's timing that was in fact in error, with the horse being physically unable to produce the change at a given instant, ... or
   The horse may be too young, too unbalanced yet, to avoid hurrying ahead once the lead change is accomplished. Though athletic and obedient to the rider's aids, a lack of time and adequate preparation in schooling may be at fault.

One mark of a higher level horse is performing

the flying change correctly, quietly, and without scooting forward after the change is made.

The horse that cross-canters behind after changing leads will be physically unable to correct this until the next stride. The period of suspension at the next cantering stride will have to occur before the change behind can be made (although some horses change in front, and then gracefully catch up behind as they begin to canter away on the new front lead).

The greater the horse's schooling, longitudinal agility and ability to come back softly to your hands and shift his weight to the rear, the greater will be his ability to perform precise and seemingly effortless flying changes of leads. If you have no particular reason to teach the flying change at this time, delay this exercise until later in the course of

intermediate schooling. You should, however, teach the flying change before schooling for the rollback.

Pictures 170, 171 and 172 are intended to sum up several of the points concerning the flying change of leads. The flying change cannot be illustrated with a single still photograph. Study these photographs, read the captions and review this section until you understand how the movement is correctly performed.

THE PIVOT

The pivot and the turn on the haunches performed from the halt are mechanically the same exercise. Only the quality of movement differs,

Picture 170. Performing the flying change of leads. *This horse was circling to the left on the correct inside lead. At the point when this picture was taken, the rider has just requested a flying change of leads to the (new) right-hand lead, and is subsequently asking the horse to begin to turn to the right. The new right-hand lead is beginning correctly from the outside (left) hind foot, the diagonal pair of legs (right rear and left front) have already been established, and the new leading leg (right front) has been advanced to take the leading leg position. The rider, recognizing that the new right-hand lead has been established, is just beginning to turn the horse in the direction of the new lead.*

Picture 171. A flying change of leads with a disunited canter. *A flying change of leads from the right to the left lead is being performed. However, in this case the horse has changed correctly in front (the new left front leading leg has been established), while not changing correctly behind. The rider is turning the horse in the direction of the new lead since the front leading leg is correct, but he will ask again with his right displacing leg at the next stride of the canter in order to also establish the correct lead behind.*

and the difference boils down to how fast the turn on the haunches is performed. When the turn on the haunches is performed with speed, to demonstrate the horse's lightness, handiness and ability to cooperate rapidly with the rider's aids, the movement is termed a pivot.

For the pivot, greater energy in movement is required as the horse rotates his forehand around his stationary hindquarters. The usual movements for the pivot are a quarter turn on the haunches (with speed), or a half turn on the haunches (with speed). The pivot is always performed from the halt, and it never involves a full turn on the

haunches since this would technically be classified as a spin.

Performing the pivot rapidly has nothing to do with rearing and throwing the head, neck and shoulders to the side and around the hindquarters. While a rapid half turn on the haunches can be made in this manner, the movement is unacceptable and places extreme strain on the pivotal leg.

The horse should rotate his forehand to the side quickly, and with energetic but relatively flat strides. In essence, he smartly paddles the forehand to the side, describing an arc around the stationary hindquarters. As the turn is made, one

Picture 172. The flying change of leads. *This photo provides another look at a correctly-executed flying change of leads. The flying change has been made during the period of suspension—an instant before this photo was taken. The horse had been circling to the left on the correct left lead, and was subsequently asked for a flying change of leads to the right-hand lead. At the instant shown, the new lead has been correctly established with the left rear leg comprising the first beat of the new right lead canter. The next beat of the canter will be the diagonal pair of legs—right rear and left front. The final beat of the canter on the new right lead will then be the right front leg itself. Note that the rider is maintaining the horse in a straight attitude (head to tail) as the lead change is performed.*

forefoot will nearly always be in contact with the ground (Picture 173) as the opposite forefoot steps to the side and in the direction of the turn being made. At certain points during the pivot, both front feet will actually be in contact with the ground (Picture 174).

While the forehand of the horse will elevate during the pivot (Picture 175), rearing and throwing the horse's weight to the side is inappropriate. A horse that rears in order to pivot is probably resisting the rider's overuse of aids—heavy, aggressive hands—and showing a lack of adequate preparation by earlier schooling.

A greater tendency of the horse to shift his weight rearward, rocking back on his hocks, should be evident in the pivot compared to the more methodical and slower turn on the haunches. The pivotal leg should usually be set well forward of the opposite hindleg. The horse should look in the direction in which he is pivoting (Picture 176).

Whenever you begin to work some horses at the pivot, away from the rail or arena wall, they will begin to halt with their hindlegs essentially parallel to one another; they simply refuse to set their

Picture 173. The pivot. *Mechanically, the pivot is the same as the turn on the haunches per-formed from the halt, which is taught at the elementary level of schooling. However, the pivot involves more rapid turning, greater energy, greater lightness and handiness in the horse. The movement is performed by "smartly paddling" the forehand in an arc around the stationary hindquarters. While the pivotal leg (the left rear leg in this picture) must remain stationary during the turn, the horse is permitted to raise the pivotal leg (and then put it down again in the same place) as the turn is executed. The pivotal leg may be raised and then re-grounded as many times as necessary during the turn, but the pivotal leg should not step for-ward, backward or to the side. The opposite hind leg simply walks around the pivotal leg, in very small steps, as the horse rotates his forehand to the side. A quarter- or half-turn is the movement usually performed.*

pivotal leg forward (Picture 177). These horses will make a quick, last-minute adjustment of their pivotal leg once the rider indicates the actual direction of the turn to be made. Actually there is nothing wrong with this so long as you continue to use your own legs and your knowledge of the horse's sequence of legs to attempt to set the pivotal leg in direction of the turn which you plan after halting the horse. In other words, don't simply leave everything to the horse that has learned to be clever with his hindlegs; continue to ride effective-ly, to ask for the halt when the pivotal leg is next to be advanced. Continue to use your own urging leg on the side of pivot as you halt to encourage the horse to bring his pivotal leg forward as he stops.

Even at this level in the horse's education, you will still want to use two hands on the reins most of the time while you are schooling for the pivot. Use a bearing rein, not a tight indirect rein across the neck, to move the horse's forehand in the direction of the pivot.

Picture 174. The pivot. *The pivot is a flat exercise. Again, it is not performed by rearing and throwing the horse's mass to the side and around the stationary hindquarters. At points during the pivot, both front feet will actually be grounded. The pivot leg in this picture is the left rear leg. The horse is appropriately crossing his front legs in preparation for the next step to the side with the forehand.*

Use your right bearing rein for a pivot to the left (Picture 176) and your left bearing rein for a pivot to the right. Also use your opposite leading rein to discourage the horse from becoming sluggish or reluctant to turn (Picture 176, again). Alternate periods of tension and release, rather than pulling steadily with this leading rein as you might have done in trying to perfect the turn on the haunches earlier in schooling. If the horse is perfectly willing to respond to your bearing rein, hold the leading rein loosely. But be ready to act with the leading rein if the horse loses his willingness to pivot rapidly.

Use your holding leg to assist the horse in turn-ing and to assist him in moving his forehand to the side. Regulate the speed of the pivot by increasing or decreasing the pressure of this leg on the horse's side. Generally, you will use your holding leg most actively as the pivot is first begun, and quite actively as the horse approaches the midway point of the pivot. Use your weight to the inside of the turn if this assists the horse in turning rapidly and smoothly (Pictures 173 and 174). Use your inside urging leg actively if the horse attempts to back as the pivot is begun.

A final note. The term *offset* can be used in place of *pivot*. Both mean the same thing; they are the same exercise.

Picture 175. The pivot. *While the horse should indeed elevate his forehand in preparation for beginning the pivot, rearing and throwing his mass to the side is inappropriate. The horse in this picture is correctly beginning a pivot to the right, using the right rear leg as the pivotal leg.*

THE SPIN

The spin and the pivot are very similar exercises. The quality of movement for both is identical, and the use of the rider's aids in producing either of these exercises is the same. The differences, however, are:

1. The spin is performed as a full turn on the haunches (with speed), whereas the pivot is performed as either a quarter or half turn on the haunches (with speed).
2. The spin may be performed from the halt, the canter or the walk. The pivot is always performed from the halt.

The spin and pivot are so similar in their quality of movement that one cannot tell the difference between the two exercises from a still photograph. All of the qualities of movement cited for the pivot apply to the spin; it is only the degree of turning which differs.

To perform the spin from the halt, execute a pivot, but continue the pivot beyond a half turn; continue pivoting until at least one full turn on the haunches has been performed. Perfect one full turn at the spin first; then practice spins of one and a half, two, and even three full turns.

Schooling for the pivot should be well in order before the spin from the halt is taught. The spin is a very tiring exercise for any horse. Generating this type of momentum from the halt can only result in fatigue whenever you practice this movement too frequently.

Practicing the spin is fun, but don't overdo it. Emphasize quality of movement in cooperation with your aids, rather than seeing how many times you can spin, or how many rapid revolutions the horse can make. Fatigue from too many spins increases the likelihood of injury to the horse, mostly strains and sprains of the joint capsules and ten-

Picture 176. The pivot. *This picture illustrates both how the horse should look in the direction in which he is pivoting, and an extremely soft use of the rider's right bearing rein and left leading rein to begin to teach a young horse to pivot to the left.*

dons of the pivotal leg. Fatigue may lead the horse to a variety of resistances to performing the exercise: walking out of the spin, disobedience to your bearing rein and active holding leg and rearing and throwing his bulk to the side.

Performing it from the walk or canter is a soft way of teaching the spin because some forward momentum is preserved; the horse does not have to generate the type of momentum required to spin from the halt.

To perform the spin from either the walk or canter, place the horse on a circle. Continue walking or cantering in circles of increasing small diameter. This amounts to winding the horse down along a circular path until the diameter of the cir-

cle becomes so small that only a spin can allow the horse to continue hs circular motion. At this point use two hands on the reins. Use your bearing rein and your leading rein to the inside of the spin to induce the horse to continue moving in a circular pattern by rotating his forehand to the side. Use your outside displacing leg to assist the horse in moving his mass to the inside, and also use your weight to the inside. Both you and the horse should be looking in the direction you are turning.

Like the pivot, the spin is a flat exercise. The horse that must elevate his forehand completely off the ground, rear and throw his bulk to the side, demonstrates a very poor quality of movement for the spin. As in the pivot, one forefoot

Picture 177. The pivot. *Some horses, after being taught the pivot, will be reluctant to set their pivotal leg far forward. These clever horses wish to be able to begin the pivot rapidly in either direction.*

should nearly always be in contact with the ground, and at points during the spin both of the forefeet will actually be grounded momentarily.

Generally, a smooth fluid spin, with the horse's weight carried largely on the hind limbs, requires a very deep forward setting of the pivotal leg in advance of beginning the spin.

All of the pictures given for the pivot are models as well for performing the spin. As I have said, the spin and pivot are really the same exercise. It is only the degree of turning which differs (a quarter or half turn for the pivot, and a complete full turn or more for the spin). In still photographs differences between the spin and pivot cannot be detected.

THE ROLLBACK

The rollback is a rapid half turn on the haunches, performed from either the walk or the canter. The term *turn on the haunches* is used here

in preference to the term *pivot* since the movement of the rollback is usually a continuous one, with the half turn initiated before the horse has completely halted. As you will recall, the pivot technically is always performed from the halt.

Although the rollback from the walk is primarily a schooling exercise, it also serves as preparation for the faster, more demanding, rollback at the canter. To perform the rollback at the walk, the rider checks with the reins to slow the horse's forward speed, and performs the rollback (turn on the haunches) in the direction of the pivotal leg which has been established. The horse walks or canters away just as the turn has been completed.

To perform the rollback at the canter, the rider canters into the rollback on a particular lead, and performs the rollback in the direction opposite to this lead (a half turn on the haunches to the right from a left lead and vice versa from the right lead). The horse canters away just as the turn is completed. As with any of the movements requiring a turn on the haunches (pivot, spin or roll-back), a pivotal leg on the side to which the turn is to be made should be established before the turn is begun.

The rollback is ideally performed as a continuous movement with the horse never *completely* halting during any portion of the movement. The half turn on the haunches executed as part of the rollback differs from any of the movements discussed so far because the horse *is permitted to elevate the forehand* off the ground as the turn on the haunches is performed.

The rollback is designed to save time, ground or both. For this reason, the usual movement is performed at the canter. The horse also canters away after completing the required half turn on the haunches. The cutting horse represents a model of sorts for the usefulness and practicality of this movement. Any working stock horse cannot get along without the rollback, and most reining tests require this movement to be performed. Even polo ponies (attired in English tack) rely heavily upon the rollback as one of their basic movements.

Teaching the rollback should not pose a particular problem at this stage of the horse's schooling. It is only a matter of putting all the pieces together as a continuous movement: a quick and obedient downward transition; a rapid half turn on the haunches just before halting with aids used as in the pivot; and finally, a quick and obedient upward transition just as the turn is completed. None of these individual exercises should be new to you or the horse. It only remains to show the horse what is required by way of the total picture, putting all the pieces together so the rollback is performed as a continuous movement. Checking, turning and cantering away should all flow together providing the impression of continuous movement.

Employing a barrier such as the rail or wall of your schooling area is a useful technique when first acquainting the horse with the rollback. Performing the rollback *toward* such a barrier encourages the horse to shift his weight rearward, to shorten his entire frame and to elevate the forehand as the half turn is performed. So long as you make sure that the pivotal leg nearest the barrier is set to bear the horse's weight before turning, and that the turn is performed with the hindquarters stationary, this method of introducing the horse to the rollback is usually quite useful.

Insuring that the pivotal leg (closest to the barrier) is grounded appropriately is largely a matter of your correct timing in checking, before asking for the turn toward the barrier; it is a matter of developing a feel for this particular movement through practice, and by mentally following the sequence of legs at whatever gait precedes the rollback. The pivotal leg to the inside of the rollback should never be grounded behind the other rear leg as the turn is begun; only a clumsy turn, one requiring the overuse of your reins, will result in this instance.

Keeping the horse's haunches stationary as the turn is made is as much a matter of safety for the horse as it is a matter of performing the movement correctly. Allowing the horse to perform a turn on the forehand while he is still in motion or allowing him to walk out of the rollback with his hindlegs increases the likelihood of strain or injury to the legs.

The Use of Aids in the Rollback

As you check the horse's speed in preparation for the rollback, remember to use your legs actively at the girth to secure good engagement of the horse's rear legs up under his body. As the rollback is begun, use your holding leg in the usual manner as you would for a turn on the haunches, pivot or spin, and continue the active use of this leg as the turn is completed in order to assist the horse in securing the correct lead as he canters out of the rollback in the opposite direction.

Use your weight to the inside of the rollback. For instance, to the right side for a rollback to the right. Also, discontinue the use of your weight to the side as the rollback is about to be completed. You should have your weight equally divided between your two stirrups as the horse completes the turn and prepares to canter away. Remember to look in the direction of the turn being performed; your own eye control is vital.

Once the horse understands the rollback, it is unnecessary and often abusive to continue to employ your reins as a means of generating the rollback once the half-way point in the turn has been reached. This is particularly true where a barrier is employed to assist the horse in learning the movement. Rather than actively using your reins in turning the horse all the way around, rely on your leg, weight and eye control to complete the last portion of the turn. The horse will necessarily elevate the head and neck and shorten his entire frame as the turn is begun. This attitude of the head and neck will persist until the turn is at least half completed. At this point, the horse will again extend his head and neck in preparation for cantering out of the rollback. Maintaining tension in your reins as the turn is completed may only result in bumping the horse in the mouth as he naturally extends his head and neck. A bump in the mouth at this point is not much of a reward for a horse that has obediently performed a difficult movement.

The rollback is performed from the walk or canter, but not from the trot. In fact, the rollback cannot be performed from the trot. If you think about the diagonal pairs of legs employed for trotting, and the spread between the two hindlegs at the trot, you will see why the rollback cannot be accomplished from this gait. You may see people jog into the rollback, and jog away from it, but you will notice that they will halt or nearly halt before actually performing the turn itself. At any rate, the sequence of legs at the trot will be broken before the rollback is attempted.

Teach the rollback at the walk before teaching it at the canter; this is a logical order. Some riders teach the rollbck at the walk first, and they also add that you should walk into the rollback, perform the half turn and walk away. I agree. Walk into the rollback, perform the half turn, but as to whether to insist that the horse always walk away is questionable. If the horse normally likes to canter away quietly, I would not insist upon his walking instead.

If you succeed in bumping him in the mouth in trying to preserve the walk after he has performed the required turn, you will discourage him from willingly performing the movement again. After teaching the rollback at the walk and permitting him to canter away if he so chooses, begin the rollback at the canter, but in this case, always canter in and canter away.

The question of leads inevitably comes up when the rollback is taught at the canter. The correct leads are:

1. You canter into the rollback on the left lead, and rollback to the right side. The horse should then canter away on the right-hand lead after performing the necessary half turn.
2. You canter into the rollback on the right-hand lead, and rollback to the left. The horse should then canter away on the left lead.

All this provided you continue to use your outside holding leg actively behind the cinch as the turn is completed. Your weight is again in the center of the saddle as the turn is completed; and your eyes are looking ahead.

Pictures 178, 179 and 180 illustrate the three phases of the rollback: the check, the half turn on the haunches and the first stride out of the turn.

THE SLIDING STOP

This is not at all difficult to teach or perform, provided the horse's schooling at the intermediate level is reasonably complete. The sliding stop is merely a rapid transition from the gallop to the halt. The horse must cooperate with the same aids used by the rider to produce any good transition.

In describing this movement, I will tabulate its important elements and the necessary actions of the rider. If you are a little uneasy about teaching your horse this movement, review your intermediate schooling to this point. In addition, attend a few reining competitions as an educated observer.

First, a few important points about this movement:

Sliding plates are *not* necessary to perform the sliding stop. Regular horseshoes are perfectly adequate to begin teaching this movement You will want the horse shod in sliding plates for actual competitions.

Moving on the line is vitally important in performing this movement. The horse must be straight head to tail whenever he is asked to stop rapidly and slide. He must gallop forward in a straight line prior to the slide; he must remain straight as he slides and stops.

An increase in speed—a burst of acceleration—should immediately precede the request for the sliding stop.

The rider produces the sliding stop as follows:

1. To begin your straight run in preparation for a slide, do the following:
   (a) Ask for a canter departure in the normal manner, but
   (b) Compress the horse and regulate his forward speed. Ask for a tendency toward central balance, great engagement and impulse. Your legs should say *go,*

Picture 178. The rollback, the check.

but your hands should say *slow*.

2. Next:
   (a) Allow the horse to lengthen his head and neck. Allow him to lengthen his entire frame, to shift his weight forward for the purpose of increasing his forward speed almost to a gallop.
   (b) Second gear; establish a fast, forward-balanced canter.

3. Finally, just before asking for the sliding stop:
   (a) Ask for a sudden burst of speed: ask the horse to gallop.
   (b) Use more urging leg, and also move your rein hand forward toward the horse's ears to say "Yes, move out, accelerate."
   (c) High gear: establish a gallop.
   (d) This is your last chance to make sure that the horse in on the line. Make sure that you are in the center of the saddle, that your weight is divided equally between your stirrups and that the horse is straight head to tail.

4. To ask for the sliding stop:

   (a) As the horse just begins to attain his peak acceleration, ask for the sliding stop. Use your aids in the normal sequence:
      1. Weight
      2. Voice
      3. Hands and legs
   (b) Your sequence of aids for the halt and slide will consume some time, and this time will vary from horse to horse.
   (c) However, note that the entire sequence of weight, voice, hands and legs must be completed during the time that the horse has both back feet off the ground, in order that he can obey your command to halt promptly by advancing both hind feet forward simultaneously (Picture 181). The horse cannot advance his hindlegs simultaneously, parallel to one another, if one of them is already grounded at the instant you ask him to halt.
   (d) Both back feet are in fact off the ground at the time that the horse's leading leg passes underneath his body and

Picture 179. The rollback, the half turn on the haunches.

leaves the ground. You will have to adjust your timing, in completing the sequence of aids for the halt, to coincide with this event.

The Use of Aids in the Sliding Stop

First, use your voice authoritatively but not loudly. Utter one *Whoa*.

Then, use your weight to insure that:

1. You are in the center of the saddle as you begin to tuck your seat underneath you and brace your back.
2. Your weight is divided equally in the stirrups.
3. Your head is up and you are looking straight ahead.
4. Your free arm is relaxed and ready to assist

you in maintaining your balance as the horse suddenly shifts his weight to the rear in order to stop and slide.
5. You do not inadvertently use your weight to one side or the other, causing the horse to move off the line as you are in the process of requesting the halt.

As you begin to use your weight as a clear signal for the horse to slow his forward speed, also employ urging legs, just in advance of finally checking with the reins.

1. Close your legs evenly on the horse's sides just before using your reins to ask for the halt to help insure that the horse will bring his legs well up under himself—grounding them parallel to one another as the slide is begun.
2. Attempt to maintain a good position of

Picture 180. The rollback, the first stride away.

your lower leg throughout the slide. This is not always easy due to the rapid shift in the horse's center of balance from front to rear. If you must grip with your thighs or pinch with your knees, do so rather than having your upper body collapse forward or backward.

3. If you have to grip with your thighs or pinch with your knees, your heels will rise, your toes will point downward and you will also push yourself up and slightly out of the saddle. All of this reduces the effectiveness of your use of weight. For these reasons, a good lower leg position is important, but squeezing with the thighs, or pinching with the knees is still preferable to losing your balance and interfering with the horse's efforts to stop and slide.

Finally, your hands ultimately ask for the stop. Employ two direct reins of opposition in the following manner:

1. First, close your fingers on the reins, and move your forearm directly to the rear to perform the check.

2. Your forearm should be moved back smoothly, closing your elbow joint, as you maintain the forearm approximately parallel with the horse's back.

3. As the horse obeys your rein action by setting the back feet to begin the stop and slide, reward his obedience to your rein aid by releasing the rein tension. As the slide progresses, you may have the opportunity to check and release several times to prolong the slide. Releasing the rein tension during the slide also encourages the horse to walk ahead with the front feet as the rear feet continue to slide—a superior form of this entire movement of stopping and sliding.

One reason that the gallop precedes a request for a slide is that the period of suspension, when no hindfoot is on the ground, is longer than for any other gait. You therefore have more time to use your aids for requesting the stop. A second reason is that, if you want your horse to slide a fairly long distance, you must have a good bit of speed coming into the stop.

Picture 181. The sliding stop. *To perform the sliding stop correctly, the horse must be on the line as you ask for the halt, and he must bring both back legs forward and parallel to one another as he prepares to slide and halt* on a straight line.

Practicing prompt halts and teaching the horse to shift his weight to the rear at the walk and trot is fine, but attempting to produce a mini-version of the slide at these gaits is not. At the walk, one hindfoot will always be grounded as you ask the horse to halt; advancing both hind legs simultaneously becomes a physical near-impossibility for the horse. At the trot, although a period of suspension does exist, the spread of the diagonal pair of legs makes sliding very difficult.

Some riders use slick spots in an arena to help school for the sliding stop. Providing that the area to be used is not too slippery or wet, this method may be used to give the horse the idea of what is expected. It is important not to scare the horse. Ask softly and expect only a short slide. This tactic should be used only to introduce the horse to sliding. Even a single sliding stop on wet footing may be all that is necessary to give the horse the initial idea; he learns he can stop suddenly with a drastic lowering of his croup and not fall over backwards.

One of the problems with using wet, slick foot-

ing involves inadvertent injury to the horse: fractures of the pelvis. I have even seen horses pull back while tied (not short enough) and sit down in what seems to be a very gentle manner. The result is a fractured pelvis—a more common injury than many horsemen believe.

Picture 182 illustrates the essence of an excellent sliding stop.

LOW JUMPING

In no way does the following discussion try to encompass any of the "how to's" for the working hunter or open jumper classes. We are only concerned here with jumping single, low obstacles—one to two feet high—in a western saddle. You will find such obstacles in practically any trail class, or when riding outdoors. If you try to apply this discussion to jumping higher obstacles or courses of obstacles in an English saddle, you are likely to end up with a frightened horse and injury to yourself, the horse or both.

Listed below are five reasons for schooling your horse to jump low, single obstacles. Low jumping can provide:

1. Another way in which to develop agility in any horse. A horse that jumps must shorten and lengthen his frame and jump off his hindquarters.
2. A means of coping more successfully with the jumping obstacles found in show ring trail classes.
3. An ideal means of developing an independent hand and seat as part of a rider's good position. Jumping can be very similar to roping in this respect.
4. A nice diversion, but still a schooling exercise, for horses that tend to become bored or sour easily.
5. A means of handling logs and low obstacles found when riding outdoors for fun.

Jumping can be broken down into four phases: *approach, take-off, flight* and *landing*.

Approach

1. See Picture 183. The horse may approach low jumps at either the ordinary trot or an energetic lope. The gait you choose depends on what your horse will be asked to do after the jump. If he must slow down or stop soon after jumping, a trot should be your choice; otherwise, a lope with impulse is fine. For low jumping, the horse does not need much speed, but he must have some energy or impulse to his gaits as he approaches the obstacle to be cleared.

The horse's approach to the jump should be stabilized—an even speed at the trot or lope. The horse should not quicken his pace as he nears the jump. A comfortable pace for horse and rider should be established well before you approach the obstacle, and maintained until take-off.

The term *fence* means any obstacle a horse jumps. The term does not literally mean a fence made of wire, wood or stone. It signifies an object to be jumped, no matter how low or how high.

During the approach to the fence, the horse may

Picture 182. The essence of an excellent sliding stop.

Picture 183. The approach. Horse: *In this instance the approach to the jump is being made at the ordinary trot—an energetic forward-moving trot that should neither increase nor decrease in speed as the obstacle to be jumped is approached.* **Rider:** *The rider is correctly looking ahead and beyond the obstacle. His upper body is inclined slightly forward and he is with (not ahead or behind) the forward motion of the horse. His seat is out of the saddle. His heels are down and his lower leg supports his upper body without the necessity of muscular gripping with the inner thighs or knees. The reins are loose. This design of position is correct. Additionally, the rider has a hold on the mane to prevent erratic changes in his upper body position should he inadvertently lose his balance as the jump is actually performed. Loose reins and the rider's hold on the mane will nearly preclude any possibility of the horse being bumped or jerked in the mouth with the bit as the jump is executed.*

slightly lower and lengthen his head and neck.

2. The rider should first establish an even pace at either the trot or canter. As you ride to the jump, rise into the standing position with your torso inclined slightly forward. Your weight should be well down into your heels and your hips, knees and ankles must remain relaxed and flexible. Keep enough leg on the horse to maintain the speed of the gait during the approach. Check with your hand if the horse quickens, or use your legs more strongly if he slows down on the approach. Allow the horse to lower his head and neck, and maintain loose reins throughout the jump. The rider should look up and beyond the jump.

Take-Off

1. See Picture 184. The horse begins the take-

off when he breaks the cantering or trotting sequence of legs used to make the approach. In other words, the act of jumping is not just a bigger or longer stride of the gait.

Take-off begins when the horse simultaneously grounds both hind legs. These grounded legs should be parallel to each other in order to allow the horse to best push himself up and over the fence with his hindquarters. As both hindlegs are grounded, the croup sinks and the hocks are bent; the forehand is elevated completely off the ground to form an angle sufficient for the horse to clear the jump. As the forehand is elevated, the horse begins to fold his front legs up and back toward his chest.

A good take-off relies on the horse grounding both back legs parallel to one another in preparation for pushing off and leaving the ground to jump. In reality, many horses jumping for the first time tend to ground their back legs one ahead of the other and in any manner they can. They begin jumping essentially by pushing themselves up and off the ground using only one of their legs at first; with experience, they begin grounding both hind legs parallel to one another, pushing off equally with both hind limbs. For the horse that canters to the jump, the last front leg to leave the ground as he elevates his forehand will be the leading leg of the canter during his approach to the jump.

2. As the horse prepares to leave the ground— as he rocks back on his hocks and elevates his forehand—the rider should maintain the quiet standing position established on the approach. As the horse rocks back and elevates his forehand, the rider should close both of his lower legs enough to maintain his balance and position. Grip equally with knee and inner calf, but do not pinch with the knees alone or your lower leg may swing backward, causing you to lose your balance to the front. As the horse's neck elevates and comes back toward you, allow the horse to close the angle between your torso and his neck. Continue to maintain a forward position, letting the horse do the work. Grab the mane if you need some help. Do not lean forward any more than on the approach.

Picture 184. The take-off. Horse: *Both hind feet have been grounded and the forehand has been completely elevated so that an angle sufficient to clear the fence is achieved. It only remains for the horse to push off with the hind legs to become airborne. Three particular points about this picture should be noted. First, the horse correctly shortens the entire frame of the head and neck (compare this to Pictures 183 and 186). Second, although the front legs are folded unevenly at this moment, both front legs will be folded equally as the jump proceeds (one front leg always leaves the ground before the other). Third, remember that experienced jumpers (and those required to jump substantial heights) will correctly ground both hind legs parallel to one another during take-off. Inexperienced jumpers (or those required to jump low obstacles) often tend to ground one hind leg ahead of the other as in this picture.* **Rider:** *the rider's upper body position remains the same as in Picture 183. However, he has now let the horse (through elevation of the forehand) close the angle between the rider's upper body and the top of the horse's neck. The rider's design of position during take-off is correct. His lower leg position is very nearly impeccable. He still maintains a hold on the mane and continues to look ahead and beyond the jump.*

Just allow the horse to close the angle. If you lean forward too far, you may end up with the saddle horn striking your chest.

Continue to look ahead. Keep the reins loose, because in just a moment the horse will need to extend his head and neck freely, and a severe jerk in the mouth with the bit may convince the horse that he never wants to jump again. If you are not sure how loose to maintain your reins, jump using a plain snaffle until you have a better feel for just how far forward the horse might extend his head and neck as he leaves the ground.

Flight

1. See Picture 185. The horse begins the flight phase at the time both rear feet leave the ground, and it continues as the horse describes an arc as he travels up, over and down over the far side of the fence. While the horse is in the air, his front legs are folded beneath him until they pass over the jump, at which time they begin unfolding in preparation for the landing. During flight, the horse's hind legs are also tucked up (bent at the hocks) as they pass over the fence. The horse extends his head and neck forward and slightly downward during the flight phase. The flight phase ends whenever the horse's first forefoot touches the ground on the landing side of the fence.

2. The rider should follow forward with the reins during the flight phase to insure that the horse is not accidentally jerked in the mouth as he extends his head and neck. Better yet, if you are not quite ready to do this, just allow sufficient looseness in the reins so that the horse will not be bumped with the bit. Be sure that you do not sit down on the horse, or fall back with your torso during this phase of the jump. If you are not careful to prevent this sort of thing, you will bang the horse on the back, and this type of abuse will generally result in an unwilling jumper or one who continually hits the fence with his hindlegs.

Picture 185. The flight. Horse: *The horse's rear legs are nearly straight; the hocks are fully extended and sufficient "push" by the hind limbs has been accomplished to initiate the flight phase. In a moment both hind feet will leave the ground. Note that as the flight phase begins the horse again begins to extend the head and neck.* **Rider:** *The rider's position design remains correct. He is applying muscular grip with his inner upper calves in order to maintain his lower leg position.*

In order to stay off the horse's back (and this does not mean lots of daylight between you and the saddle), keep your weight down in your heels and keep your lower leg underneath your own center of balance. In order to stay with the motion of the horse as he jumps and avoid falling back onto the saddle with a plop, round your back slightly to avoid the saddle horn and lean forward a little more than you did at take-off. Pushing your rein hand up the horse's crest will help you stay forward with your upper body and will allow the horse plenty of room to balance himself with his own head and neck.

Keep your body centered over the middle of the saddle. Do not lean to one side or the other. Again, keep looking ahead.

Landing

1. See Picture 186. The horse begins the landing phase when his first forefoot touches the ground on the landing side of the fence. The horse should canter away from the fence for at least a stride or two, no matter what gait was used on the approach. This is a normal occurrence. If you must suddenly pull a horse up to a halt, walk or trot immediately after jumping, you can be prepared to do so. Let him canter on for a stride or two, however.

As the horse descends to the ground, he will often raise his head and neck in preparation for landing. The normal sequence of legs for landing is:

Picture 186. The landing. Horse: *Landing occurs when the first forefoot touches the ground (in this case, the left front). The ''fork'' defined by the horse's left and right front legs at the instant this photo was snapped is typical of the attitude of the horse's forelegs during landing. Note how the horse extends the head and neck; had the rider not maintained loose reins during the previous phase of the jump, the horse would have surely been bumped rather severely with the bit at this point.* **Rider:** *This rider remains basically correct in his position. He continues to look ahead. He has good depth in his heels to absorb the concussion of landing. He has released his hold on the mane (recognizing that he is in no danger of losing his balance at this point). He is prepared to give forward with his hands and arms should the horse extend the head and neck even further. It may seem that he is sitting in the saddle a little too soon, but he is not—his seat is just touching the saddle and he has not really applied any weight to the horse's back at this point.*

1. The first forefoot contacts the ground.
2. The second forefoot is grounded ahead of the first.
3. The hindfoot diagonal to the first forefoot grounded is next to touch down.
4. The remaining hindfoot is grounded slightly ahead of the previous hindfoot.

The horse canters away on the lead represented by the second foreleg to be grounded. If this was the left front leg, then he will canter away on the left lead. During the first stride away from the jump, the horse may lower his head and neck to assist himself in catching his balance.

2. The rider, upon landing, should take care not to catch the horse's mouth with the bit or sit suddenly upon the horse's back. You should allow your hips, knees and ankles to absorb the concussion as the horse lands; and you should remain in the standing position until all four of the horse's feet are on the ground again. If you do these things, abusive riding can be avoided and the horse will not feel that he has been punished for jumping.

As the horse unfolds his front legs and reaches for the ground, the angle between the horse's neck and the rider's torso will increase. This is fine, but do not sit back or down completely until the horse is on the landing side with all four feet on the ground.

Schooling for Low Jumps

There are six points you should understand about schooling for jumping single, low obstacles:

1. As you practice, if your horse quickens when you take the standing position in preparation for the approach, circle to steady him. Make your approach the next time around, or the next. Be sure that your leg does not slip back as you stand. The horse may interpret this as a request to increase his forward speed, or to canter if you were previously trotting.

Picture 187. The use of ground poles. *Trotting or cantering over ground poles is good preparation for teaching any horse to jump low obstacles. When using ground poles, maintain a correct design of position. Have the horse maintain an even pace before and after the stride over the pole while on loose reins.*

2. Begin your schooling for low jumping with a pole on the ground. Trot, then canter over the middle of the pole in both directions, until the horse maintains a steady pace on both sides of the pole. The horse's stride should not be broken as he trots or canters over the pole. Practice this in the standing position with loose reins (Picture 187).

3. After the horse is steady over the ground pole, begin jumping very low objects. An X jump is an inviting type of obstacle for the horse to learn to jump (Picture 188). These X's encourage any horse to jump across the center of an obstacle rather than crookedly. After practicing over X's, the horse can jump horizontal bars (Picture 188) and other low obstacles.

4. With regard to fence construction, every jump should have a ground line (Picture 189) on the approach side. The ground line should be set out about one foot from the base of a fence two feet high or less. These ground lines will help the horse in gauging his take-off spot as he approaches the fence. If left alone, he will soon find the spot that is the most comfortable from which to begin the take-off. Obstacles should be constructed of fairly heavy poles, generally four to six inches in diameter, with no sharp corners.

5. To avoid having the horse balk at the fence by attempting to run to the side and around either end, place your obstacle next to the rail or wall of your schooling area. At least running around one side will have been precluded.

6. If the horse runs around the fence to the left, for example, punish the disobedience with your left leg and with split reins across the left side of the neck. If the horse refuses the jump by stopping outright in front of the fence, punish him with both of your legs by kicking simultaneously with both at the cinch. Don't permit him to attempt to jump

Picture 188. Jumping X's. *Jumping these fences is a nice way to introduce both horse and rider to jumping. Jumping X's encourages the horse to jump over the center of obstacles. Practicing with X jumps generally should precede jumping obstacles like the horizontal rails shown in Pictures 183–186.*

Picture 189. Ground lines. *Employing a ground line like the white pole in this photo makes learning to jump a more comfortable experience for the horse. Ground lines assist the horse in determining a safe take-off point for each jump. Additionally, these same ground lines may assist the horse in gauging the height of the obstacle to be jumped and the effort required to safely clear a given obstacle.*

the fence flat-footed from a halt as you do this. Hang onto the reins as you punish him with your legs. When you have made your point, back calmly, twelve or fifteen feet, and ask him to trot forward and jump the fence. Keep a firm urging leg on him for this second try. After jumping the fence, return to a stabilized trot or canter and a normal approach if you wish to continue practicing.

The mechanics of the jump relate closely to two other important exercises. The actions of the hindlegs during take-off closely parallel what is required to produce a good sliding stop, and the sequence of legs upon landing is very close to the way in which the horse manages his legs when performing the rollback from the canter.

Chapter 8

ADVANCED RIDING AND SCHOOLING

This chapter attempts to answer three questions:

1. Who is an advanced rider, and how does one become an advanced rider?
2. What is an advanced-level horse, and how does one make such an animal?
3. What are the advantages of riding and schooling on the advanced level?

The answers to these questions may seem more philosophical than practical, but as you read them, you will begin to appreciate just how advanced the advanced level of riding and schooling is.

Who is an advanced rider?

Perhaps the advanced rider is you or I—or maybe neither of us. Perhaps, as a ten-year-old girl might tell us, it is her friend who rides in the advanced riding class at their summer camp. Perhaps it is the rider in the advanced class at the local stable where riding lessons are given. Perhaps it is the college student enrolled in a class entitled Advanced Riding Techniques in her college riding program. Perhaps it is you who have just won a ribbon in a pleasure class at a major national stock show.

As you read this book, you may have said to yourself, "Well, what this man is proposing is rather difficult and exacting. I felt that I was riding and schooling at the advanced level when he was only half through the section on Intermediate Schooling."

If this is your reaction, then I am thrilled. One of the things I set out to do has been accomplished: to put riding and schooling in a demanding, international perspective for you.

An advanced rider is one who is capable of ob-taining the best possible performance from any horse, at any level of schooling, by riding that horse with the control techniques that are understandable to the horse at his particular level of schooling, whatever it might be.

While the advanced rider does not need to have a picture-perfect position in accomplishing all of these things, he must have an extremely functional position which makes it easier for him to get a particular lesson across to the horse. Even for the advanced rider, it is difficult to maintain an excellent position all of the time, and this is especially true whenever he must school many green horses each day. Because horses are so unpredictable, sometimes a functional position, a good working position but not necessarily a show ring position, is preferable for riding and schooling during a long day in the saddle.

What all riders on the advanced level have—what some of the rest of us occasionally lack—is the ability to remain always perfectly in balance with the horse's forward motion and to use their aids correctly and efficiently in a soft way, and one that is most understandable to the horse. In effect, the advanced rider can always keep his center of balance over or nearly over that of the horse. The horse and rider are always, in a manner of speaking, going in the same direction, provided that the horse remains reasonably obedient and cooperative. The rider is never ahead, or behind, the forward motion of the horse.

A rider at the advanced level, regardless of the horse's particular level of schooling, can stay out of the horse's way as he willingly *tries* to respond promptly to each of the rider's aids. In this way, the advanced rider is seldom inadvertently abusive to the horse. He never gives the horse conflicting aids. For instance, the rider's hands never say slow, while his legs or weight distribution say go

237

faster. This clear and unconfusing use of aids by the advanced rider is a matter of a secure position—a good working position—and correct and efficient use of aids.

A rider who can always remain in balance with the horse's forward motion, one who can stay out of the horse's way, and one who has a good working position with correct and efficient use of aids, is a rider who is very soft. The advanced rider is a soft rider, and these riders most often have the horses that are themselves very soft, precise and relaxed in their performances.

However, take note. Being a soft rider does not mean that they hesitate to correct a horse's mistakes for the sake of always remaining soft. Quite the contrary is true. These same soft riders are quick and efficient when punishing disobediences by the horse, but then, almost in the same breath, they can return to soft and sympathetic riding. The ability to punish a horse at exactly the instant when he will understand why he is being punished, and the ability to return to the lesson at hand almost casually is one characteristic that makes advanced riders so efficient in their schooling, and therefore successful in the show ring.

The rider on the advanced level has developed, over a long period of time, a sensitive feel for what is occurring beneath him as he rides. This sensitivity *originates* with a perfect understanding of the mechanics of the gaits, and the various exercises and movements the horse is called upon to perform. However, for the advanced rider, an understanding of the mechanics of the gaits and various movements has become *second nature.* This understanding has progressed from a mental understanding to a physical feeling. This highly developed sense relating to the motion of the horse allows the advanced rider to correct defects, and overcome weaknesses in the horse's performance without overriding or underriding the horse. In this way, softness is maintained (by not overriding), while effective results are achieved (by not underriding).

This is the essence of riding at an advanced level. Are you one of these advanced riders? You may well be, if:

1. Your position astride the horse is secure, and
2. You can maintain a good working position while always remaining in balance with the horse's forward motion, and

3. You can employ your aids correctly and efficiently, in teaching the horse a new lesson as well as in providing timely punishment for disobediences, and
4. You understand all of the mechanical aspects of forward motion presented in this book, and you can begin to feel these events as you ride, and
5. You never employ conflicting aids while riding or schooling, and
6. You can remain soft in your riding as you take a green horse from the elementary level of schooling through the intermediate level of schooling, as presented in this book. If you have all of these traits, you are probably ready to *begin* riding on an advanced level.

These six points reflect a high standard of performance for the rider. If you feel that perhaps you cannot ride quite to this level at this time, although your riding may be really quite good and unabusive, you will naturally want to know how to ride at a higher level. To become more advanced, you can:

1. Ride or study with someone who will share their years of experience and who will discuss all of the aspects of riding and schooling that they know well.
2. Ride many different horses at all different levels of schooling.
3. Understand how the horse moves mechanically, and how different qualities in the horse's forward movement are desirable in allowing him to perform at his best. Riding, reading, thinking, studying and watching others ride will all help.
4. Concentrate much more than most riders care to do as they ride and school horses. Concentrate on your position, your use of aids and the movement of the horse underneath you.
5. Place yourself mentally in the horse's position as you ride; especially when teaching new lessons to the horse.
6. Read, discuss and watch others ride. Listen to the other riders, and think hard about what they say. Sort out the logical from the illogical. Keep what makes sense, and discard the rest. Recognize that riding and schooling do change, not only in style and manner of dress, but in theory and knowl-

edge. Take advantage of educational enrichment opportunities whenever you can: clinics, new books, guest lecturers and guest instructors.

What is an advanced level horse?

Very simply, he is a superior animal in terms of his disposition and his natural quality of movement. He is one that has been schooled through the intermediate level of schooling as I have presented it in this book, one that is ready, when mounted by an advanced rider, to refine his overall performance even more.

When I say that the advanced horse is one that has completed the intermediate level of schooling, I will make three qualifications. You may omit the spin, but not the pivot. You may omit the sliding stop, but not good downward transitions, prompt and square halts. You may omit low jumping as an exercise.

The intermediate level of schooling must be completed in its entirety before more advanced schooling is begun, so that sufficient cooperation with your aids may be learned by the horse, and so that sufficient agility (and the ability to maintain central balance, at least for short periods of time) is present. However, omitting the three exercises just mentioned will not seriously impair the horse's ability to begin advanced schooling. If you do not need these three exercises for events in which you compete, omit them if you wish. By doing this you will save some additional wear and tear on the horse's legs.

If your schooling at the intermediate level is in order (with or without the three exercises just mentioned), you may wish to begin advanced schooling. In this case, what will you hope to gain? The answers are:

1. The best possible performance from each horse. A greener horse, one who is a little younger and perhaps a little more athletic than your own mount, may still outperform you for certain events, however.
2. Better upward transitions. At this point in schooling you will simply demand that an excellent quality of movement be maintained from the last stride of a slower gait through the transition to a faster gait.
3. Better downward transitions. At this point in schooling you will demand that the horse employ direct flexions of the head in softening all of his downward transitions, including transitions to the halt.
4. Better halts. The quality of the horse's movement will be maintained until he has come completely to rest, at attention, squarely.
5. Smaller circles while maintaining all of the good qualities of movement which you would normally demand when performing larger circles. Teach the volté (discussed later).
6. Greater cooperation in taking the correct lead. At the advanced level of schooling, this includes taking *whatever* lead the rider requests. Obediently cantering on the wrong lead is an exercise called the counter-canter (discussed below).
7. Better flying changes of leads, if these have not already been perfected during intermediate schooling. At the advanced level, greater steadiness is required in the flying change. The horse should never scoot forward immediately after executing the required change to a new lead.
8. A better turn on the haunches from the walk. The back legs should maintain the sequence of the walk while the front legs cross one in front of the other as the horse turns to the side.
9. Semicollected gaits for purposes of increasing the horse's overall longitudinal agility, regardless of whether you have an interest in showing California-style pleasure horses.
10. The pivot, spin and rollback performed without resistance by the horse.

The Counter-Canter: This is definitely an advanced exercise. For one thing, it can be dangerous to horse and rider because falls (though not likely) can occur. Simply put, the counter-canter involves cantering on the wrong lead (purposely) in obedience to the rider's aids. A counter-canter while circling or turning to the right requires that the horse canter on the left lead. A counter-canter while circling or turning to the left requires that the horse canter on the right-hand lead.

Performing the counter-canter demands that the horse obediently take and maintain whatever lead is requested by the rider. Obedience to the rider's aids is the crux of the matter—the benefit of higher levels of schooling.

The counter-canter is requested with the same sequence of aids which is normally employed for beginning any canter, but in this case the rider requests the outside rather than inside lead. Again, this constitutes a test of obedience to rider's aids. Otherwise, there are only two practical benefits to this particular exercise.

Clearly, the first benefit is in increasing the lateral agility of the horse. The second benefit of this exercise is for reining horses that have become a little ring sour: they begin to dive inward, speed up or anticipate the rider's request for a flying change of leads while performing the standard figure eights required by most reining patterns. For these horses, demanding the counter-canter gets them listening hard for the rider aids.

When teaching the counter-canter, remember to keep your circles fairly large and your turns not particularly sharp. Remember, a fall is possible when turning while cantering on the outside lead. If you teach, consider the liability factor if you include this exercise for your higher-level students.

When first teaching the counter-canter, remember that the horse will be a little unbalanced as he turns on the outside lead. Maintaining a very steady working position is necessary. Don't lean, or attempt to use your weight laterally as he turns or circles on this false lead. Employ your outside leg at the cinch to maintain the outside lead, but don't lean or otherwise unbalance the horse while he is performing this difficult movement.

At first, use an outside indirect rein, or even an inside direct rein, in order to encourage the horse to look slightly in the direction of his outside leading leg. Later, after he understands this movement, and has become accustomed to turning and circling while maintaining the outside lead, you may begin to ask that he move on the line with his head and neck. He should look in the direction in which he is turning while also maintaining the required lead.

The Volté: This is no more than traveling around a very small circle. The volté is a circle 6 meters across, a little over 21 feet. Teach the horse to walk, trot and lope the volté. Insist upon good engagement and movement on the line as he does this.

Performing the volté will increase the horse's lateral flexibility. It also increases his longitudinal flexibility by promoting direct flexions of the head, and a greater shifting of his weight to the rear. Be careful, however. Too much practice at the volté tends to excite and overly animate some horses. Performing a volte at the canter is occasionally a requirement of trail classes.

What are the advantages of riding and schooling at the advanced level?

Schooling any horse to the advanced level can be a rather touchy proposition. You cannot merely assume that because you invest the time in advanced schooling, your particular horse will always come out on top in the show ring. Indeed, he may be beaten by a less schooled horse that is simply more athletic or one that tires less easily.

Advanced schooling is no guarantee of winning in the show ring. However, if you pick very special horses with superior physical ability, excellent conformation and dispositions, you will be much happier with your efforts at advanced schooling. Indeed, such horses should excel over less well-schooled, but physically equal rivals. You should think about this point whenever you contemplate spending the time, energy and money to school a horse at the advanced level.

Who really *needs* to ride on an advanced level? Only two, or perhaps three, types of riders.

The first type is the professional who makes his living riding and schooling horses. Here the economic benefits are clear; better schooling, faster and more efficient schooling, the ability to leave holes in the horse's education when economics dictate and the skill in the show ring to help the horse get around these deficiencies in schooling.

The second type of rider, or professional horseman, who needs to ride on the advanced level, is the professional riding instructor. Obviously, if you teach, and intend to take any rider to a capable, intermediate level, you must ride just a notch higher—at a very high intermediate level, or preferably at the advanced level.

There is a third type of rider who may feel the need to ride at an advanced level. He or she is neither a professional trainer, or a professional riding instructor. This rider is simply a highly educated amateur, one who wishes to get the best possible performance from any horse. Perhaps, in the final analysis, he or she is then the only one, within a huge population of riders, who is truly interested in a higher standard of performance just for the sake of excellent riding and schooling, and for what can be accomplished on the western performance horse.